GOING
TOO
FAR
enough

GOING TOO FAR

enough

AMERICAN CULTURE AT CENTURY'S END

HENRY SOUTHWORTH ALLEN

SMITHSONIAN
INSTITUTION
PRESS
WASHINGTON
AND
LONDON

Essays © 1987, 1988, 1989, 1990, 1991, 1992, 1993
by the *Washington Post*
Reprinted by permission

Editor: Jack Kirshbaum
Designer: Linda McKnight

Library of Congress Cataloging-in-Publication Data

Allen, Henry.
　Going too far enough : American culture at century's end /
Henry Southworth Allen.
　　　p.　　cm.
　Includes index.
　ISBN 1-56098-367-1 (alk. paper)
　　1. United States—Civilization—1970–　　2. United States—
Social life and customs—1971–　　I. Title.
E169.12.A3752　　1994
973.92—dc20　　　　　94-21531

British Library Cataloging-in-Publication data available

Manufactured in the United States of America
00 99 98 97 96 95 94　　5　4　3　2　1

⊗ The paper used in this publication meets the minimum
requirements of the American National Standard for
Permanence of Paper for Printed Library Materials
Z39.48-1984.

Cover: Fireworks photograph by Jeff Tinsley, Smithsonian
Institution. Image of car from Classic Status Stamp Company.

to my late, sweet father

also named henry southworth allen

sailor, sail on

contents

acknowledgments

These are just a few of the historians and anthropologists who have tried for years to teach me what a culture is: Jackson Lears, Jeffrey Meikle, Elaine Tyler May, Lary May, Conrad Kottak, Lou Marano, and Skip Rappaport.

These people understood what it is to be patrons: Katharine Graham and her son Donald Graham, who have built the *Washington Post* into a great newspaper, and done it with a breathtaking, almost offhanded, blend of savvy, instinct, and the sort of confidence that endures—maybe even finds amusement in—eccentric feature writers with bad authority problems. Executive editor Leonard Downie Jr. and managing editor Robert Kaiser continue the tradition. The generosity of all of them in making this book possible has been enormous. And once more, my thanks to Mary Hadar, editor of the *Post*'s Style section, who gave me world enough and time. And to my assigning editor, Janet Duckworth, who knows that God is in the details.

These have been people who proved that grace, angels, and blind luck exist: Mark Hirsch, Curt Suplee, Joel Garreau, Sidney Blumenthal, Jeffrey Frank, Larry Stern, Harry Boyte, Peter Braestrup, Peter Dunne, Alex Cruden, Bill Smart, Bob Stark, Lucy Clark, Jim Webb, Michael Jerace, the United States Marine Corps, Richard Restak, Carole Horn, Steve Weissman, the late Ted Wood, who could listen even better than he talked on those sails around Chebeague Island, Aunt Cissie Lindemann, Merrill Leffler, and B. J. Clark, who killed himself, thereby making the world infinitely more complicated and somewhat less possible; all of the sources who have given me so much time and help; almost all of the readers who have written me letters; almost all of those who think they should be on this list but aren't; my children Nicholas, Peter, and Hannah Rose, who are the best teachers I'll ever have; my sister Julia and my mother, Mary.

Many of these have joined in a seeming conspiracy to forestall my self-destruction, especially my beautiful and mysterious wife, Deborah Allen, who saved my life but doesn't see any point in going on and on about it.

What a strange country this is—stranger than China, stranger than Atlantis, probably. It is rich, it is new, it froths with possibility, and still we fret over what we've squandered and betrayed.

"O lost, and by the wind grieved . . ."

Robert Bacon, a Harvard athlete and then a partner of J. P. Morgan, went off to World War I saying: "The world—our world—is not lucky enough to be snuffed out as was Pompeii. We have got to go through a long sickening decadence." At the close of the same century, an author named Bill McKibben wrote in *The End of Nature* about the shame "of realizing how much more we could have done— a sadness that shades into self-loathing."

We delight in confessing that we have fouled our own nest and grovelled before the altar of Mammon. We are sinners in the hands of an angry God, and, being Americans, which is to say the offspring of both Adam Smith and John Calvin, we are always on the lookout for a good deal on redemption.

Hence the vision-quest quality of our vacations, space travel as proof of American righteousness, the belief in the redeeming powers of art, and the worship of demigods such as Albert Einstein and the melancholy Wyeths. Save us, O save us. We preach a crusade we call The Good War, a fact not lost on Communist Vietnam's Gen. Vo Nguyen Giap, who once pointed out: "In war you must win."

American culture believes in the healing virtue of landscape and the miracle of invention. We have a Hindu-sized collection of mythical figures—Mickey Mouse, John Kennedy, the yeoman farmer, Zsa Zsa Gabor. We believe in the sacramental power of guns, the sanctity of little white towns in New Hampshire, and the proposition that the secret of success is knowing how to go precisely too far enough.

"Tomorrow we will run faster, stretch out our arms farther . . ."

We hunt for Edens—a summer house, the wilderness, a past when the Anglo-Saxon ruled—with the puzzled dignity of lost dogs. We expect salvation to issue from the White House or nuclear physics. We play our parts in rituals—the Miss America pageant, trash recycling, taking our children to *Fantasia* or the Fourth of July fireworks. And, very strangely indeed, we are a culture that believes happiness is the normal state of human affairs, a belief that is contradicted by most of philosophy and all of history.

We search for meaning at the same time we pretend that everything, as Joe Friday used to say on *Dragnet,* is just the facts, ma'am. I started wondering about this paradox when I was a Marine in Vietnam, where meaning was everything but we kept thinking the facts would win it for us. Afterward, I would read Michael Herr, who knew what the war meant because he understood culture. He understood the Marines as a culture, the war as a culture, the media as a culture, and, God help us, irony as a culture. What a smart guy.

I've been saved from journalistic entropy, I hope, by hooking up with a lot of smart guys through the years, especially the kind of academics who understand both culture and what Gregory Bateson meant when he said that "information is a difference that makes a difference." I would also like to mention my wild surmise, silent in a bookstore in Washington, on first looking into cultural history as written by the late Warren Susman. Meanwhile, I've been more than saved from academic daintiness by taking part in the epistemological mud-wrestling match that has been the best of American journalism (and my living) ever since the 1960s, from the White House to Saudi Arabia.

Anyway, a nation that has strewn anthropologists across the continents has next to nothing in its libraries about the meaning of the rituals, taboos and totems that constitute its own culture: state fairs, Batman, mass insanities, lost cities, J. Edgar Hoover, parades, bus stations, which is to say a palimpsest of meanings and symbols floating over us like one of those mammoth American flags waving over a Cadillac dealership—most of them proudly hailed by a country that rarely stops to think about them at all.

This book thinks about them. That's the point of it.

part one

lost moorings, busted compasses

lost moorings, busted compasses

America is like a barroom drunk. One minute it brags about its money and muscle, and then for the next hour it bleats into its beer about failure and hopelessness—from Mr. Big to a pitiful helpless giant, half-full to half-empty, strutting to fretting, a huge, lumbering manic-depressive going from Carter's malaise to Reagan's morning again in America to George Bush warning us: "You face a choice, whether to turn the clock back and return to . . . the malaise days." Which America seemed to return to anyway, hence the election of Bill Clinton, the Man from Hope. On and on.

Right now, we're in a bleating phase.

Bleat, bleat, bleat. The governing class—media, academia, appointive politicians, lawyers—is whipsawed by a nasty combination of puritan dread and WASP-rot nostalgia, of compost-heap righteousness and self-loathing wistfulness. So they bleat that we deserve whatever punishment we get. After all, America has raped Mother Nature, dishonored its Founding Fathers, abused its children, forgotten its past, and mortgaged its future.

The way the bleatists see it, Americans don't have problems, they have national crises, which keep adding up in commission reports to "a nation at risk," as if a quarter of a billion people living in the strongest, richest, freest, and most generous country in history were going to vanish tomorrow into the La Brea Tar Pits. In John Updike's *Rabbit at Rest,* the protagonist considers that "there has been a lot of death in the newspapers lately . . . everything falling apart, airplanes, bridges, eight years under Reagan of nobody minding the store, making money out of nothing, running up debt, trusting in God."

Everything becomes a sign that things are getting worse. A *CBS News* report reveals the tragedy of the "hidden homeless"—people who are forced to live with relatives. Once these situations were called "families," but now they're proof of decline. Fears of decline have produced books by the declinists, who have been answered by the anti-declinists, who may be right, but they have to admit that American pessimism is so rife that they had to write their books to keep us from bringing on decline with self-fulfilling prophecies.

The barroom drunk raves on and on. Listening to him is the price you pay for hanging out at Club America, where one minute our good is crowned with brotherhood from sea to shining sea, and the next it's nothing but bitch-goddesses and hogs with both front feet in the trough. Manic/depressive, half full/half empty.

America is a strange country.

In *Tales of a New America,* Robert Reich, Bill Clinton's secretary of labor, wrote:

> Celebrate our triumph over savages and evil abroad! Rejoice in the opportunity open to each of us to gain fame and fortune! Admire our generosity and compassion! See how we have overcome vested privilege! But the same stories can be cast as rebukes, exposing the great gulf separating what we are from what we want to become, or how far we have fallen from an ideal we once achieved. The world is succumbing to tyranny, barbarism, and devastation while we stand idly by! Hard work and merit are sabotaged by convention, chicanery, and prejudice! We are selfish, narcissistic, racist, indifferent—look at the poor and hungry in our midst! Our democ-

racy is a sham, and everything important is controlled by a cabal at the top!

Or is it just possible that there's something new in the national character?

Media reports have indicated a generation grown so narcissistic and selfish, "so enamored of ourselves, that we are dissatisfied if our explorations bring us face to face with any image but our own." It is a generation marked by "desire for stimulants and narcotics . . . fear of responsibility, of open places or closed places, fear of society, fear of being alone, fear of fears, fear of contamination, fear of everything, deficient mental control, lack of decision in trifling matters, hopelessness . . ."

So the answer is no, there is nothing new. Those quotations were taken from popular publications of a century ago.

As early as the 1830s, Tocqueville looked at America's upper classes and saw that "a cloud habitually hung on their brow, and they seemed serious and almost sad even in their pleasures" because they "never stop thinking of the good things they have not got." In 1854 Thoreau assured his place in *Bartlett's Familiar Quotations* with: "The mass of men lead lives of quiet desperation." In 1881 a book called *American Nervousness* popularized the term "neurasthenia," a disease that affected "civilized, refined and educated" people, said the author, George M. Beard, with a set of symptoms that sound like a combination of depression and the "Chronic Fatigue Syndrome" (CFS) that would appear a century later.

On the other hand, the *New York Times* said on January 1, 1900, in a lead editorial: "The year 1899 was a year of wonders, a veritable annus mirabilis, in business and production. . . . The outlook on the threshold of the new year is extremely bright." In the 1950s, Bruce Bliven wrote in *Twentieth Century Unlimited* that "half a century ago, mankind and especially the American section of mankind, was firmly entrenched in the theory that this is the best of all possible worlds and getting better by the minute." The change in fifty years, he said, was "the alteration in the moral climate from one of overwhelming optimism to one which comes pretty close to despair." But that statement itself was made half a century ago! Surely the desperation level couldn't have increased again at the same rate he described.

After World War II, America was living through an "age of anxiety," in W. H. Auden's phrase. *Time* magazine reported that "in the uneasy air of 1951's autumn, a sense of wrong stained the air like smog." (What was that all about?) Then came conformity, Norman Mailer's "cancer gulch," the '60s "games" played by "plastic" people, and in the 1970s, Jimmy Carter's "malaise." In the 1980s, you couldn't avoid hearing about all the people stricken by CFS, a disease in which fevers, lymph-node swellings, night sweats, diarrhea and muscle pain got together with mood swings and panic attacks. One woman with CFS had a dog who'd gotten it too. And let's not forget hypoglycemia, post-traumatic stress disorder, premenstrual syndrome, postpartum depression, seasonal affective disorder, psychic numbing, holiday depression syndrome, and midlife crisis.

In *The Diseasing of America,* Stanton Peele asks

> What has given us the idea that we are so impotent and helpless? Why have we become enmeshed in dysfunctional, exaggerated fears about our environment? Why have we decided that we—and our children—cannot control even our own emotions and behavior? . . . Why have we become so afraid that addiction is everywhere and that we are out of control of our eating, shopping, lovemaking, gambling, smoking, drug taking, menstrual cramps, feelings after birth, anxieties and depressions, and moods of all kinds?

"America is an underachiever in happiness, when you compare us to countries who are poorer than we are," says Ronald Inglehart, author of *Culture Shift in Advanced Industrial Society*. He points out that according to life-satisfaction surveys, "the Irish are happier than Americans, even though they're much poorer." So are a lot of countries. In fact, some Americans get more unhappy the richer they get. "Once protests were a working-class phenomenon. Now it's the upper-middle and upper classes who do the protesting, particularly the post-materialists for whom quality of life and self-expression are important issues—younger, more educated people."

O well-bred bleatismo—the educated people being the ones more prone to the strange belief that the natural state of mankind is happiness. Such a belief begets big-time bitching.

If a certain fretful gnawing and desperate exhaustion have always been American traits, perhaps it's not the quality of our desperation but merely the quantity that has changed in recent years. Even after allowing for changes in the way we diagnose clinical depression, and for the fact that mental illness isn't kept secret anymore, a lot of psychiatric epidemiologists think there's a lot more depression in America, an increase of two to three times, an increase far greater than increases in schizophrenia, panic disorder, and phobias. Almost anything could be causing it: food additives, viruses, media overload, political cynicism, nastiness as a sort of new etiquette of public discourse.

Frederick Goodwin, a psychiatrist who has run both the Alcohol, Drug Abuse, and Mental Health Administration and the National Institutes of Mental Health, sits in his twelfth floor office and says:

> Vulnerability to depression is a constant. It doesn't change. But the incidence of depression has increased since the 1960s and the age of onset has lowered. What might explain it? There were the traumas of the early and mid-1960s, and fundamental changes in society. There was a loss of the compact between people and government. Gender differentiation broke down. There was a doubling in the divorce rate. We now are seeing the first generation of kids coming to adulthood who were not raised by their mothers. We are seeing adults who survived because of advances for kids who used to die in infancy, adults who might have survived with somewhat compromised nervous systems. We've had a decreased impact of religion and patriotism, and an increase of cynicism about public institutions. We had a tremendous increase in mobility after World War II. External sources of self-esteem were stripped away. Allan Bloom [author of *The Closing of the American Mind*] has cited in-

creasing moral and cultural relativism. It's hard to get an anchor. A lot of depressed patients cannot forget injuries, and the legal system plays into that with its concept of injury liability, and there is the politics of victim empowerment that runs the risk of reinforcing that way of thinking. It is useful to say there is a certain contagion factor here, and it affects the whole society. Hopelessness and inability to believe you can change things are part of depression too, and since 1964 we've seen a tremendous drop in research and development as a percentage of gross national product, a drop in investment in roads, bridges and education. That would reflect a general loss of confidence in the future.

Or let's reverse the thesis and say that maybe it's not the quantity of desperation but the quality that has changed.

In 1900 it was easier to believe in the Doctrine of Progress. At century's end, a sense of stasis has set in. Progress has gone the way of World of Tomorrow articles in *Popular Mechanics*. Nostalgia has replaced expectation. After a century of astonishment at upheaval and invention, Americans put their ears to the ground and hear nothing more than their own heartbeats.

There are so few frontiers left of any kind, mechanical, artistic, political, whatever. Americans like to know there's something happening out there. But it feels like nothing is happening. If it weren't for the gunfire, you'd have a hard time telling the difference between America and Canada. It's like the feeling you have in a 3 A.M. South Dakota motel room as you keep turning the television dial and all you get is stations signing off with "The Star-Spangled Banner."

The agents of change—good and bad—have lost mana. No wonder drugs, no Commies, no thirty-hour work week, no Nazis, no Eisenhower grin, no Joe McCarthy capturing the minds of Mr. and Mrs. Front Porch U.S.A, no beatniks or Maoists charming American children out of their sensible shoes. No panics over LSD in the reservoirs. No romance of a hip and mysterious black culture offering wisdom and intoxications beyond white imagining. There is little Secret Knowledge anywhere, in the way that it once lurked in psychoanalysis, sex (remember the *Kamasutra*?), existentialism, Marxist di-

alectic, Asian mysticism, the CIA, psychedelic drugs, and the high culture of Lionel Trilling and the *Partisan Review* crowd. We do put
faith, however, in the virtues of wilderness, the mysteries of comput-
ers, and the miracles of psychopharmacology such as Prozac. But hipness—the acute awareness of the existence and propriety of change—
has become the attribute of marketing consultants like Faith Popcorn.

"A shortage of trends" in the clothing business, said the *New
York Times* in all seriousness. A cultural entropy has set in. Jean-
François Lyotard writes in *The Post-Modern Condition*: "This is a
"period of slackening—I refer to the color of the times . . . One listens
to reggae, watches a western, eats McDonald's food for lunch and
local cuisine for dinner, wears Paris perfume in Tokyo and 'retro'
clothes in Hong Kong; knowledge is a matter for TV games." Plus
c'est la même chose. Irony is all.

College graduates of the 1950s and early '60s believed that literature, abstract art, foreign movies, and modern jazz would save them
from "conformity" and rumpus-room philistinism. They are disappointed now, and their children can't begin to understand why T. S.
Eliot or Ingmar Bergman were once saints and prophets. There's no
place to track down saints, either. No Paris in the '20s, Spain in the
'30s, New Mexico in the '60s. The Revolution isn't happening anymore. Culture heroes are niche-marketed—Michael Jordan for bas-
ketball fans, Madonna for Madonna fans, Donald Trump for fans of
crass mega-spending, before he lost so much money. It's hard to think
who embodies the national spirit in the manner of Jesse Owens,
Charles Lindbergh, Babe Ruth, Ernest Hemingway, Amelia Earhart,
Albert Einstein, or Henry Ford. For years the press clamored for another Hegelian hero who would stand for a new America the way
Kennedy did. Imagine their disappointment when it turned out to be
Ronald Reagan. The fault is not in the stars but in ourselves.

Invention is our due, frontiers are our property, the future is a
cornucopia. After the American Revolution, we also counted it as a
basic right to start anew, to purify, to release man's natural goodness
in the manner of the French Revolution, to create the New Man and
let a thousand flowers bloom. Because they are the most violent-

thinking and inauthentic people in America, intellectuals saw the Revolution as the last, best hope, a sort of god to them in the 1960s. It never quite arrived, though it seemed to spend a lot of time hanging out just around the corner. Any second now . . . As Rosa Luxemburg had promised: "You stupid lackeys, your order is built on sand. Tomorrow the Revolution will raise its head again and proclaim to your sorrow amid a brass of trumpets: I was, I am, I shall always be."

Be what? Take a program of suppressing unions, exalting motherhood and the family, abandoning price controls, rejecting government attempts at modernization, simplification of the tax code, moral tightening, erasing the national debt, and recovering the national glory after a lost war, and you are talking about both the Republican platform in 1980 and the agenda of the French Revolution in 1789.

The Revolution is over. Dead. Forgotten—although there are still people in America waiting for the Day When Those Who Are Just Will Arise to Claim What Is Theirs. Think of the Idaho Nazis arming themselves with ring-mounted .50 caliber machine guns against the Night When They Come Pouring Out of the Cities Looking for Our Women and Our Canned Goods. Think of the doomsday ecologists, the pimply freaks of the World According to Clearasil, the disgruntled postal clerks, the insane oilmen brooding over racial genetics, all waiting for the fabric of society to run like a nylon stocking—bureaucrats staring out windows of corporations, government offices, cars in traffic jams, houses in perfect suburbs—and dreaming of the day when it all goes up in smoke, huge chunks of mirror-wall office buildings vaulting through the air, fires all night, and power lines dangling. The famous will be forgotten and grass will grow in Wall Street. Every mountain and hill laid low! What a comforting fantasy for the powerless, the meaningless, the lifeless, the adventureless.

It's over. Once in a while the Revolution hovers in the imagination for a moment in the manner of the Virgin Mary appearing over a parking lot in Waxahachie, Texas. But it dwindles away. In Nicaragua, for instance, when the Sandinista revolutionaries lost to a democratic coalition in an election, the American revolution-groupies known as the "sandalistas" wept in public.

One of the great lures of the Revolution was its belief in the natural goodness of man and its rejection of the concept of natural depravity. At century's end, however, America was undergoing a reinvention of Original Sin by the latter-day puritans known as environmentalists, whose religion combines the tones of Unitarianism and Druidic animism. It is also a religion whose scientific liturgy conceals the fact that it is dealing in guilt, redemption, days of reckoning, self-loathing, just about anything else you might hear from any preacher good enough to go on TV and sweat, cry, and speak in tongues at the same time.

The operant deity is kindly old Mother Nature as redefined for a new faith, a kvetch who makes you feel guilty for eating Big Macs, dumping half a pint of paint thinner down the cellar sink, driving to work instead of riding the bus, and riding the bus instead of riding a bicycle. Then she makes you feel even guiltier for not feeling guilty enough.

Go ahead, use that deodorant, don't even think about me, God knows I'll be gone soon enough, I won't be here to see you get skin cancer when the ozone hole lets in the ultraviolet rays.

She weeps, she threatens, she nags.

Go ahead. Burn my rain forests, kill my dolphins, drive on my dunes, wear my mink coat. I'll be gone soon enough.

She's the wounded matriarch who plays helpless one minute and announces she's selling off the summer place the next.

The way you've treated me, why should I leave it to any of you?

She's right, you know she's right.

There have been a lot of different Mother Natures in America. The Puritans saw her as a howling witch. The settlers of Virginia saw her as fertile Lady Bountiful, begging to be seduced. Landscape painters of the nineteenth century gave us a Mother Nature as sublime and transcendent as Athena, bearer of power and wisdom. Inventors and scientists saw her as a guardian of secrets. Walt Disney came up with a coy, dimpled fairy godmother who sent bluebirds with a picnic basket if you got lost in the woods.

Now it's a Mother Nature who's remarkably like the storied

guilt-mongers of American movies and novels, a sort of combination of Joan Crawford in *Mildred Pierce* and Mrs. Portnoy in *Portnoy's Complaint*—a disappointed, long-suffering martyr who makes you wish, at least for her sake, that you'd never been born.

In *The End of Nature*, Bill McKibben writes about the shame "of realizing how much more we could have done—a sadness that shades into self-loathing." In *Appalachian Wilderness*, the late Edward Abbey writes: "We are none of us good enough for the world we have." *Environmental Action* magazine warns that even Mother Nature's most devoted children may not be devoted enough: "Wilderness lovers beware. Your next Vibram-soled step could be fatal. Not to you, but to the wilderness." An ad for population control shows a picture of a smiling baby, and describes what a burden he'll be on poor Mother Nature: "He is a disarming little thing, but he begins to scream loudly in a voice that can be heard for 70 years. He is screaming for 26 million tons of water, 21,000 gallons of gasoline, 10,150 pounds of meat, 28,000 pounds of milk and cream, 9,000 pounds of wheat. . . ." Ah, yes, "slimy, beastly life, eating and drinking," as Thoreau said.

You aren't my children. Better my own children should die than they should behave like that.

Mom, please.

It used to be that only white Western males were the wicked children, and aborigines were the good children. A weeping Indian brave was the centerpiece of a TV ad about pollution, and a smiling one has been featured in an ad for biodegradable trash bags. Now everybody's guilty, all the way back in time. Smithsonian Institution Secretary Robert McCormick Adams has said: "More than two-thirds of the native land birds of the Hawaiian archipelago are now extinct, for example, with more than half apparently having disappeared of prehistoric human pressure, long before the arrival of Captain Cook." In the *Los Angeles Times*, a National Park Service biologist writes:

> I know social scientists who remind me that people are part of nature, but it isn't true. Somewhere along the line—at about a billion

years ago, maybe half that—we quit the contract and became a cancer. We have become a plague upon ourselves and upon the Earth. It is cosmically unlikely that the developed world will choose to end its orgy of fossil-energy consumption, and the Third World its suicidal consumption of landscape. Until such time as Homo sapiens should decide to rejoin nature, some of us can only hope for the right virus to come along.

James Lovelock, who developed the Gaia Hypothesis describing the Earth as a self-regulating organism, warns that Mother Nature is a vengeful type who "will play some dirty tricks and hit us with some new weapons."

It used to be, Mother Nature loved us, forgave us, cleaned up after us. Now she's deer ticks wasting us with Lyme disease and coyotes attacking children in Los Angeles suburbs. The ocean heaves medical waste at vacationers. The earth pumps radon gas into basements, causing lung tumors. Once, Mother Nature said not to worry about sexual taboos. Then she came up with herpes, chlamydia, endless mutations of gonorrhea, a rise in syphilis rates, and, finally, AIDS, which some eco-activists of the bulldozer-sabotaging variety have called nature's "payback."

I know, you laugh at me, but I'm not as helpless as you think.

Eco-moralist/farmer Wendell Berry writes: "Our industrial accidents, so-called, should be looked upon as revenges of Nature. We forget that Nature is necessarily party to all our enterprises and that she imposes conditions of her own. Now she is plainly saying to us: 'If you put the fates of whole communities or cities or regions or ecosystems at risk in single ships or factories or power plants, then I will furnish the drunk or the fool or the imbecile who will make the necessary small mistake.' "

Whence comes this guilt, this despair, this haunted, angry, mystical, brooding, stoical, self-righteous, self-loathing, fatalistic, passive, resentful, and misanthropic tone that takes on the grandeur of a combination of *Paradise Lost* and the *Götterdämmerung*? Environmentalism arose in Germany, Britain, and North America, in cultures that had once practiced the pagan mysticism of the woodlands, and among the sort of people who celebrate the birth of Jesus Christ by bringing a tree into the house and decorating it like an altar.

William Temple Hornaday, director of the Bronx Zoo, wrote in 1913: "All members of the lower classes of southern Europe are a dangerous menace to our wildlife." It was the Anglo-Saxons who "have an inherited love for oaks and heathers," said John Muir, a founding father of American environmentalism. As late as 1957, the dean of birdwatching, Roger Tory Peterson, would say that "many of our first-and-second-generation immigrants, drawn from Europe's marginal populations, are enjoying prosperity for the first time and perhaps have not had time to develop judgment."

It's a short step from loathing other people to loathing yourself. George Perkins Marsh, another nineteenth-century environmental prophet, said: "Man is everywhere a disturbing agent. Wherever he plants his foot, the harmonies of nature are turned to discords." Gifford Pinchot, a conservationist and friend of Teddy Roosevelt, said: "Wherever the white man, and especially the Anglo-Saxon, sets his foot, the first thing he does is take the cream off the country." This song is still being sung. In 1966 historian Lynn White told an audience of scientists: "By destroying pagan animism, Christianity made it possible to exploit nature in a mood of indifference to the feelings of natural objects." Edward Abbey takes that indifference and turns it around: "The finest quality of this stone, these plants and animals, this desert landscape, is the indifference to our presence, our absence, our coming, our staying or our going." Or Larry Gray, an artist and member of the North Coast Environmental Center: "My attitude is that if the human race self-destructs, something else will take our place. . . . it might be some wonderful tree that takes over. The landscape will stay on."

I don't worry about me, I worry about you, but a lot of good it does.

In the '60s, hip Americans moved back to the land, looking to *The Whole Earth Catalog* for advice on how to build log cabins, geodesic domes, or yurts, heat them with Defiant woodstoves, and light them with Aladdin lanterns. They raised too much zucchini—you could hear it creaking in the sun as it grew. This was the simple life. They had to be rich to live it, or grow a lot of marijuana, or be writers who'd write articles urging the simple life on people who would have to write articles themselves in order to live it. Like a lot of fads, it was a sort of pyramid scheme.

Environmentalism became commodified. The ecology staff car went from a Volkswagen Beetle with a daisy pasted on the back to an old step-side pickup to a Jeep Cherokee with a bumper sticker reading "Think Globally, Act Locally." *Vogue* magazine warned that "our world is going to hell in a handbasket," but "who says social consciousness can't be fun?" Celebrities got into it: Meryl Streep, Michael Keaton, Kevin Costner, Robin Williams, Quincy Jones, and Barbra Streisand appeared on an "Earth Day Special" on ABC. Corporations announced tree-plantings, kayak races, claims of biodegradability, and so on. Merrill Lynch offered investors its "Eco-Logical Trust 1990." This was America, all right: guilt and the fast buck, self-loathing as a way of life. The sort of people who can smack their lips while they dine on their own livers had found the cozy thrill of apocalypse, doom, and a Mother Nature only they could love.

Go ahead, I'll be gone soon enough. I just hope you live that long.

Nothing is possible, everything is real. That was the grim environmental news. The religion that fought off this sort of apocalypticism used to be the cult of inventing, which preached that everything was possible, though inventors needed a little more time to make it all real. If we turned the planet into a carcinogenic lump, we'd build rockets to take us to other planets. Or we'd wipe out cancer with wonder drugs. This was the religion that faded as environmentalism arrived, but there was a time when inventors were heroes, even saints, in a lost paradise of gizmo gods: Edison, Salk, Fulton, Carver, Wilbur Wright, Orville Wright, Morse, Franklin, Goddard, Tesla, Colt, Marconi, Ford, Goodyear. Once, these men were giants in the land. They built better mousetraps. The world beat paths to their doors. "The

American invents as the Italian paints and the Greek sculpted. It is genius," said a European visitor to the Centennial Exposition of 1876.

A century later, with almost half of U.S. patents going to foreigners, America's inventors are people who build better portfolios, pectorals, or media hype; who come up with $150 sneakers, the home equity loan, and elevators that talk. And the inventors are anonymous. Companies invent things. Marketing people invent things. The insane Tokyo salarymen invent things. You wonder if our giants began to vanish when Americans began telling each other that inventing wasn't worth it: folktales of Gillette suppressing the thousand-shave razor blade or Standard Oil hiding the plans for a hundred-miles-per-gallon carburetor in a safe deposit box. Indeed, if a giant pops up, he may face years of lawsuits over patent infringement by corporations. A robotics inventor named Jerome H. Lemelson testified before Congress in 1979: "Company managers know that the odds of an inventor being able to afford the costly litigation are less than one in ten; and even if the suit is brought, four times out of five the courts will hold the patent invalid. When the royalties are expected to exceed the legal expense, it makes good business sense to attack the patent. . . . What all this means to the inventor is that he either quits inventing or he licenses foreign."

No more miracle tales of Thomas Edison, the Wizard of Menlo Park, working so hard he had to catnap on the laboratory floor. No more Samuel F. B. Morse, abandoning a brilliant but unrewarding career as a painter to send "What hath God wrought" in dots and dashes from Washington to Baltimore in the first telegraph message. No more horses bolting as Nikola Tesla's generators sent lightning ripping out for ten miles from his laboratory. And, after decades of being milled down to homogenized and socialized pabulum by American public schools, no more Teslas epitomizing the ideal of the nineteenth-century romantic genius by saying, "Originality thrives in seclusion free of outside influences beating upon us to cripple the creative mind. Be alone—that is the secret of invention: Be alone, that is when ideas are born."

Imagine picking up *Scientific American* and seeing someone say, as a writer said in 1896, that this is "an epoch of invention and progress unique in the history of the world"; that there has been "a gigantic tidal wave of human ingenuity and resource, so stupendous in its magnitude, so complex in its diversity, so profound in its thought, so fruitful in its wealth, so beneficent in its results, that the mind is strained and embarrassed in its effort to expand to a full appreciation of it." Once, the patent office was one of the biggest tourist attractions in Washington, but that was a century ago when they still had a hall full of working models in the space that now holds the National Portrait Gallery. It was called the Museum of Models then, full of coy miniatures with their unnerving precision. It had pillars and groined ceilings, like a shrine. There was no dream too big or small— endless variations on the theme of steam engine, typesetter, drill, still, valve, sled, reel, camera, fire alarm, gin, press, reaper, lock, lathe, lamp, sewing machine, automobile, adding machine, pinball machine, stove, phonograph, telephone, pump, playpen, paper bag maker, unicycle, bicycle, tricycle, washing machine, clothespin. The period from 1864 to 1873 may have been the golden age of the clothespin, in fact, with sixty-two patents issued. You would think that a clothespin would be self-evident, that its form would follow clearly from its function but there are enough clothespins in government storage that you can see how long it took humanity to get it right. It took a while. Dexter Pierce, of Sunapee, New Hampshire, came up with a simple split piece of wood in 1858. He is the Edison of hanging it out to dry.

"It is the obviousness and simplicity of the machine as a symbol of progress that accounts for its astonishing power," Leo Marx writes in *The Machine in the Garden*. Witness the panic of hope that erupted when two cold-fusion scientists in Utah said they'd figured out a way to make unlimited electricity in a fish tank.

Once, artists, writers, and political thinkers were inventors and scientific tinkerers: Leonardo, Samuel Johnson, Thomas Jefferson. Abraham Lincoln patented a device to float ships off sand bars. Actress Lillian Russell patented a trunk. Maybe what's needed is celebrities taking up inventing as their new cause, sort of like the environment or homelessness. The problem here is that environmentalism and war have taken the glamour out of a lot of technology. It is now ecological heresy to say, as the *American Journal of Science* said in 1840, that "Man is indeed lord of creation; and all nature, as though daily more sensible of the conquest, is progressively making less and less resistance to his dominion." Modern architecture no longer aspires to build Le Corbusier's "machine to live in." The Wizard of Oz is exposed as a mere inventor. The last believers in the power of the individual engineer may be the girls who spend Saturday mornings watching their boyfriends writhe around under cars. Then again, there was an "Invention–New Product Exposition" in Monroeville, Pennsylvania. It featured American inventions such as a noiseless alarm clock (it vibrates under your pillow) and a guitar strap for both left- and right-handed musicians. And there was a throwback to the old days—a water-powered engine designed by the man who invented the computer floppy disk and the digital watch. His name is Yoshiro Nakamutsu. He is known as "the Edison of Japan."

With the end of the Cold War, salvation through mechanical invention subsided into quaintness. It had once meant so much that America and the Soviet Union used it as a battlefield, with the Soviet Union claiming that a Russian had invented radar first, the telephone first, and so on up to the space age, when the Russians stunned the Americans into despair by putting a satellite in space first. Immediately, students started learning Russian and sneering at American technology. Thirty years later, one of the ironies revealed by the end of the Cold War was that socialism had not only failed to build much in the way of technology, but it had turned Eastern Europe into a toxic-waste dump while doing it. It also turned out that the seventy years of Revolution hadn't built anything resembling the New Man. We were right all along, as it turned out. We won the Cold War. We should be happy about this. We were not all that happy.

Was it because the hero at the victory celebration was Mikhail Gorbachev—the leader of the losing side? Was it because the end came with what Václav Havel called the "velvet revolution" rather than anything that looked like the apocalyptic fireballs, final conflict, enemy within, godless hordes, and either massive armed uprisings or massive armed down-puttings we've expected for generations? It's easy to talk about it as something that came and went, like gasohol, but it lasted forty-five years. Less than a third of the people in America were born before it started. Two-thirds of America's housing units have been built since. Perhaps it's more fun beating Nazis in satanically well-tailored uniforms than Soviet bureaucrats in lumpy suits. No war-crimes trials this time. And no disgrace for sympathizers of the losing side. Quite the reverse, for some reason—note the current reputations of the Hollywood Ten, Jane Fonda, William Kunstler, etc. In this Age of the Victim, power is bad and weakness is good, and therefore there's no virtue in being the only superpower left on Earth. Leftist intellectuals are uneasy because it wasn't the American flag that America planted in Moscow, it was the golden arches of McDonald's. The *London Observer* commented: "In the strange encounter between American fast food and state socialism, the richest irony is that the service ideology of an American corporation is a more reliable bearer of egalitarian ideals."

Pigging out: If the French image of popular devotion to freedom is Delacroix's painting of "Liberty Leading the People," the East German image seemed to be footage of "Hans Carrying the VCR." Amusing, but not inspiring. This may be why television coverage of the demolishing of the Berlin Wall fell flat. People stopped looking for mushroom clouds every time the noon siren went off down at the firehouse, and the journalists kept saying how "historic" it all was. But nobody cared much. It was like the old *New Yorker* cartoon where one counterman holds up a hamburger the size of an inflatable wading pool and the other one says: "So you just cooked the biggest hamburger in the world. Now what?"

With the end of the Cold War it was easy to worry that America would see a dwindling of: its birthrate, home building, standard of living, respect for corporations and science, quality of roads, energy of music and the brilliance of art, the clarity of a two-sided worldview, and a belief that the federal government can bring about full civil rights. Then again, there's been a dwindling of all those already. And there's no need to look rich, tolerant, and progressive in front of the world if there's no other big country out there competing for hearts and minds. Lost moorings. Busted compasses. No telling the sheep from the goats. One even senses nostalgia for the Cold War, from left-wingers who based their either-or thinking on it, to right-wingers who saw communist conspiracies and subversion everywhere.

It was a way of thinking. Every Cold War kid who went to college learned the word "dichotomy" before the end of freshman year. (With extra credit for using "Manichaean" or "the contradictions of capitalism.") You were either part of the solution or part of the problem, on the bus or off the bus, establishment or antiestablishment, culture or counterculture, pro-war or antiwar, hip or square, long hair or short hair, under thirty or over thirty. Better Red than dead, said "ban-the-bomb" advocates in the early 1950s. Vice President Spiro Agnew said in the late '60s that thanks to the "nattering nabobs of negativism" we were a "polarized" nation.

The political bloodlines got thinner. Communism produced anti-communism, which produced things like McCarthyism and the paranoia of the John Birch Society, which in turn produced the anti-anti-communism that became a staple of American liberalism, which in turn provoked the anti-anti-anticommunism of, say, Irving Kristol, the godfather of neoconservatism, which in turn no doubt inspired Charles Peters, editor of the *Washington Monthly,* to make his attempt to become the godfather of neoliberalism. On and on.

Meanwhile, the Final Conflict became the Fine Old Conflict. Overnight, symbols became souvenirs: the mushroom-shaped cloud, the Third World, Norman Mailer, brainwashing, William Buckley, Sputnik (and all the other niks—beatnik, peacenik, no-good-nik), McCarthyism, the military-industrial complex, seeing who blinks first, the Rosenbergs, duck-and-cover drills, the button, the Evil Empire, "Who lost China?," fallout shelters, throw-weight, NATO, SEATO, ANZUS, SAC, CIA, Carl Sagan's nuclear winter (when "the living will envy the dead," as Khrushchev said), James Bond, *Dr. Strangelove,* and so on. Much of it going, much of it gone.

The Cold War wasn't there anymore, and people began to realize what it had given us.

Suburbs, for instance: "City planners back in the '40s and '50s talked about the creation of the suburbs in explicitly Cold War terms," said Elaine Tyler May, who wrote *Homeward Bound: American Families in the Cold War Era*." The idea was "to decentralize the population and industry, and if you got people out of the cities, you'd reduce the threat of class warfare that might be communist-generated. William Levitt [builder of Levittowns] said that 'A man who owns his own home cannot be a Communist—he has too much to do.'" Even dating was redefined as a courtship ritual leading to the early marriage and big families that were encouraged as a bastion of warmth in the Cold War.

Four-lane highways: Without the Cold War we might not have had the National System of Interstate and Defense Highways, which was pushed hard by Eisenhower in part because he wanted to be able to evacuate cities in case of nuclear attack.

Corporate culture, experts, and scientists as heroes: In *Recasting America*, Lary May wrote that with the arrival of the Cold War, "public opinion polls no longer recorded strong antimonopoly sentiments. Instead, politicians and businessmen spoke with one voice in praise of the modern corporation and an affluent society. . . . Across the country, a modern symbol of that ethos arose as architects constructed skyscrapers built in the 'international style,' which celebrated the power of technology."

Abstract expressionist painting as a symbol of freedom: The government sponsored art shows overseas. *Life* magazine made a hero of Jackson Pollock. Critic Clement Greenberg wrote: "The main premises of Western art have at last migrated to the United States, along with the center of gravity of industrial production and political power."

Them: This is a country that likes to have a Them to worry about, real or imaginary. Traditionally, we created our Thems right here at home: Indians, Catholics, Jews, anarchists, white males, black males, walking-time-bomb Vietnam veterans. But happily, for the last forty-five years, the big Them has been thousands of miles away. "Them Russians, them Russians, them Chinese and them Russians," as Allen Ginsberg wrote.

Civil rights: "The civil rights issue arose in 1948 largely because of the report of the Civil Rights Commission which Truman had appointed in December 1946—and because of a threat of war which had suddenly become more imminent," Michael Barone wrote in *Our Country*. Truman integrated the armed forces two weeks after he was nominated at the 1948 Democratic convention. The establishment line was that we had at last become a society of classless consensus— just like Russia, only better. Daniel Bell wrote a book called *The End of Ideology*. Seymour Martin Lipset said in 1960 that "the fundamental political problems of the industrial revolution have been solved."

Now what?

While we win and get poorer, we're watching the communists surrender in order to get richer. There is a logic at work here. It reminds you of the idealistic American flier arguing with the 107-year-old brothel proprietor in Joseph Heller's *Catch-22*, which was one of the books that defined the Cold War mentality, even though it was set in World War II. " 'You put so much stock in winning wars,' the grubby iniquitous old man scoffed. 'The real trick lies in losing wars, in knowing which wars can be lost. Italy has been losing wars for centuries and just see how splendidly we've done nonetheless. France wins wars and is in a continual state of crisis. Germany loses and prospers.' "

There was another line of thinking that said we could end up richer, but sadder. Calling the triumph of democratic capitalism "the end of history," a former State Department analyst named Francis Fukuyama wrote that it will be "a very sad time. The worldwide ideological struggle that called forth daring, courage, imagination and idealism will be replaced by economic calculation, the endless solving of technical problems, environmental concerns and the satisfaction of sophisticated consumer demands."

Consumer demands were one of the battlefields of the Cold War. In 1959's "kitchen conference" in Moscow, Nixon and Khrushchev visited an American exhibit at a fair. Nixon "cited figures to show that the 44 million families in America own 56 million cars, 50 million television sets, 143 million radio sets and that 31 million of those families own their own homes," he recalled in *Six Crises*. When Khrushchev attacked the Captive Nations Resolution, Nixon tried to change the subject to color television. When Nixon brought up freedom of choice, Khrushchev "changed the subject back to washing machines, arguing that it was better to have one model than many." If the Russians represented godless materialism, Arthur Schlesinger Jr. said, Americans stood for "godly materialism." Adlai Stevenson asked: "With the supermarket as our temple and the singing commercial as our litany, are we likely to fire the world with an irresistible vision of America's exalted purposes and inspiring way of life?"

Well, yes, as it turned out. Once more the bleating had it wrong.

In 1907 an economist named Simon Nelson Patten had preached the revelation that would shape the twentieth century: "The new morality does not consist in saving but in expanding consumption." Here you'd been earning a penny by saving a penny, and now you'd get both rich and good by spending it. Now you were supposed to jettison the Protestant work ethic, with its self-denial, its Poor Richard shoulder to the wheel. It took a while to talk people into changing their ways. Debt was a sin then, bankruptcy a frequent cause of suicide. This attitude had to go. Chevrolet ran an ad in the 1920s saying, "Ask your banker—he knows." In the picture, a stocky, middle-aged banker—the paragon of respectability—was shown counseling a young couple to, yes, borrow money to buy a Chevrolet. How exciting. An age of character became an age of personality, full of quests for experience à la Hemingway, and notions of life that became consumption items in themselves. Psychoanalysis! Art for the masses! Sincerity! Leisure! Sell the sizzle, not the steak! The idea was to be somebody, not to do something—to consume your own life, in other words. There were doubts and downturns, but the Full Employment Act of 1946 said that the benefits of the Age of Consumption were the right of all Americans. Supermarkets! Togetherness! The idea of things came to mean more than the fact of them. Progress—not turbines or toasters—became General Electric's most important product, according to its slogan. And debt became our most important asset.

But there has always been a sense of something just a bit spiritually off in the Age of Consumption, prompting spasms of penitent praise for real life, the simple life—the agrarian movement of the '30s, the small-is-beautiful and less-is-more of the '70s, the quasi-religious rituals of recycling and environmentalism, the authenticity crusades that went from the furniture of Gustav Stickley at the turn of the century to the streamlining of the New York World's Fair in 1939 to the Stickley revival of the 1980s. Simplicity is within our grasp, and the Temple of Mammon shall fall. The problem here is that people liked the Age of Consumption. It was a little like the Cold War—it organized lives, told people who they were, and gave them status, friends, and an idea of the future. Out of the entropic masses of middle-class America it raised new tribes. Daniel Boorstin writes: "Old-fashioned political and religious communities now became only two among many new, once unimagined fellowships." Next to the Presbyterians, the Swedes, the Democrats, or the tenant farmers, we created communities of Camel smokers, Humphrey Bogart fans, skiers, Revere Ware cooks.

By the 1950s the consumer communities had already become so well defined that middle-class friends tended to buy the same cars, go to the same sort of places on vacations, send their kids to the same colleges. Marketers knew that if they gave the middle class a choice of widgets priced at $20, $30, and $40, the $30 widgets would sell the best. Then urban critics began to attack the suburbanites for their ticky-tacky houses lined up in rows, their tail-fin cars, their "midcult" taste, their "conformity." The late 1960s brought a revolt against all this, and as the '70s wore on, marketers began to notice a strange shift in consumption patterns. People were ignoring the middle-priced items in favor of either the top or the bottom of the line, producing a pattern that industrial designer Cooper Woodring called the "sacrificial enhancement" syndrome: "We've all become very unpredictable. I don't want average in anything. For example, I might eat at McDonald's and drive a Lexus—sacrificing good restaurants to enhance my driving. I might wear a Ralph Lauren sport coat and bluejeans."

The new thing was niche marketing, with sales pitches aimed at smaller and smaller segments of the population—black urban professionals, single women 18–35, and so on. Soon, everything you bought came with memberships in ever-tinier clubs—the Volvo Society, the Loyal Order of the Reebok. It's hard to run a suburban middle class this way, seeing that sacrificial enhancement is the way outsiders act—the cowboy with $500 boots and a $7.98 shirt, for instance, or the Greenwich Village bohemian with a $5,000 Hasselblad camera and 5,000 cockroaches. People advertised that their middle-class lives as commuters weren't their real lives—their bumper stickers read I'D RATHER BE . . . sailing, rock-climbing, in Key West. They wore clothes that bore advertisements for their manufacturers, creating ad hoc communities of Polo people, Nike people, Brooks Brothers people.

At century's end, Americans found themselves working harder and harder to pay for their faith that things will keep getting better and better—economist Juliet Schor wrote that the average American worker puts in 163 more hours a year than twenty years ago. Most Americans expected their children would grow up to be worse off, economically. The promise of ever-increasing material happiness that kept us loyal during the Cold War had been broken. For the first time in a century, America seems to have no bohemia, no underground believing that the future is theirs. Is it possible that with their own commodity fetishes and quests for authenticity they were much the same as the bourgeoisie they thought they were fighting? Was it all driven by the Cold War anyway?

Americans get cranky and bored and then they get renewed, as if the great national snake had shed another skin: Cold War anxiety, the death of God, the dilemma of Vietnam. In the American cosmology, change is a birthright, like happiness. So Americans could be comfortable rushing once more into the sort of future that provokes words such as "Truly this is almost a miraculous era. What is before us no one can say, what is upon us no one can hardly realize. The progress of the age has almost outstripped human belief." Once more, we could find ourselves "drowning, as it were, in a maelstrom of conflicting, confusing and cacophonous ideas. Colliding visions rock our mental universe. Every day brings some new fad, scientific finding, religion, movement, or manifesto." The first quotation is from Daniel Webster, who wrote it in 1847. The second is from Alvin Toffler, author of *Future Shock*, and he wrote it in 1979.

What we need is a good Cold War. Dichotomies. Culture. Counterculture. Wonder drugs. The biggest hamburger in the world. Moorings. Compasses.

part two

back to the garden

Supposing the Last Day on Earth to be a festival—and why not?—it could look like a state fairgrounds at the end of a blue and perfect afternoon. There's a quarter moon over the Ferris wheel. Flags snap above the racetrack. There's a chill in the air, which makes the smoke from the pit barbecues smell good. There's a lot of noise—the crowd, the barkers, the industrial clatter of the Tilt-a-Whirl, the sheep bleating like strangled cynics. Things have a suspended quality—is it the noise? the wind? A horse skitters sideways in the horse ring, and dust streams from each hoof. An old woman waits for the guess-your-age man to guess her age, knowing that he's going to be right. Things seem to be culminating: harvest, blue ribbons, the horribly delicate sashay of a Duroc pig whose last stop before the slaughterhouse is the swine judging. There's a glory to it all. Then faces all over the fairgrounds start lifting.

"Look," people say, until everybody is looking up past the Ferris wheel. They are looking at hot air balloons, which are rising over the fairgrounds. There are more than a dozen of them, and they shine in the evening sky like ornaments in search of a Christmas tree, silent and final. They make you think that if humankind were coming to an end, and we could be reborn on some other planet by sending out seeds the way a dandelion or a milkweed does, those seeds would look like hot-air balloons.

It's all so lovely it hurts: the balloons, the dwarf Hotot rabbits with their mascara eyes, the Worcester County Farm Queen with her quick, sad smile like the smile of a woman who has to say no but is sorry she can't say yes, or two thousand Maryland farmers and spectators rising to applaud the 4-H choir after it sings Lee Greenwood's "God Bless the USA."

Fairs are one of the great institutions of American life, a medium in themselves like television or print—they educate, they entertain, they make us think we've seen truths of sorts.

"I come here to get away from the garbahhhge," says a woman who sits with her sister in the grandstand of the race track. She is working on the racing form and a draft beer. She is glad to see the end of a long, hot summer. "You can smell fall in the air. It's time to move on."

Down on the track, the thoroughbreds pace through the dirt with the heavy twitch of legs meant only to run, not pace. They are sleek and awkward. They look like aristocrats roused by revolutionaries in the middle of the night.

"God, they're pretty," the woman keeps saying as she counts her losses. "But it takes more than pretty."

This is one of the truths that fairs bring home: It takes more than pretty. There's a reality to fairs. This is why they seem a little strange in America, nowadays. In the Land of Secondhand Man, where reality is a theme park and life is a beach, when everything is shrink-wrapped and sanitized for our protection, the state fair is a throwback. Right here, standing in front of you, mooing, this is an Ayrshire cow. That is comb honey, these are farmers, and your horse just lost. Your strawberry jam just won a blue ribbon. Your age has just been guessed, precisely. Your pig fetched 56 cents a pound at auction. Reality. A lot of us aren't used to firsthand experience, this being a country where people will drive 3,000 miles past 10,000 American small towns so they can tour the small-town Main Street at Disneyland, a country where the word "authentic" means "reproduced," as in the Australian dusters that get sold to our educated elite in catalogues. We have a hard time telling the real thing when it gets put right in front of our noses.

"Are those real?" says a teenage boy. He is not a farmer—you can tell because he has an earring shaped like a lightning bolt in his left earlobe, and not many of the farm boys at this fair wear earrings. Also, he is asking his question about fruit and vegetables. He seems to be in considerable distress about this. Are they real? Why does he ask? What's in front of him are not *Guinness Book of World Records* walnuts the size of shrunken heads. They are just fruit and vegetables on white paper plates. They are laid out on long tables . . . home-grown red bartlett pears, blackberries, Chinese chestnuts, tomatoes, Stayman apples, cushaw melons, patty pan squash, sugar baby water-melons, Katahdin potatoes, eggplant, okra, banana peppers, kale, cantaloupe, hubbard squash, butternut squash, crookneck squash, pecans and hickory nuts, cobbler potatoes, endive, zucchini, Rome apples, Jonathan apples, nectarines, red cabbage.

"I didn't think any of these things were real," the boy says. "They look . . . like in pictures."

If he'd walked into the building and seen full-color computer-enhanced photographs of bush lima beans or cayenne peppers, he would have known exactly what he was looking at. But here, first hand, with no Good Housekeeping Seal of Approval, no Sunkist or Chiquita Banana stamped on a plasti-rapped serv-u pak, all these fruits and vegetables look so real they look fake—it seems that only an illusion could look so authentic, like the Disneyland Main Street. The organizers of the fair understand this. Next to the vegetables is a display of firewood, a cord of firewood, 128 cubic feet. That's all. It is there not to compete for a blue ribbon but to educate the city dwellers who have never seen a cord of wood. They may think they've seen one, they may even think they bought a cord of wood from that lean-faced guy in the pickup truck last fall, the guy with the USS *Coral Sea* baseball hat and the T-shirt that said "The More I Know About Women, the More I Love My Truck." This guy stood next to his truck and pointed to the wood in the back and said: "It's about a cord." Except the memory of that cord seems about half as big as the cord of wood stacked up at the state fair.

At the Farm Queen contest, ignorance about farming seems to have driven the contestants crazy. They walk down a runway while a woman plays "Someone to Watch Over Me" on the piano. They wear formal gowns—some of them have made the gowns themselves. A guy in a tuxedo asks them questions about how to teach children about agriculture, how to educate urban dwellers, and girl after girl keeps making a speech that winds up in a tone of peeved wonderment: "We feed America!" It takes more than pretty to win here too.

Originally, it went the other way. American agricultural fairs took urban modernity to the farmer.

"Their 18th century founders believed that science could elevate farming along with every other human endeavor, and they tried to diffuse its light among the folk who worked the land. Fairs were a means of diffusion, supposedly one of the more effective, because they combined practical demonstrations of new methods, displays of improved livestock, and competition for premiums," writes Donald B. Marti in his definitive *Historical Directory of American Agricultural Fairs.*

Fairs are ancient and widespread—it's possible that the only country with no tradition of fairs was Japan, before it was opened to the West. The church sponsored religious fairs until about the fifteenth century, then abandoned them because they had grown too tawdry and commercial. Market fairs replaced them, though they declined toward the end of the eighteenth century. It took Americans, who have always understood the necessary bond between self-improvement and capitalism, to come up with the modern fair, where farmers could be fed the fruits of the Enlightenment and the Industrial Revolution.

The secret was competition—contests and prizes for everything farmers produced, from hay to homespun. Some of the first American fairs of this kind were held in the District of Columbia by the Columbia Agricultural Society, a group of local gentry. James Madison attended one in his homespun inaugural suit. The first state fair on the modern model was in Syracuse in 1841. By 1858 about 900 agricultural societies were holding fairs, and by 1913 there were more than 2,500 fairs in America, probably not much different than they are today, except for the electric lights. Like the fifteenth-century churchmen, Americans have been troubled by moral decay and honky-tonkery at the fairs. Newspapers of the 1840s and 1850s feature letters decrying the evils of horse racing and, worse, of "female equestrianism"—women racing sidesaddle. The *Boston Cultivator* wrote in 1858 that if "one of the fair contestants" knew "what was witnessed by thousands of rude men, unless we have greatly mistaken her character, she would blush for shame."

The trouble was, it was hard to get the farmers in to be educated without the bait of fun. Livestock shows with no midway draw a tiny fraction of fairs. On the other hand, the fair has to police the midway to keep out carnival stuff, the strippers, or the ever-popular freak shows featuring such favorites as the lobster people or the Man from Borneo who eats money (no slugs or Canadian currency, please).

Anybodyanybodyanybody, don't walk on by, give it a try, when the balloon pops you win a prize, one thin dime, one tenth of a dollar, slip it in, slide it in, how 'bout you now, two rings wins, we got a winner, right here, anybodyanybodyanybody, guess your weight, guess your age, I miss a few and I get a few, nobody's easy . . .

For all the fat clouds of aroma from the fried dough stands, and the flashing lights and screams from the Zipper or the Pirate ride, or the winners wandering around carrying huge stuffed animals, there's a starkness to it all.

At the High Striker, the men line up to try to drive a piece of metal to the top of a pole with a wooden mallet.

"C'mon, Wayne," the crowd yells.

Wayne takes off his shirt to reveal an assortment of tattoos and flesh the color of fluorescent light with muscle drifting somewhere beneath. Wayne takes up the mallet, taps the spot he's supposed to hit, and looks at the words climbing up the pole: MOMMA'S BOY, SISSY, HUFF 'N' PUFF, WHAT A WHIMP, LIVER LIPS, SWEET PEA, OLIVE OIL, POPEYE, HULK, ALMOST A MAN, or SUPER OCK. It's supposed to be SUPER JOCK, but the J fell off, up there on top of the pole. Wayne spits on his hands, puts his tongue between his teeth, turns his hat around backward, checks his wallet, which has a chain on it and is linked at the other end to at least forty-seven keys that hang next to his knife holster. He tries to dig his feet into the asphalt. This is the voodoo of male might.

"C'mon, Wayne."

He brings the mallet around in a terrible swift circle that passes about two inches to the right of the spot he's supposed to hit, and he hits the asphalt. A clean miss. None of his friends says a word. They know Wayne, and they know better. He'll swing again, of course, and ring the SUPER OCK bell on both tries. He'll even win a cigar, but it's that first swing he'll remember.

It takes more than pretty. This is the message of the fair, from the intimations of sausage among the squinty splendor of the Yorkshire Crosses and Chesters sprawled in their stalls in the hog shed to the losing tickets scattered at the race track like the confetti of a parade you hold when your army is defeated. One look at a cow tells you that, too, dairy cows in particular. They look like elk that held their breath and then melted—the gothic height and narrowness of their hipbones, the dropsical collapse of their bellies, and the way their hooves seem to lag when they walk, and leave the ground a second too late, and then they lift their heads and offer up a wildly pointless moo. Pigs, on the other hand, have a ballistic precision to them, like projectiles in some stop-action photograph in which they have just touched the target, which accounts for their flattened noses. Lambs come very close to getting by on pretty, especially in the judging of the Shepherd's Lead, in which little girls in wool dresses they made themselves lead their lambs around a ring—lambs they have sheared and carded until they get perfectly smooth and start to glitter a little, like the blankets you get in cheap motels.

These kids look you in the eye, size you up, and talk straight.

Did you know you were going to win with your Hampshire wether, Erika?

"Yep."

What kind of flowers are those in your hair?

"Fake."

It's as if they haven't gotten the word from Phil Donahue, Dr. Joyce Brothers, Ann Landers, and the Amalgamated Psychologists and Magazine Pundits of America that adolescence is a stormy and alienated time of when the best you can hope for is pretty.

"You can usually pick out the farm kids," says Rhonda Long, who is fifteen, and the daughter of a Black Angus breeder on the Eastern Shore of Maryland. "They have a lot of responsibility. My brother Rance is sixteen and we drive all over the country showing cattle. He dropped me off here and I'll stay in a motel for the next ten days."

She wears a red knit shirt and pearl earrings. She is brushing two cows that have been collecting championships so fast she can't count them.

I'm bringing the hair up, bringing it forward to make her look longer, and show off the bone structure. These'll never get slaughtered. We breed them by embryo-transplanting them. This one here, Lively Lady, say, she'll come in heat twelve times a year and produce eight to fifteen embryos every time. We buy the best quality semen, inseminate them, and nine days later you give them a spinal block and you go in and you flush them with 500 cc of saline solution. You filter that, and search it, then plant the fertilized eggs in recipient cows—lesser cows that have good milk for feeding the calves. You don't flush every month, you only do it two or three times a year, and sometimes the heat goes off regular—the weather, or they'll get sick. They'll be with us a long time. They get rinsed off twice a day. They stay in a heated barn in the winter, sometimes an air-conditioned barn in the summer. It's hard to give you a price on them because farmers always make a deal, it might be $20,000 and the first flush, that kind of thing.

The question is, how do we breed more Rhonda Longs? How is it possible not to think that if it were, in fact, the Last Day on Earth and those hot air balloons were leaving for another planet, and you had to pick people to go on them, and start the world all over again somewhere else, you would probably have Rhonda Long very high on your list of candidates?

You pull up to the summer house after driving all day Saturday in the heat. You look around. None of the neighbors are back from swimming yet and the front-walk petunias look neglected in the glare—there's a festive but deserted quality to things. You open the door. The house is hot. The cleaning woman, who lives in the village, closed all the windows that morning in case there was a thunderstorm.

"Open some windows!" everybody says.

The heat is full of the smell of blankets, sand, mildew, a freshly swept fireplace and damp couch cushions. There is a buckled map hanging on the wall. There is a pile of the last tenant's newspapers next to the fireplace. There is a sense of possibilities. You turn on a light, and turn it off again. You turn on the cold water, which runs hot. Then you carry your suitcase upstairs.

Your bedroom is very hot. You open the suitcase. You packed it only last night, but it looks like an ungainly time capsule from another life. You wonder why you brought those dress shoes. You sense that once again, you won't finish that copy of *Anna Karenina*. You don't care. You like not caring because it means you are starting to be On Vacation. All happy summer houses are alike—you never wear your dress shoes or finish *Anna Karenina* in any of them. You pull out a bureau drawer. You smell the parched wood and the old shelf paper thumbtacked to it, a smell that is ancient and utterly personal, like the smell of the double-ended wooden spoons you once ate Dixie Cups with.

This smell lasts till you open the window. The wind fills the room instantly, like a cool noise. You look at the excellent sky over the tree-tops. You hear a flag rolling and snapping, with the hollowness that sound gets near water. You breathe deeply. You take off your clothes. You put on your bathing suit. You have every intention of going swimming before dinner. Just for a moment, though, you lie down on the unmade bed. You close your eyes. You make a mental note to water those petunias. You are in your summer house. You are asleep.

Summer houses are where you believe that you become the Real You, and the rest of the year you're a ghost in the unreal city, wandering around like somebody looking for a car lost in a shopping center parking lot. Back home you get mail addressed to "Dear Occupant," "Dear Student," and "Dear Lucky Winner." You work in places where you have to wear a picture of yourself on a card hung around your neck so people will know that you're you. You go to schools that train you to take tests that show how well they trained you to take the tests. You are a sort of statistical ectoplasm. Everything is rules.

At the summer house, everything feels like tradition instead, even if you've never been there before: drinking drinks you will never drink anywhere else (brandy shrubs, Pimm's Cups), Mom always going first in the outdoor shower so she gets the sun-warmed water, playing Parcheesi on rainy days, using jelly jars for drinking glasses.

Everything is permitted (as long as you hang up your bathing suit and don't track sand in the house) and everything is real. Your parents won't let you take a bus at home, but here you can take the boat all the way across the lake to town. You feel like a kid in a Disney movie, orphaned and entitled at the same time, wanting nothing more than the blond hair and the impossible tans of the summer carpenters, who have great trucks and beach parties (which, as it turns out, are not quite as great as you'd thought they'd be).

Summer houses are tiny cottages on motorboat lakes, jostling with all the other cottages in a kind of laundry-flapping, lotion-sticky, barbecue proximity that verges on the sexual. They are mammoth old brown-shingled dowagers groaning in the wind off the ocean. They are Adirondack camps with rusting screens that stick out like beer bellies, and Minnesota lake houses that have no locks on the doors. They are the gloomy dinosaurs of Mantoloking, New Jersey, asleep amid the hydrangeas. They are cabins, camps, lodges, farmhouses, A-frames, ex-barns, not so much built as moored on the edge of dunes, lakes, valleys, cliffs, harbors, and national parks. They are more Northern than Southern, more Eastern than Western, not so much architecture as an opportunity for metaphysical multiplication of porches, decks, and outdoor staircases. They are cottages with locks that are stiff from the salt air, and very old cars cooking inside closed garages. They are group houses where you bridge the psychic gap between fraternity parties and the vacations you will someday take your children on. They are rental houses with the mysterious owner's closet, which is locked until you find the key and open it one rainy afternoon to find only some canned tomatoes, a butterfly collection, and a bottle of Old Mr. Boston sloe gin.

They have pasts, instant history: the crayonned j'accuse you find under a porch cushion—"Susan is a liar"—or the old man at the boatyard showing you a walrus skull he pulled up in a fishing net. Who was Susan, when was the walrus? There are the Indians, animals, and primeval cataclysms that left their names on these places: Chincoteague, Seal Cove, Mackinaw Island, Crater Lake, Thunder Mountain. You return to a tribal comity. Instead of asking for my binoculars, you ask for the binoculars. Not my air mattress but the air mattress. Everyone's. The tribe's. You all pick blueberries. You all shoot the .22.

"Your mother is the shot in this family," you tell the kids, putting the tin cans back on the fence posts.

"It's not true," she says. "You say that every year."

"It's true!" the children shout.

With an air of bewildered and dutiful modesty she knocks down each can, even the little orange juice can, with one shot. Everyone cheers.

"You're all such fools about this," she says. "Every year."

They are houses on islands in Maine where a north wind brings down light so intense it seems on the verge of fragmenting into chunks the size of ping-pong balls, a light that also creates shadows with a pleasantly alarming coolness. In September, these houses are shut for the winter, sometimes in a ritual known as an "Augusta closing," in which you turn the mirrors to the walls, put a stone in the toilet, put newspaper up the chimney and cover the lampshades, although nobody is quite sure why anymore, any more than they know why it's called an "Augusta closing."

They are where: You find a faded forty-eight-star flag in a drawer and raise it every morning. You eat corn on the cob and taste the mosquito repellent on your hands. You fall in love on purpose. You save your dog from drowning. You sit out on the porch on a starry night, the whole family singing "The Battle Hymn of the Republic." You secretly paint your nose white with zinc oxide and look in the mirror to see if you look as good as the lifeguard, and you don't. You feel you have betrayed something not because you lost your retainer but because you had to go back to the city to replace it.

They are houses you rent one after another, a new one every summer until all the rusty hibachis, thundering shower stalls, and landlady-needlepoint samplers become the same.

They are houses you go back to year after year.

"It never changes," your father says as you drive through town, past the five-and-dime with its beach chairs and umbrellas out front, past the Dairy Queen where you always buy a cone for the dog too.

"They painted the windmill at the miniature golf course," your mother says.

"Well, dammit, it needed painting," says your father, who is irritable in the manner of sentimental men.

"But they didn't even have a windmill last year," your brother says, thus beginning a debate on which miniature golf course you're talking about, and is miniature golf the same as Putt-Putt, and if so what is pitch 'n' putt? This debate will become a sly running joke through the whole stay at the house, where, fortunately, nothing has changed (as your father notes in a voice that invites no contradiction) except for some new planks in the porch, and still more copies of Reader's Digest Condensed Books on the mantel.

They are where you fall deepest into the ur-illusion of America, which is that you can endlessly invent and reinvent yourself. You bring along your old brushes and paints from college, and the skirt you used to paint in, and suddenly the colors don't turn to mud and the trees and houses don't look like they're floating. Is it possible that you're really an artist after all? You make the mistake of asking your husband.

"Remember those pictures we saw at the art gallery?" you ask. "Isn't this every bit as good as they are? Really. I want to know. Tell me why it isn't."

"Beats me," he says.

They are a sort of duty-free zone for drinkers, a place where the back-brain demon-philosopher of alcoholism lets them have all they want. "Sun's over the yardarm," they say at noon. Or they tear open the beers as soon as the tennis game ends. Or they wait all day for cocktail hour.

After a while there arises the tocsin of ice rattling in empty glasses.

"Freshen that up for you?"

"Just a dollop?"

"How about a dividend?"

The children watch their parents drink. They don't understand the chemical smugness their parents feel, and sense a sudden happiness in them instead, something attained and enshrined out there in the adirondack chairs, under the maple tree. They believe this happiness will be theirs too, when they grow up.

Summer houses are the last WASP outposts of johnnycake breakfasts and cold-water plunges; houses that were built as desperate nineteenth-century attempts to hold onto strengths and virtues that only remain now in the attic as ghosts hovering over old oars, Mercer Beasley tennis rackets, a broken banjo, and albums of sepia photographs glued to black paper with "corners"—pictures of men standing on a long-lost yawl, puffing out their chests; of a beefy cook and the feebleminded daughter she always claimed was her niece.

The families try to keep them going as much out of noblesse oblige as anything else, even though they bitterly resent how America fails to appreciate its rich. As years go by, the winters come to be full of phone calls debating a new roof, and is there any sense in trying to fix the sailboat? And what with the taxes and the burglary last winter, wouldn't it be easier to sell the place? The anguish! Whole childhoods will vanish, along with the ultimate promise of a summer house—that it will always be there to redeem the gray dwindlings of modern life. But ultimately, it goes on the market. And no one in the whole family has the money to buy it.

What happened to their strength, their virtue and, oh, their money?

Summer houses are where: You see a copperhead behind the springhouse and feel the whole world go hard, wise, and dark on you as you back away from it. You lie awake listening to the weather-vane goose spin its wings in the dark. You vow that this time you will not turn back into a ghost of yourself when you get back to the city, even though you know you have vowed this before. You compete to see who can imitate the local accent best. You roll up a straw rug to sweep, and you see perfect little rows of sand. You will remember the feel of the lawn —bristly, because you walked on it barefoot. You will remember the smell of the house—a combination of mothballs, caramel, pine trees, citronella, and the faint vegetable breath of that slow sink drain with its brass screen.

You go to the inn for dinner.

"We eat here every summer," your sister says to the waitress. "And I always have a milkshake."

"That's nice, hon," the waitress says. "What flavor you want this year?"

Ah, the locals. Kind as they may be, there is a tightening in their eyes when they see you have taken the romance of the summer house so far that you believe you belong to this place, that you spend eleven months of the year somewhere else, but you live here.

You say: "Someday, I want to winter over here. It must be beautiful."

They say: "Maybe so. I spend as much of it as I can in Florida."

The locals warn you not to go clamming or musseling—the red tide is in, bearing hideous disease. You are grateful until you notice that the red tide has a strange way of coming in about the time the summer people arrive, and leaving when they leave.

The locals keep breaking the faith—building condominiums or putting a neon sign on the store. Even if you own property, you can't stop them, because the town meetings are held over the winter, when you aren't there. Sometimes their children go off to college and end up living in the Unreal City, and in a voice carefully modulated to avoid condescension, you congratulate them. But you are sick at heart. Don't they understand?

As it happens, they ask the same question about you.

There is often an offspring of a rich family, usually a boy, who flounders for a while in the city and then asks to try living in the summer house year-round, and be a carpenter, a fisherman, a potter. This is very romantic. It is also a symptom of the disease known in the Northeast as "WASP Rot." If he sticks it out, the whole winter, with the pipes freezing, the wires down in the blizzard, the chainsaw broken, the locals will look at him come spring with grudging acceptance and think: "His family must be disappointed in him."

Summer houses are where you believe you are who you are and the world is what it is, but then you have to leave.

The last morning comes. It is always the same. Breakfast is no good. The dog runs away. Down at the store there is a goodbye said to a lifeguard, a goodbye accompanied by lifted eyebrows and the word "Write."

You stack the newspapers by the fireplace. You count your film canisters, knowing that the pictures will puzzle you yet again with their pallid failure to limn the sunset after the thunderstorm, or the potato race at Old Home Day. You note with regret that you never watered the front-walk petunias—this omission somehow shows you don't have as much claim on this place as you'd hoped. Did you pack your dress shoes? Your copy of *Anna Karenina*?

The dog is found. The woman from the village arrives to clean.

"We hate to leave," you say.

"You've had nice weather," she says. "Right up till today."

"Oh, we have. But this morning the radio said thunderstorms."

"I'll close all the windows," she says.

They all wanted out, we all want in.

"Here the fortunate ones through money or influence or luck might obtain exit visas," says the narrator, just after the shot of the globe turning in its Nazi-ridden agony. "But the others wait in Casablanca and wait and wait and wait."

It's the others we envy, strangely enough. We want to be waiting with them in Rick's Cafe Americain, pawning rings, lighting cigarettes and drinking Veuve Clicquot. We want to be wry and existential, with prices on our heads and bodies worth putting a price on.

We want pasts worthy of Humphrey Bogart's white dinner jacket and whiskey despairs.

"What is your nationality?" asks the Nazis' Major Strasser.

"I'm a drunkard," says Rick.

"And that makes Rick a citizen of the world," says Captain Renault, played by Claude Rains.

Now, more than half a century after it came out, *Casablanca* not only shows us the past we wish we had, it is part of the past, itself. It makes us nostalgic not only for the good-war glamour it portrays, but also for all the times we've seen it before. It lets us savor a no-exit hell a little like college, full of a sense of nostalgia and destiny at the same time. O lost Edens! O the glamour of doom! *Casablanca* makes us jaded sophomores again, declaring ourselves world-weary and corrupt, but always seeing our natural goodness peek through in the end. It's a world where the air is heavy with poignancy and alarm and we could live every moment as if we're in love.

We want to be freedom fighters in Ingrid Bergman's satin gown and diamond ear clips. We want to believe in nothing, like Sydney Greenstreet's Ferrari, swatting flies while he buys and sells human lives amid the mystical corruptions of what used to be called the Orient. We want to believe in everything, like Paul Henreid's Victor Laszlo, the resistance hero.

"If we stop fighting our enemies, the world will die," Laszlo says.

"What of it?" asks Rick. "Then it'll be out of its misery."

"Do you know how you sound, Monsieur Blaine? Like a man who's trying to convince himself of something he doesn't believe in his heart. Each of us has a destiny. For good or evil."

Casablanca takes the idea of a spiritual quest in the desert and gives it irony and a table in a nightclub. It has more redemptions than TV evangelism. Sluttish Yvonne may go out with a Nazi, but when the band strikes up the *Marseillaise,* she's singing. Corrupt Captain Renault redeems himself with a lie. The lost love between Bogart and Bergman is found again in a paradox worthy of a Shakespeare sonnet: "We'll always have Paris." And we believe it! Who can not get goose bumps just thinking about him drinking away in the small-hours cafe, saying, "She's coming back. I know she's coming back." And then not only does she come back, a miraculous white aura in the doorway, but we believe that too, the impossible dream of every spurned lover.

Here is the secret of *Casablanca* as a great American movie: In a country where Heaven is a dream of endless second chances, all of these major characters get to have their cake and eat it too, their love affairs and their purity, their money and their principles. Everyone a winner! Door prizes for all!

It is one of the great accidents in movie history. Everything could have gone wrong and almost nothing did. Ronald Reagan and Ann Sheridan were supposed to get the parts of Rick and Ilsa. An alternate ending had Ilsa staying behind while Victor escaped to America. Ruin lurked in every story conference. Warner Bros. took no particular interest in it, and ticket sales were moderate, but it won three Academy Awards. The higher-brow critics looked on it with amusement. James Agee wrote: "Apparently, 'Casablanca' is working up a rather serious reputation as a fine melodrama. Why?"

It might not have acquired its cult status if it hadn't been for the assassination of Kennedy, with his witty tough-guy appeal, and the Vietnam War, which made us hunger for a time when there were things worth dying for. It got to be such a staple at the Brattle Theater in Cambridge, Massachusetts, that the bar in the basement was named the Blue Parrot, after the cafe where Greenstreet swats those flies. Alienated Harvard students watched it over and over, memorizing the great ironic lines and marveling at a world where a good war was possible.

Alastair Cooke once said that Bogart was "the romantic democratic answer to Hitler's New Order. . . . He is the first romantic hero who used the gangster's means to achieve our ends." Kenneth Tynan wrote that "the Bogart cult in its present form—classless and international—dates from the Cold War. We trusted him because he was a wary loner who belonged to nobody, had personal honor . . . and would therefore survive."

In 1992, with both the Nazis and the Communists safely in the dustbin, Bogart survives splendidly by merely being so American. Like Jay Gatsby, he has a mysterious past with a lost love. Like Huck Finn, he lights out for the territories. Like a Hemingway hero, he has been wounded. He has retreated to an ideal boy's world of utter independence—no family, no love, no past or future, just Bogie and his pals. It's this world that Ilsa destroys when she walks into the cafe on the arm of Victor Laszlo and brings back the pain of lost love in Paris.

Dooley Wilson, who sings "As Time Goes By," tries to save Rick: "We'll take the car and drive all night. We'll get drunk. We'll go fishing and stay away until she's gone."

Fishing! He is playing Jim to Bogart's Huck, trying to shield him from the corruptions of the world and the ambiguities of womankind. As for Bergman's Ilsa, she embodies the martyrdom of misunderstanding—if only Rick knew the truth, he wouldn't have suffered so, but she couldn't tell him the truth. She is guilty and innocent at the same time, a paradox she illustrates with every sigh, every look of pained bewilderment.

How astonishing that unlike the other beauties of half a century ago—Crawford or Garbo, say—Bergman has not hardened into a hieroglyph, an anachronism that makes the people of the past seem like some tribe whose taste in women is a little laughable. No. Bergman has stayed fresh, maybe because beauty to her is more of a verb than a noun. She never seems quite sure how she's going to react to the next line. She is eagerness and fatigue, passion and self-consciousness all at once. Until she appears, the movie is a strident and timebound melodrama. But of all the gin joints in all the towns in all the world, she walks into Rick's, redeeming not just Rick and a conquered Europe but the whole movie. Suddenly Rick's sorrow is more than a plot device. The movie acquires a languid, flickering resonance like an aquarium in a darkened room—or is that just the wonderfully dramatic lighting, and all the tricky camera angles through the Moorish masonry and exotica?

For Ingrid Bergman, civilization is a tragedy that must be borne, kind of like being married to Victor Laszlo, who is the secret villain of *Casablanca*. Yes, he is the handsome, noble hero of the resistance, the suave, principled hope of millions enslaved by Third Reich tyranny. But Victor is to Ilsa what Ashley Wilkes is to Scarlett O'Hara. He's the son every mother is supposed to want and is slightly disgusted to get. Of course, we admire him, we wish him well, but his future is foreclosed by his horrible European maturity. To the extent that we like Ilsa, we're glad to see him cuckolded by Rick, and to the extent that we share Rick's cynicism about Ilsa, we're glad to see her sentenced to a lifetime with Victor.

To the extent that we distrust romantic love as a virtue, we are delighted to see everyone reject it in favor of higher principle, as in

Rick's line to Ilsa that "the problems of three little people don't amount to a hill of beans in this crazy world. Someday you'll understand that." The movie makes us feel virtuous, in other words. American audiences love to feel virtuous.

But we get to have love too, or at least the characters do. Like Romeo and Juliet, Tristan and Isolde, Rhett and Scarlett, Rick and Ilsa can never be united—can we really picture them living in some suburb, with the kids, the lawn? No. True romantic love is doomed by definition. The sword has to lie between Tristan and Isolde.

At the end, the eternal Huck Finn boyhood is preserved when Rick walks off into the fog with his new sidekick Captain Renault, saying "Louis, I think this is the beginning of a beautiful friendship."

We'll always have *Casablanca*.

wasps

Once in a while, some white knight arises in America to save the WASPs from their despair, but he succeeds only in getting hammered on till even his friends laugh at him—Elliot Richardson running for the Senate, Endicott (Chub) Peabody losing elections in both Massachusetts and New Hampshire, or John Lindsay as mayor of New York.

There was a day when the WASPs ruled, and everybody else was the exception that proved their right to rule. But for the past century they have been slinking back into a kind of seedy twilight like another American archetype, the Indians, until they exist largely as a collection of legends—*The Great Gatsby,* the old-boy founders of the CIA, Skull and Bones, the Lodges speaking only to the Cabots—along with bestselling exploitations such as *The Official Preppy Handbook* and souvenir stands such as Ralph Lauren's Polo stores.

WASPs are fair game. No one worries about offending WASP ethnic sensitivities, any more than they worry about offending Gypsies or the Welsh when they say someone gypped them or welshed on a bet. The clichés of the WASP live on, smoldering in a sort of dump fire of the American soul, fueled by grudges—of Catholics against Protestants, Western farmers against Eastern money men, one side of the tracks against the other, immigrants against Brahmins, the valley against the hill, Southerners against Yankees.

In a book called *The WASP Mystique,* Richard Robertiello and Diana Hoguet wrote: "Fantasies of spankings, shame and public humiliation . . . seem particularly common to WASPs." Would they have considered writing such a thing about any other ethnic group? In *Miami and the Siege of Chicago,* Norman Mailer wrote that WASPs "were the most powerful force in America, and yet they were a psychic island. If they did not find a bridge, they could only grow more insane each year, like a rich nobleman in an empty castle chasing elves and ogres with his stick." In 1971 Michael Novak, now a neoconservative at the American Enterprise Institute, wrote in *The Rise of the Unmeltable Ethnics* that WASPs were so out of touch with reality of their power that the solution was: "To wit, let every WASP lady by law, in yearly ritual, in full public gaze, strangle an abandoned cat with no other assistance but her bare hands. Let every WASP male wring the neck of a chicken until its head pulls bloodily free, or in some other way, sticky with felt violence, get the feeling of changing history and mastering the environment."

The word didn't even come into common circulation until the 1960s, when a sociologist named E. Digby Baltzell, at the University of Pennsylvania, picked it up in his book *The Protestant Establishment.* It got popular fast—its hint of petulant insect violence was irresistible, and it appealed to the sort of minds that categorize people by their handwriting or astrological sign.

In a short story called "Winter Dreams," F. Scott Fitzgerald wrote: "He knew the sort of men they were—the men who when he first went to college had entered from the great prep schools with graceful clothes and the deep tan of healthy summers. He had seen that, in one sense, he was better than these men. He was newer and stronger. Yet in acknowledging to himself that he wished his children to be like them he was admitting that he was but the rough, strong stuff from which they eternally sprang."

Envy is the hatred of something you want, the resentment of something you admire, a contradiction that will destroy itself if given a chance. Not only have non-WASP Americans envied WASPs, but the WASPs have pulled off the neat trick of seeming to envy themselves, feeding as they do on the New England boiled dinner of both self-loathing and smugness. This sort of contradiction is what Fitzgerald epitomized in *The Great Gatsby* with the effete brute Tom Buchanan, who has a "harsh, defiant wistfulness." And: "Not even the effeminate swank of his riding clothes could hide the enormous power of his body. . . . It was a body capable of enormous leverage—a cruel body."

There aren't very many of them. According to 1988 data gathered by Chicago's NORC (National Opinion Research Center), 13.7 percent of Americans say they are of English and Scottish origin—for comparison, about 12 percent of Americans are black. Even when you count people both wholly and partly of English ancestry, they total about 50 million, about the same as people who define themselves as wholly or partly German. They are not that rich, taken as a whole. Granted, 9.9 percent of households of English or Scottish ancestry have incomes over $60,000 a year, compared with 8.1 percent of all American households. But median household incomes in the 1980 census place WASPs—at $16,746—behind eleven other groups, six of them usually considered to be minorities. One reason is that a lot more white Anglo-Saxon Protestants live in trailers in Appalachia than houses in Greenwich, Connecticut. But no one thinks of these people as WASPs. (Lower-class white Anglo-Saxon Protestants aren't called WASPs. They are called hillbillies, crackers, swamp Yankees, white trash, or rednecks.)

This is not to say that WASPs haven't wielded power culturally, politically, and financially, but most important, the WASP is a stereotype, a bit of American mythology, like the cowboy, the Indian, the yeoman farmer, or the scrubwoman who puts all of her children through medical school. The word summons up good breeding (horses, roses, people) and things that are right (people, addresses, forks); a people graceful under fire and awkward on the dance floor; a

world of alcoholic crypto-Brits with their monograms in little yacht-
ing flags on the sides of their station wagons; Ivy Leaguers ashamed of
any mark higher than a B-minus; Puritans venting their ids on fox
hunting; thin-lipped debutantes with last names for first names (Whitney, Paige, Kendall), and God as a sort of Julia Child without the
sense of humor; a world of scholars of crossword puzzles and ge-
nealogies, of a careless, even shabby ur-Yankee elite beating the rest of
us over our heads with their modesty, prudence, thrift, and sense of
entitlement.

In *Love Story,* a 1970 movie that depends on the audience's un-
questioning belief in the WASP myth, Ali MacGraw, playing Jenny
Cavalieri, tells Ryan O'Neal, playing Oliver Barrett IV, that she can
tell he went to prep school because he looks "stupid and rich." Then
she echoes the yearning and resentment of millions of Americans
when she says: "Why is it I suddenly wish my name were Abigail
Adams or Wendy WASP?" And: "I love not just you but your name
and your numeral. They're part of what you are."

In the 1973 movie *The Way We Were,* blond, blue-eyed campus
hero Hubbell Gardner writes a short story called "The All-American
Smile." It begins: "In a way he was like the country he lived in
everything came too easily to him." In the course of the movie, which
chronicles the troubled romance of WASP Hubbell, played by Robert
Redford, and Jewish Katy Moroski, played by Barbra Streisand,
Hubbell will write a novel titled "A Country Made of Ice Cream." He
takes Katy to a party, saying with ironic WASP self-consciousness:
"We can all be decadent, eat eggs Benedict and vote Republican."

Sydney Biddle Barrows, New York's "Mayflower Madam," told
the women in her brothel to dress as if their grandfathers were taking
them to lunch at "21"—the WASP as sexual fetish! *The Official
Preppy Handbook,* by Lisa Birnbach, is a guide to tribal ritual and
trappings: things to monogram, things not to monogram, twenty
slang terms for drunkenness, how to acquire the right accent and
throw a tailgate picnic, and where to buy a camel's hair coat. Designer Ralph Lauren, a Jew from the Bronx, has created a temple to
the myth of WASP country life in the old Rhinelander mansion at

72nd and Madison in Manhattan. He has decorated it with worn oriental rugs, wooden-shafted golf clubs, brass telescopes, tattered leather suitcases, a worn-out teddy bear on a wicker bed, photographs of college rowers, old boxing gloves, a tartan Bible for $500, a battered 1920 pith helmet (O, lost empire) for $135, all of it having the air of something doomed from the start and knowing it.

In the late nineteenth century, Boston patricians saw their bloodlines falling back under waves of immigration. One of them, Sen. Henry Cabot Lodge, argued that immigration would cause "a great and perilous change in the very fabric of our race." Francis A. Walker, president of MIT, despaired that control of America was being taken away from "those who are descended from the tribes that met under the oak trees of old Germany to make laws and choose chieftains." In 1903 John Dos Passos, father of the novelist, could still say: "The twentieth century is par excellence the Anglo-Saxon century. . . . It is now manifest that to this great race is entrusted the civilization and Christianization of the world." But when the immigrants took control of the cities, rich WASPs tended to respond by either hiding on Fifth Avenue or fleeing to suburbs such as Far Hills, New Jersey, or the north shore of Long Island. They adopted wholesale an image of English country life that led them to be pretend-farmers on country estates. (In the movie *Wall Street,* greed-freak Gordon Gekko, played by Michael Douglas, says: "That's what you've got to remember about WASPs—they love animals but hate people.") They changed, in the formulation of Baltzell, from being an aristocracy with a mission of ruling well to being a caste seeking only to protect its own prerogatives while it mourned its former glory. Robert Bacon, a Harvard athlete and then a partner of J. P. Morgan, went off to World War I saying: "The world—our world—is not lucky enough to be snuffed out as was Pompeii. We have got to go through a long sickening decadence."

In the 1920s a number of books such as *The Passing of the Great Race,* by Madison Grant, had a vogue that provoked this passage in *Gatsby*: " 'Civilization's going to pieces,' broke out Tom violently. 'I've gotten to be a terrible pessimist about things. Have you read

'The Rise of the Colored Empires' by this man Goddard? . . . It's up to us, who are the dominant race, to watch out or these other races will have control of things. The idea is that we're Nordics . . . and we've produced all the things that go to make civilization—oh, science and art, and all that. Do you see?' "

The cure was the ordeal, a sort of grail quest in search of yourself. Teddy Roosevelt tested his manhood as a cowboy in the Dakotas and a Rough Rider in Cuba. Rich young WASPs were keen indeed on World War I, forming the Lafayette Escadrille and fighting and dying in large numbers. At St. Paul's School in Concord, New Hampshire, a monument to those who died in that war shows an Angel of Death of such voluptuosity that one senses the school and its upper-class supporters were grateful for the slaughter—that the war had redeemed them in their own eyes.

One St. Paul's WASP who died a heroic World War I flier was Hobey Baker. According to one account, Baker was such a gentleman when he played hockey at Princeton that he refused to believe that anyone would foul him. "On the rare occasion when he was forced to admit he had been deliberately fouled, he was driven to tears." George Bush was a heroic World War II flier who left Connecticut to compete with the oilmen of Texas—but still he was called a wimp in the 1988 presidential campaign.

Another example of the hero-wimp: In a turn-of-the-century short story by Frank Norris, two men are in love with the same girl. One is Jack Brunt, "a tower of leathery muscles ... a man whom other men, children and some women like," and the other is Wesley Shotover, blond and blue-eyed, with "almost the face of a girl, smooth, guiltless of beard" and the character of a frivolous type who smokes cigarettes, eats chocolates, and drinks vermouth. But Brunt has bad heredity, including an immigrant grandfather, while Shotover's ancestors moved among the Founding Fathers. When a gang of opium-crazed Chinese attacks the porch where both men sit with the girl they love, the muscular Brunt retreats inside the house while the well-bred Shotover drives them off with a whip.

Blood tells, is the message. How loathsome. But of course that's a lot of the message that anybody is sending when using the word "WASP." No one objects to the racism or ethnophobia, however, because WASPs are too useful an enemy to ruin by describing them with the delicacy we reserve for other ethnic groups. Americans feel much more comfortable analyzing people by ethnicity instead of class. Talking about class smacks of Marxism, and it goes against the superstition that America is a classless society. Better to be a racist than a communist. Hence the usefulness of "WASP," which uses ethnic and religious terms to describe what most people think of as the upper classes, along with the middle-class people who got to America early, and defined the ethos we still live with.

Now they all feel a little displaced, superannuated, awkward. They're proud that they built America, proud of their links with England, but they've learned to be ashamed of that bad business with the Indians and the slaves, the mill town strike-busting, and so on. WASPs used to brag about their footprints on Plymouth Rock. Now, it's only for the clowns and hustlers of WASPery, in the manner of George Plimpton—author, amateur sportsman, professional WASP— going on television and using his Locust Valley lockjaw accent (and much-touted Mayflower roots) to sell popcorn.

Then again, only another WASP would find George a bit much, so what difference does it make?

Notes from Randolph, New Hampshire, taken on the porch of a brown-shingled house in a valley beneath Mounts Madison and Adams.

The notes are taken on a yellow pad braced on the arm of a wicker chair equipped with footrest and swing-out highball caddy. An extremely strenuous hike up into those mountains has been planned, even announced, but now that the rest of his family has gone off swimming, the hiker finds himself alone on the porch, procrastinating. Given the prospect of a forest of black flies, endless sweat, and thigh muscles on fire, he finds himself fascinated by the clouds.

It's a good day for them, like a spring day, back and forth from sun to rain to sun again, a sort of acuteness to things. As the old guy down at Lowe's gas station said this morning when asked for a weather prediction: "Off and on." Birches twinkle, the porch drips, there's a mildewy smell of wet moss and woods hit by sunlight. There's the sound of a logging truck way out on Route 2. After a week in this house, the procrastinating hiker has come to terms with the trucks. As Hawthorne wrote, while taking notes in a woods near Concord, Massachusetts, on July 27, 1844, and hearing a locomotive in the stillness, "It brings the noisy world into the midst of our slumbrous peace. As our thoughts repose again, after this interruption, we find ourselves gazing up at the leaves, and comparing their different aspect, the beautiful diversity of green."

Or the clouds. Fortunately, the clouds are particularly diverse today. They rise over the ridgeline like periscopes, the hiker decides. They sneak up the side of the mountain with the desperate sensuality of a dog pushing its way onto a couch, an inch at a time. They back over the summit with cautious horizontality, like a mechanic on a dolly rolling himself under a car.

Very interesting. The air is nice and fresh, like air you breathe through a screen window after a thunderstorm when there are little squares of water in the screen. A bird lifts from an evergreen next to the porch. There is the sound of a logging truck down on Route 2, an anxious noise, up and up as it climbs the hill toward Gorham, a chord with no resolution, the sonic equivalent of a worried shrug. After a while it's quiet again, except for the wet rush of a small wind through the trees.

There is hiking to be done, but there are also clouds arcing over the mountains like sheep jumping over a fence in a cartoon version of what you imagine when you're trying to get to sleep. This is noted on the yellow pad. Clouds drag across the slope of Madison like spun glass on a Christmas tree, the stuff called angel hair, a prickly integument, little pieces snagging in the branches. Wisps at the bottom of the cloud mass race to keep up with the rest of it, the mother. Clouds move with the ridiculous invulnerability of metal ducks in a shooting gallery. Clouds slip away over the ridge like a snake disappearing into weeds.

There is the hearty, busy noise of a couple of trucks. One sounds its air horn. The hiker checks his watch. It is beginning to look like a shorter hike might be in order. Certainly at this hour it's too late to contemplate getting up above tree line, up to the rock over a mile in the air, a sort of imagined quality to it at this distance, viewed from a wicker chair on a screened porch. Besides, what if it rains again? As it happens, the sun is vanishing, gloom is gathering with a weighty, shadowless clarity that makes the sunlight that vanished only moments ago seem like an illusion, the sort of thing you're a little embarrassed to have believed in, in your youth. The wind picks up. This is reality, this gloom. How could the hiker ever have thought otherwise? Clouds come in with the proprietary air—almost angrily so—of people arriving at a cocktail party they had to fight to be invited to. And here's the fat woman at the party, spreading her arms and her mammoth caftan with the raffishness of a woman eager to prove with her vigor that she doesn't care that she was invited not only despite her fat but because of her money.

Then sunlight verges, verges, verges and suddenly it's back, strangely awkward, and the forest is divided into a million halves—all the little lights, all the little shadows. The porch drips. A bird flies. The light has the poignant quality of something you know will end, but it doesn't end.

A patch of blue appears behind Mount Madison, an impossible blue, like a rejected swatch at a dressmaker's where the customer, sitting in a chair with an edgy fascination not unlike that of the hiker on his porch, says, "I wish I could wear that blue, but . . ."

A truck gets over the top of Gorham hill and comes down Route 2 throbbing with relief, "now dying away and then reviving like the beat of a partridge, conveying travelers from Boston to the country," as Thoreau put it when he sat in his woods and heard a locomotive. He also said, "When I hear the iron horse make the hills echo with his snort like thunder, shaking the earth with his feet, and breathing fire and smoke from his nostrils (what kind of winged horse or fiery dragon they will put into the new Mythology I don't know), it seems as if the earth had got a race now worthy to inhabit it."

What more justification for truck noise could the hiker ask for?

A cloud prostrates itself before the summit of Adams with an Oriental abjectness. A cloud moves over the top of Madison with the slow thoroughness of some kind of mollusk scouring a reef for algae. The hiker looks at his watch again and considers that if he doesn't get a move on, he won't get any hiking in at all, he'll just have to join his family at the swimming hole. A cloud smears across the upper slope of Mount Madison in the manner of a deck of cards spread across a table by a magician.

The hiker notes this on his pad. A blue jay darts. The sun stays out and the afternoon acquires a sudden endless quality. There is time, perhaps, for a brisk hike. On the other hand, the water down at the swimming hole is very, very cold, and if he swims out to the float and back, he'll feel just as virtuous as if he'd climbed to Dome Rock and gotten bitten by any number of black flies. He wonders if his family has started home yet—he likes company. He wonders where his bathing suit is. A cloud skims the summit of Madison with the happy silliness of an alligator dreaming it can fly if it spreads its legs like wings and arches its back just so.

tract mansions

Tract mansions are those huge, solemn, neo–Falcon Crest, post-split-level, stately home statements that started erupting from tiny treeless pieces of former farmland all over America during the 1980s. Someday they will memorialize the frantic striving and get-mine optimism of their era the way the great dinosaurs of Victorian architecture memorialize the conspicuous consumption of a hundred years ago.

You can find them outside cities in the areas that like to think of themselves as soon to be or having once been "hunt country," places where stalks still stand in abandoned cornfields, awaiting the bulldozer. You drive out past your city's beltway, out till you get to gas stations where you don't have to pay before you pump, and they begin to appear—huge, exposed things, like beached whales, a little pathetic like a woman waiting for her date to arrive at a restaurant.

They look as if they were delivered rather than built, and they seem strangely circumscribed, sitting on no more land than it takes to hold the deck and the exhaust fans for the trilevel air-conditioning.

Who buys these things?

"We did a study that broke down our market into bulls, tigers, lambs, and owls, and we found that it's 75 percent tigers," says Susan Garmzaban, the sales manager at a house called "The Gorham," north of Washington, D.C. She describes herself as a "tiger-bull combination" and says that tigers are energetic people who like red cars and "dazzling master suites." Bulls are stately types who drive black Mercedeses. Lambs like houses that are cozy and warm, and the owls want to know everything about the wiring, the R-factors of the insulation, things like that. "The worst combination to sell to is a couple that's bull and owl. The easiest is a tiger married to a lamb."

Is there anything tigers particularly want?

"They want the ooh-ahh appeal. They want people to see that marble foyer and the pillars and go, 'Ooh! Ahh!' They want them to say, 'Wow, look what they bought!' The overall feel has to be opulent."

Where do they get their ideas of what they want?

"*Falcon Crest* and *Dallas*."

"Tara," says Garmzaban's fellow salesman, Jeffrey David.

"And Tara," says Garmzaban. "When they tour this house I point to the curving staircase and I tell them, 'This is a sort of *Gone With the Wind* staircase.'"

"The builder is trying to find the buyer's optimal level of fantasy within their budget," David says. He walks across the office and points to a drawing of the Gorham.

"The great thing about this design is that it isn't a little anything. It's got Federal, it's got Colonial, it's got Georgian, it's got Palladian, but it isn't a little one of any of them. When you drive around the suburbs, how many matchbook or cheese-box Taras do you see—little houses too small for the style? With this house, people can't link any of the styles to the size."

Ooh. Ahh. The size. Tract mansions are apt to start at around 4,500 square feet of finished space, or about three times the size of the average American new house in the 1980s, and go up. The endless space doesn't go for bedrooms—more than four is unusual—but for half-a-dozen bathrooms, his-and-hers walk-in closets, wine cellars (which are simply rooms in the basements with bottle racks) and the two-story foyers with chandeliers. They feel like museums. Rooms shift from one style to another as if they were dioramas: the family room with the rough-hewn fieldstone fireplace next to the totally electronic kitchen with the Jenn-Air grill on the Brady-Bunch cooking island next to the formal dining room with the crown molding, chair rails, and a chandelier that looks like a combination of the whole eighteenth century and a UFO. And upstairs the master bedroom with a bathroom suite that could lure Caligula back from the dead—marble and onyx and Jacuzzi and three sinks and two-stream showers illuminated by one of three or four Palladian windows in the house (the ones with paned half-circle arches on top). The outsides are usually done in a style called "contemporary traditional." This tends to be something you might also call End-of-Century Eclectic or Manor Mannerist or the Lifestyle Style. The more styles the better, all at once: not just Williamsburg, New Orleans, American Shingle, and French Provincial, but the modern suburban mutations of Gothic-Novel-Romantic, Dollhouse-Symbolic, Thermopane Palladian, Vinyl-Siding Victorian, Two-Story-Lawyer-Foyer, and Upwardly Mobile Kapow. A Tudor chimney rises past modern staggered gables with Palladian windows flanked by Victorian carriage lamps, all of it scaled up or down for impact.

Aren't oddly scaled historical references hip in postmodernist circles? What about that Chippendale scrolled pediment that sits on top of Philip Johnson's AT&T building, making it look like the sideboard that ate Manhattan? Ah, but postmodernist historical references are supposed to be ironic. Tract mansions are not supposed to be ironic. What looks even stranger to people who don't understand these houses is the way they are often set on lots so small that the garage doors have to be in front because there's no room for a driveway on the side.

They look like the houses on the hill without the hill. Like much of their era, they are prisoners of economics. If a lot costs $300,000, you can't put a little house on it and sell the whole thing for $500,000 as well as you can put a huge one on it, full of what are called "the amenities," and sell it for $1 million. This follows what is sometimes called the Rule of Four, which states that the total price has to be about four times the cost of the land. It all makes sense once you realize that the day is over when status is determined by land. Now it's the house that does it, not some piece of property whose main function is fulfilling a 1920s country-squire fantasy—the tweed, the horses, the poachers. Not that developers reject the squire fantasy, but they realize that you don't need the reality when you've got the symbol, such as that badge of rural authenticity, a mailbox—not a little metal hut from Sears, but a mailbox with a cedar-shingle roof on it. Or a mailbox made of brick. (A brick mailbox? In the language of the trade, quirky mailboxes may not be "hot buttons" like the Sub-Zero refrigerators or interior pillars, but they are "memory points.")

As always in America, it is a question of reconciling the contradictory ideals of individuality and community. This brings up the dynamo powering suburbs and tract mansions: the car. Without it, twentieth-century architects and city planners might have been able to realize their dreams of happy city dwellers riding around on mass transit, such as the monorail trains you used to see in magazine drawings of the World of Tomorrow. In short, no modern suburbs, which would mean no tract mansions. How happy the architects would have been. In *The Anglo-American Suburb*, architect Robert A. M. Stern wrote: "As the car became a central feature of American life, architects increasingly treated it as a problem rather than a virtue and abandoned the planning issues of the suburb to the developer. Even designers such as Clarence Stein, who clearly saw the advantages of the car's freedom to enable travel wherever it was desired, regarded the relationship of the car to the house as one to be hidden and subverted."

Tract mansions, on the other hand, make a virtue of the car, with three- and four-car garages on the front of the house. In fact, tract mansions get sold as if they were cars themselves, with model lines—the Gorham, the Marshall, the Emerson, the Hampstead. (A century from now, when we have another burst of mansion building, will the builders evoke the qualities of our era by naming them "The Reagan" or "The Trump"?) These model lines are decked with options—Italian marble instead of ceramic bathrooms, intercoms, garage door openers, crown molding, recessed lights, wet bars, central vacuums, libraries (often with wet bars), golf rooms, whirlpool baths, bidets, window treatments, wallpaper upgrades, and landscaping packaging.

In city neighborhoods where the old money lives, houses can gin up the required head-crushing status clout with no more than a little brass Tradesman's Entrance sign and a gas lamp. People walk past them and savor the good taste. There is no need for ooh-ahh. Out in tract-mansion country, where nobody walks and people go past at fifty miles an hour, the status cravers need the Lifestyle Style to do the same job. Just as the car created billboards where once there had been mere handbills, it created tract mansions where once a town house sufficed. The car mandated humongosity.

These houses come on with an air of hulking gravitas and a disgruntled gloom, as if they will be owned only by the kind of people the neighbors never get to know. They reflect the fact that the money and a lot of the power are out in the suburbs rather than downtown. Consequently, they have to have authority, so they end up looking like funeral homes with decks on the back, or small private military academies with three-car garages, or town halls with wall-to-wall carpeting and Jacuzzis, or firehouses with circular driveways. They have generic importance. The symbolism is so clear and huge that it can work anywhere in America.

In *Learning From Las Vegas,* architects Robert Venturi, Denise Scott Brown, and Steven Izenour sum up the attitude of the haters of suburbs—and, one assumes, tract mansions. "To them, the symbolic decoration of the split-level suburban sheds represents the debased materialistic values of a consumer economy where people are brainwashed by mass marketing and have no choice but to move into the ticky-tacky, with its vulgar violations of the nature of materials and its visual pollution of architectural sensibilities, and surely, therefore, the ecology."

Well, yes.

But no. Tract mansions are the crown of suburban creation with

their gigantic family rooms, rumpus rooms, big kitchens, and breakfast nooks. They take the idea of symbolic ticky-tacky—miniature
Taras, tiny Tudors, cast-iron eagles that stood for pioneer independence, cast iron jockeys that stood for gentry, all the pasted-on symbolism of suburbia—and blow it up huge, bigger than life. If
post–World War II housing tracts were full of little versions of big
houses, Reagan-era mansion tracts are full of big versions of little
houses.

Ooh. Ahh.

Tract mansion builders build houses the way Ralph Lauren
makes clothes. The symbolism is everything, as in Lauren's blazers
with the family crests, the polo-player logos.

"This is not a breakfast nook," a salesman named Mike Mc-
Greevy says. He aims his smile at an alcove paneled in cedar and lit by
a Palladian window. Overhead is a skylight. Rustic, classical, and
modern all going at once. "Could you call this a breakfast nook? It's a
'Hunt Club Room.' "

The house is a model. It is furnished, or, as the agents say, decorated. Past some French doors with plastic snap-on mullions is the
family room, with its fieldstone fireplace and pictures of farm animals
on the walls. But French farm animals, "Les Animaux de la Ferme,"
as the caption says. Books scattered on tables include *And So to
America, One Lucky Woman, Burnt Offerings* and *The Bottom Line.*
There is a framed picture, in the style of a family photograph, except
that the picture was cut from a magazine. It shows polo players.
There is no television, sound system, or wastebaskets. They don't
symbolize anything, so why bother? Other touches in the downstairs
rooms: gardening tools and some Ortho plant food, a bottle of 1986
Mouton Cadet bordeaux, a Buddhist statue, and "window treatments" that don't so much have a function as they make calculated
statements, like bridesmaids' dresses. There are more framed photographs cut from fashion magazines. Books include *The Particles of
Modern Physics, Sword at Sunset, The Grand Defense, The Horse-
man,* and Reader's Digest Condensed Books. The library features a
ship model, a button-tufted leather chair, an antique shoeshine box,

two antique globes serving as bookends and, on the desk, a book opened to Immanuel Kant's "Theory of Ethics." It's as if Thomas Jefferson had decided to start a catalogue company, and this was the showroom.

There are three bedrooms and a master bedroom suite. The bedrooms seem to be set up for two girls and a boy—a studious girl with a knitting basket and a copy of *Schools Without Failure* on the night table; an artistic girl with an easel and drawings scattered on the bed and fashion pictures on the bulletin board; and a boy who is scientific—a telescope, a map of the moon and a book called *Shuttle Challenger*—but red-blooded—a parachute ceiling treatment and a toy trailer truck (a White Freightliner called The Golden Eagle Express).

Inside the master bedroom area is a master bathroom suite. These suites are the hottest of the hot buttons in the tract mansion business. This one is lit by a Palladian window and a chandelier. Ooh. Next to the two-person whirlpool bath, hinting at connubial wonderland, are two wineglasses. Ahh. The four-poster bed stands beneath a cathedral ceiling and bears a breakfast tray holding a copy of *Connoisseur* magazine. On either side of the bed are books hinting that it isn't easy, living life in today's world. On one side are *How to Protect Yourself Today, How to Survive in Your Native Land,* and *Hanging by a Thread*. Hers? On the other side are *Baroni* and *Perfectly Clear*. His? On the bureaus are pictures of happy, glamorous middle-aged couples, cut from magazines.

The sitting room features a plaid couch, a wicker chair, a drop-leaf coffee table and a copy of *The House That Had Everything*.

Isn't this the American dream? This is no rejection of tradition, standards, values, taste, style, or class. Instead, it affirms, it states boldly, it shouts that all of them could be yours because they're all for sale. The Sherwood. The Jamieson. The Emerson. The Manchester. The Wynmar. The Glencairn. The River Bend. The Ashburton Oaks. The Gorham. These are the houses our great-grandchildren will remember us by.

Ooh. Ahh.

landscape

Children hate landscape.

Landscape is a religion in America, a thing of virtue throughout the social strata, from the owners of black-velvet parking-lot sunset paintings to the owners of Monets. Children don't care. It's the object of a sort of low-church worship that can be done from a car, or in an easy chair with a magazine, or at movies such as *Out of Africa*, or in museums. Children couldn't care less. The thing is, we have to learn to like it. A love of beautiful scenery—land that looks like landscape paintings—is artificial, a cultivated response.

"I'm bored," says the nine-year-old in the back seat of the station wagon.

"How can you be bored?" says Mom. "Look at the sunlight on that river! It's just like Monet!"

"River," the kid says. "Monet."

Children don't start out hating landscape, just ignoring it. They admire rainbows and moo-cows, and they keep an eye on thunderstorms, but when it comes to scenes that landscape paintings have taught us to admire, asking a child to look at scenery is like showing a dog his reflection in a mirror—no reaction.

There are exceptions to the back-seat child—John Ruskin, the nervous hero of nineteenth-century English art criticism, wrote that his love for landscape began in early childhood. "The first thing which I remember, as an event in life, was being taken by my nurse to the brow of Friar's Crag on Derwent Water; the intense joy, mingled with awe, that I had in looking through the hollows in the mossy roots, over the crag, into the dark lake." But he said he couldn't tell how common these feelings were among children, and pointed out that "the charm of romantic association can be felt only by the modern European child." In liking landscape painting, Ruskin wrote, we are "under the influence of feelings with which neither Miltiades nor the Black Prince, neither Homer nor Dante, neither Socrates nor St. Francis, could for an instant have sympathized."

The Romans and Greeks used landscape in decoration and friezes, and Pliny and Vitruvius wrote about it, but it had little stature next to sculpture and architecture. It was not high art, as it is with us. Nor was there much sense that inherent beauty, wisdom, or virtue lurked in scenery. Wilderness was something to be protected from, not protected. The first European given credit for climbing a mountain was Petrarch, in 1336. When he got to the top (Mont Ventoux, 6,427 feet), he looked into a copy of St. Augustine and was seized with guilt for having looked outside his soul for truth and beauty. St. Jerome may have gone to the country complaining of the city's wickedness, but there was little medieval interest in landscape for the sake of landscape.

Then, in Renaissance Italy, particularly Venice, a number of ideas came together: scientific interest in the material world; the concept of using perspective to give the illusion of depth in paintings; and a rediscovery of the classics, including poets such as Virgil, who extolled the pastoral life—though not landscape in the style of later writers—in the *Eclogues* and *Georgics*. There are categories of landscape beside pastoral. Kenneth Clark writes about the landscapes of symbols, fact, fantasy and ideals, for instance. There was the expressionism of northern painters from Grunewald to van Gogh, and the mighty sublimity of Bierstadt and Church. But they all go back to pastoral, and its melancholy fascination with edens, with the dream of the harmony of man and nature, and the hints of pagan hope that natural virtue might exist apart from the redemption of society or religion.

Not only is our concept of landscape and landscape painting a pastoral one, but so is our concept of America. As Leo Marx argues in *The Machine in the Garden,* American culture was founded on the struggle between technology and the pastoral ideal, as in George Inness' *The Lackawanna Valley,* where a train puffs through fields whose tree stumps show that the wilderness was there just a moment ago. We took a literary and artistic convention of shepherds, satyrs, goddesses, and peasants surrounded by streams and God's own gardens, and decided we could make it real, we could actually live like that, we could become Jefferson's yeoman farmer, or become, say, the very actual—as opposed to mythological—nudes in Eakins' relaxed and gorgeous *Arcadia.* In Europe, pastoral was largely a theme for urban artists and poets. Here it became a political program, a way of thinking, and a sort of civic religion with saints such as Thoreau. We still have the rapture of converts. Only twenty years ago, college kids were making pilgrimages to the hills of Vermont or New Mexico in the "back to the land movement." It was one of the sillier episodes in the history of an overfed ruling class, but it was the logical product of educations that had begun with their parents urging them to look out the car window at the river.

Landscape is orthodoxy, a national esthetic. Such a nasty, misanthropic esthetic it can be, too. "We had a wonderful vacation," say the hateful kid's parents when they get back from vacation. "We could sit on the porch all day and never see a human being."

In our most popular art, we find human beings less interesting, virtuous, or beautiful than trees, clouds, and hills. Among other things, the brief history of landscape painting is a history of incredible shrinking man. Michelangelo, ennobler of human beauty, couldn't understand the Flemish landscape painters. He said: "Their painting is of stuffs, bricks and mortar, the grass of the fields, the shadows of

trees, and bridges and rivers, which they call landscapes, and little figures here and there." The people get smaller and smaller. The nudes
and musicians of fifteenth-century Venice dwindle to figurines amid
the enormous trees of eighteenth-century France, and then either vanish utterly or turn into the ghostly blobs of Puvis de Chavannes or
Matisse.

On the other hand, landscape has appealed to the common man
since its beginnings. It glorified peasants along with goddesses, saints,
and satyrs; witness all the engravings and woodcuts here. As early as
the middle of the 1500s, Giorgio Vasari wrote in a letter that "there is
not a cobbler's house without a German landscape." Like democracy,
landscape rose to its current prestige in the nineteenth century, when
it also became a theme in popular fiction as well as poetry (Thomas
Hardy's moors, for instance) and inspired the notion of conservation
and national parks.

There's also an abstractness about it that appeals to the modern
sensibility, which prefers to see a world populated by principles, institutions, and forces rather than gods, heroes, or even individual
human beings. Medieval painters pasted symbols of things—crucifix-
ions, unicorns, saints—on flat backgrounds. Renaissance landscape
painters enclosed their subjects with three-dimensional space, created
according to the laws of perspective. The relationship between the
things in landscapes—a shadow mass, a blazing sunlit green next to
it, the blue of the sky against the beige of a hill—was as important as
the things themselves. Abstract painting may have jettisoned the techniques of perspective, but it retained perspective's sense of relationship.

The pastoral world is a world of proportion, a seemingly candid
and ingenuous existence where things fit in, rather than stand out, a
world where mood and tone are the goal, rather than the sort of
achievement commemorated in portraits or history paintings. Pastoral is timeless, and it is always summer. Life is one long interlude
without consequences, a fantasy of the delights of being either very
rich or very poor. As Hazlitt said of the landscapes of Poussin, it is a
world of "foregone conclusion." How pleasant. Fragonard's *The*

Swing is shallow and arrogant, but it has pastoral's glorious feeling of caesura about it, with the aristocrats gamboling beneath ridiculously tall towers of trees and clouds.

It's hard to imagine the environmental movement without this tradition. Also: armies of buses rolling up and down the East Coast on foliage tours, New York's Central Park, suburbs, national parks, beachfront houses being eaten by the Atlantic Ocean, Nepenthe restaurant in Big Sur, highway signs pointing to "Scenic Overlook," songs about sunsets, and children whining in the back seats of cars on vacation trips. Or America: Oh beautiful, for spacious skies, for amber waves of grain, for purple mountains' majesty . . .

"I'm bored," says the kid.

"How can you be bored?" says the mother. "Look at that grain, look at those mountains . . ."

New Hampshire is a fraud.

Which is to say that behind that idyll of white-steepled, sleigh-belled, town-meeting, republican-with-a-small-R America lurks a much realer and hidden New Hampshire—the souvenir hustlers, backwoods cranks, motorcycle racing fans, out-of-state writers, dour French Canadians and tax-dodging Massachusetts suburbanites who have conspired as New Hampshire has conspired for two centuries to create an illusion of noble, upright, granite-charactered sentinels of liberty out of little more than a self-conscious collection of bad (if beautiful) land, summer people, second-growth woods full of junked cars and decaying aristocracy, lakes howling with speedboats, state liquor stores that are open on Sundays, and the most vicious state newspaper in America—the *Manchester Union Leader,* which has been known to greet the birthday of Martin Luther King by describing him as a Communist dupe.

They sell the rest of the country maple syrup, lottery tickets, and Yankee sagacity the way Indians on reservations sell moccasins, bingo, and environmental wisdom. They never shut up about how close-mouthed they are. They beat you rich and they beat you poor. They do this by taking a Calvinist pride in the money they've made from one bit of luck or another—the knitting mills of the 1920s or the high-tech boom of the 1980s—and then taking on the smugness of Thoreau in defending the poverty of the swamp Yankees and shack people living back in the woods with yards full of mean dogs and broken snowmo-biles. They exhibit the ethics of Switzerland and the shrugging shabbi-ness of New Jersey. Or as Emerson wrote: "The God who made New Hampshire taunted the lofty land with little men." The question is not who they think they are, to be holding us hostage every four years with their presidential primary. Instead, who do we think they are, to let them get away with it— this white, tight, and right smidgen of a place, this myth-mongering bastion of no-tax/no-spend conservatives with no minorities to speak of and about half of one percent of the American people? As Thomas Jefferson said, after New Hampshire town meetings had attacked his Embargo Act, "The organization of this little selfish minority enabled it to overrule the union."

By now it's a tradition. It's hard to imagine a first primary in any other state. Would we have paid as much attention in 1952 if Eisen-hower had won a first primary that was held in Nevada? In Alabama? Would Reagan's primary landslide in 1980 have counted as much in Delaware? It's possible, but this would imply that two centuries of self-promotion by New Hampshirites have counted for nothing, and that television reporters stand in front of all those white-painted Grange halls and covered bridges for nothing—even if the bridge is merely the fake one that the Wayfarer Sheraton, the media madhouse just outside Manchester, put up so that there'd be a view outside its restaurant. It would imply that the New Hampshire of a billion Christmas cards holds no place in the American mind, along with the Jeffersonian vision of yeoman New Hampshire farmers like Jabez Stone in Stephen Vincent Benét's "The Devil and Daniel Webster," or the small-town America that Thornton Wilder has summed up for a million audiences in his play set in the mythical Grover's Corners, New Hampshire, and called *Our Town*.

In Dublin, Judson Hale, editor of *Yankee* magazine, says: "The image really helps." As early as 1964, when Henry Cabot Lodge won the primary as a write-in, beating Rockefeller and Goldwater, *Yankee* was noting with pleasure that "the eyes of the nation—the lens of television—and the voice of the press all focused on New Hampshire's Big Town Meeting Day."

Yankee sells a million copies a month, mostly to people who don't live in New England, much less New Hampshire. Hale also publishes *The Old Farmer's Almanac* and *Alaska* magazine. Why publish Alaska in Dublin, New Hampshire?

"Alaska is a region people dream about, just like New England," Hale says. "They say, one of these days I'm going to get a cabin out in the woods, just as they say about New England that they're going to get a little house with a picket fence by the town green."

At Dartmouth College, historian Jere Daniell calls the dream "coffeetable New England." He says: "The fascination with New Hampshire's primary is one of the products of a political transformation that began in the 1930s when rural New England was re-romanticized—that's when *Yankee* magazine was founded and a show called *Town Meeting of the Air* went on the radio." The image got another boost in the 1960s, "with the anti-Vietnam movement and people opting for the pure life in rural New England. Now we've got the immigrants from Taxachusetts. It used to be the Rhode Island types who came up here with their snowmobiles. Now it's the cross-country skiing types. Every town has to have a green now, whether they originally had one or not. If you've got a church with no steeple, you have to put a steeple on it."

The dream of New England hangs over the New Hampshire hills like an anesthetic gas, easing the pains of New Hampshire's tackiness, erasing the phone wires, the mini-golf courses, the sense of chronic opportunism that lurks behind the white clapboard purity of all those houses with dates over the doors instead of street numbers. You don't have to look very hard, though, to see the uneasy compromise of land and people that is the Granite State. From the air, in winter, at primary time, the hills of New Hampshire appear to be held together with a jagged stitchery of stone walls built over the centuries to divide the fields. Now those walls are hidden by the woods that returned when the farmers finally got all the Indians killed in time for farming to collapse. In 1850 half the state was cleared. Then the railroads brought in cheaper food from the better land to the west, and the mills pulled the young people off the farms and into towns like Manchester, and the more enterprising New Hampshirites left for points west. By the end of the century, "the racier, the more adventurous, the less stable, the more exciting and excitable, had left," says Evan Hill in *The Primary State*. And New Hampshire was on its way to being four-fifths woods. In 1889 the state's Department of Agriculture published a booklet entitled *Price List of Abandoned Farms in New Hampshire*. In 1891 a woman named Kate Sanborn wrote a book called *Adopting an Abandoned Farm,* which she followed with the even more successful *Abandoning an Adopted Farm.*

Was she any relation to Frank B. Sanborn, who published the classic *New Hampshire—An Epitome of Popular Government* in 1904? In a discussion of New Hampshire's first settlers, he evokes the free spirits you find living back in the woods in trailers and plywood shacks, the "worthy nonconformists, chiefly of the yeoman and tradesman classes, while along with such, or as a godless fringe to the pious garment, came a host of the shiftless, ne'er-do-well, or positively vicious kind, who naturally found in a new country some relief from the restraints and some respite from the fruitless toil of the fatherland."

These traits were not confined to the lower classes, says Sanborn. "The samples of gentry that came over were often of the last-named sort, undisciplined or trained in self-indulgence."

The current laureate of New Hampshire's sylvan depravity is Ernest Hebert, author of a cycle of novels set in southwest New Hampshire. Driving on back roads to Keene from Hanover, home of Dartmouth College (motto: Vox Clamantis in Deserto—A Voice Crying in the Wilderness), Hebert says: "There may be more woods here now than there have ever been. The forest is transforming itself back to what it was when the white man arrived, and maybe before that— the Indians had a sort of slash-and-burn agriculture. The nature of the landscape says a lot about the people who live here. It's a messy forest, and as a result, people have messy yards."

He has turned off the main road to illustrate his point that the candidates and the media never see what are known as the swamp Yankees. In a town called Sullivan, he points out the tar-paper-and-plastic shanties with coonskins nailed to the sides. Wood smoke pumps into the air. Inhabitants stalk with ancient resignation through yards studded with truck axles and boats full of snow. There is junk everywhere. There is an atmosphere that reminds you New Hampshire sells more beer and distilled spirits per person than any other state, though a lot of it goes to outsiders. As Hebert writes in *The Dogs of March* of an unemployed millworker named Howard Elman: "Birches, a score of junk cars, a swing on a limb of a giant maple, a bathtub in the garden, a gray barn, a house sided with fading purple asphalt shingles, a washing machine riddled with bullet holes—to Howard, these things were all equal in beauty. He saw no ugliness on his property. As nature felled weak trees and scattered fallen leaves, so Howard Elman dispensed with machines that would not work. To his eye, his yard and field beyond were one."

Woods and squalor: In a debate in *New England Monthly* over the merits of the two states, Vermonter Richard Ketchum wrote that "New Hampshire is the one that looks like a summer camp that's closed for the winter, the one where you drive for hours through dark pine and spruce forests without glimpse of man or beast, the one where you can't tell if it's night or raining or if you're just lost in the woods." The odd thing about the debate was that the praise of New Hampshire by poet Donald Hall made it sound worse than Ketchum's damns. Hall wrote: "New Hampshire, my New Hampshire, is inhabited by real people who drive pickup trucks with gun racks and NRA bumper stickers . . . Beginning in June, Vermont drones with the sound of string quartets, while over here, motorcycle gangs converge on Loudon. (The rest of the year in New Hampshire it's the same noise, now performed by chain saws and snowmobiles.) . . . In New Hampshire, the state supper is beans and franks, and every recipe begins with salt pork, Campbell's cream of mushroom soup, and Miracle Whip."

Escape the woods, and you find yourself back in the uneasy land of three-lane highways scattered with sand and bordered with soft ice-cream stands and mini-storage warehouses (those cairns of transiency); portable signboards advertising Liv Bait 4 Sale; weathering neocolonial shopping centers with gilt-lettered signs offering The Bear Facts, the Ped'ling Fool, Hair It Is; and the palimpsest of three hundred years of history—streams that run black in the piney gloom next to highways that run under railroads that lead to rivers that once floated logs past the mills now bearing the generic name of FOR LEASE, and of course those stone walls that wander out of the snowy woods like lost old people. In Europe, the history blends. Here, it looks raw and mechanical. Rising above all of it are the white steeples of the churches erected despite the reply of one crowd resisting an early Puritan evangelist: "Parson, we came hither to fish."

Boston's Robert Lowell has written:

In this small town where everything
is known, I see His vanishing
emblems, His white spire and flag-
pole sticking out above the fog,
like old white china doorknobs, sad,
slight, useless things to calm the mad.

It's a tradition for out-of-staters to define what New Hampshire is. And why not? Like the state itself, the concept of "native" is an elusive reality—half the people who live there were born somewhere else. Early on it was artists such as Thomas (*Voyage of Life*) Cole, who arrived in the White Mountains in 1827 and called them "emblems of nature's purity." In 1855 George Shattuck, a Boston physician with a summer place outside of Concord, New Hampshire, gave the land for the founding of St. Paul's School, one of the elite boarding schools that is meant by phrases such as "old boy network" or "St. Grottlesex." The high WASPery of St. Paul's also evokes what historian John Higham has called "the image of America that Anglo-Saxon intellectuals cherished. The tradition of racial nationalism had always proclaimed orderly self-government as the chief glory of the

Anglo-Saxons—an inherited capacity so unique that the future of human freedom surely rested in their hands." That New Hampshire is 98 percent white links it in some minds with the tradition of English freedoms, and in others with an America that can still define moral and political attributes by race or national ancestry.

In 1899 the state government instituted Old Home Week, a sort of homecoming to celebrate the rural values that had been lost not just in New Hampshire but in America. Also, the idea was to give tourists and summer people more romance to believe in and spend money on. Soon, the air fairly creaked with self-consciousness. Nowadays New Hampshirites are even self-conscious about being self-conscious—witness a history published in cooperation with the New Hampshire Historical Society that admits that "the state is somewhat culturally self-conscious, in the manner of New England states generally." Bookstores have hefty stocks of books about New Hampshire, the picture books that show nothing of the snowmobiling gun nuts, the books with titles like *How to Talk Yankee,* and of course the collections of Yankee jokes.

"Lived in this town all your life?"

"Not yet."

Even Robert Frost, a Californian who became the state poet, acknowledged self-consciousness as a basic theme of the New Hampshire mind when he concluded his "New Hampshire" by saying:

I choose to be a plain New Hampshire farmer
With an income in cash of say a thousand
(From say a publisher in New York City).
It's restful to arrive at a decision,
And restful just to think about New Hampshire.
At present I am living in Vermont.

At present, too, an important part of America's future is determined every four years by a state that holds less than one percent of the votes cast for president in the Electoral College. Liberals wisecrack that it is a nice place to visit, but you wouldn't want to have a handicapped child there. There is neither sales nor income tax. Teach-

ers' salaries are lower than in almost all the other states. As for yeoman virtue, less than 1 percent of the state's income is from farming,
and at the end of the 1980s it was the fourth most industrialized state
in the union. Its state government is a running joke, inside the state
and out, with a governor who serves a two-year term and a legislature
of more than four hundred people—"the fourth or fifth biggest in the
world," New Hampshirites like to boast. They also point out that it is
also one of the weakest, because of the dominance of the town-meeting system in running the state. One former governor, Meldrim
Thomson, wanted to arm his National Guard with nuclear weapons,
and he flew the flag at half-staff at Easter.

The state's Democratic Party is so lifeless that in 1986 it had to
dredge up a former governor of Massachusetts, Endicott Peabody, to
run the required doomed race for the U.S. Senate against Warren
Rudman. Since the labor strife of the 1920s and '30s that ended with
the owners of the textile mills taking their mills to the South, there
has been little in the way of labor kingmakers to focus New Hampshire politics. There is no powerful bishop or veterans' lobby or television station or major league team to rally around.

New Hampshirites complain now that the old New Hampshire
can only be found north of the White Mountains, up empty roads
past paint-peeling houses, the Old Man of the Mountains (possibly
the least inspiring famous rock formation in America) and through
Franconia Notch, past the birches and pines and maples that mix together in forests that are somehow lush and spare at the same time,
up past towns so little and isolated that gift shops are big advertisers
on the radio. "Don't forget Valentine's Day."

Up there are towns like Littleton, with the solidity of, say, the
1950s, before television and self-consciousness had a chance to melt
everything into air. There's a slow, heavy ease to Littleton, shoe factories, an abrasive mill, and a joint called the Coffee Pot with vinyl
booths and two old guys nursing cups of coffee at a Formica counter.

"It's changed," says Floyd Ramsey, a retired schoolteacher. "People here are starting to drive like people from the city, they pull out in

front of you like Massachusetts people, when they've only got a block to drive."

The other old guy says nothing. He rubs five days worth of beard. He bares a small number of teeth, none of which oppose the others. Is he a relic of the closed lumber mills? Of some backwoods trailer life? Is he a half-moronic casualty of all the changes that have made the noble, Emerson-reading Yankee farmer merely a thing of legend?

Then he starts to talk, this codger of seventy-four, whose name is Norman Danneman, and you realize you've been had.

"You have a limited geographic area with X number of people in it," he says with the aplomb of an MIT sociologist, "and when you get an increase in X, you get congestion, you get a change in behavior."

Is this some kind of joke he plays on the out-of-state journalists who come through every four years?

Beat you rich, beat you poor, beat you smart, beat you dumb. And they know they're doing it.

part three

If Jack Kennedy had lived . . .

Imagine the changes as he grew old: his neck swelling like Frank Sinatra's, his gorgeously hooded eyes gone so fleshy they'd look tired and sly. His hair would seem old-fashioned, a relic of the '60s the way Ronald Reagan's hair was a relic of the '40s. Maybe he'd have made a good elder statesman like Averell Harriman, propped up on a Georgetown couch by an ambitious wife.

But he wouldn't be our Jack Kennedy, the Jack Kennedy who hovers in the American psyche like a hologram, a national idea the way Mt. Rushmore is a national monument. Even Reagan and the Republicans invoked Kennedy as if he were motherhood or the flag. Politicians on all sides wanted to be Kennedy-esque, with floppy-forelock haircuts and baby-grand smiles. You can imagine Kennedy laughing at them the way he laughed toward the end of his life, showing some lower teeth, the sides of his mouth stretching out far enough that the corners turned down a little, not just sardonic but self-consciously sardonic. He once said: "Bobby and I smile sardonically.

Teddy will learn how to smile sardonically in two or three years, but he doesn't know how yet."

It was a matter of style, not substance. Jack Newfield of the *Village Voice* attacked Lyndon Johnson as the "Antichrist" even though Johnson was actually enacting the programs that Kennedy had only talked about. Reagan may never understand how Kennedy people could hate him for cutting taxes and raising military spending at the same time, when Kennedy did the same thing.

As it happens, every new administration has disappointed the old Kennedy people: aging Hamlets in pin-striped suits, the best and brightest at law firms, dinner parties, and endless book signings, exiles with the ennobling fury of people who never feel the need to explain anything to anybody. They had hoped to constitute what James Reston once hailed as "a new class of public servants who move about in the triangle of daily or periodic journalism, the university or foundation, and government service."

The Kennedy White House spawned a giddy elitism based on a blend of potential, a look, and a certain crispness of attitude, as if the principles of undergraduate popularity had been inflated into a political philosophy. The Kennedy people were too fast for the State Department, too smart for Congress. There was a premise that one or two acutely excellent people in the right place at the right time could change the world, Peace Corps–style or James Bond–style. It was a government of "informal consultation, anti-bureaucratic, round-the-clock vigils, the crash program, the hasty decision, the quick phone call," as Victor Navasky has written. Much slamming of phones and smoking of little cigars. Much conspicuous intelligence. "There's nothing like brains," Kennedy said once. "You can't beat brains." He scared us out of our middle-class Eisenhower complacency, and filled the air with a sense of edgy possibility. If existentialists had saints, he might be one, finding truth in action, not contemplation. In a campaign speech, he said: "I don't run for president in the 1960s because I think it will be an easy time. I don't. I think it will be a very dangerous time for us all."

Much has been made of Kennedy's charisma, Irishness, war heroism, and media manipulation. But what lingers in the backbrain of American culture is more basic. To begin with, he was madly good looking. When you see the old footage of him now on television, it feels like your head moves when you follow him across the screen. Lovely: He runs on a lawn during a touch football game, enthralled with the chaos downfield; or campaigning on a Boston street, he turns away from an old couple and flicks his hand back toward the man as if to say everything from "Thanks" to "You and me, pal" to "We'll be looking for you at the polling place." Perfect. It was the kind of move Richard Nixon never, ever made, not once. Six feet one-half inch tall, 170 pounds when he was assassinated in 1963. Brown hair, blue eyes. That slight hunch to his shoulders, increasing with age and the pain of his back problems, a posture that gives him a preoccupied air, which in turn makes whatever he's doing look as if his attention just has been caught, a gift.

A fabulous head. Like California hot rods of the early '60s, the scalp raked forward, a muscular momentum with no particular destination. His eyes squinted a little, as if in surprise or second thought, and a lot of white showed under the irises, hinting at exhaustion or appetite. He was one of those rare men on whom eye bags look good—a piquant contrast to his teenager's hairline—and he was the only president who ever looked good in sunglasses, which he wore a lot, tapping into the iconography of the Age of Cool, when sunglasses suggested a fashionable alienation. The lips were just full enough to hint at insolence, and his smile was thrillingly ambiguous, four thousand teeth placed in just such a way that his S's would whistle a little, yet another of his arresting little acutenesses, along with that strange accent that for all the fat flatness of the vowels seemed to be in a hurry. The chin was terrific, curving out and a little up, as if the whole face might just soar away, any second.

A dangerous face. It had moments of stillness that were menacing, or a little sly, as if he had a piece of gum in his mouth and didn't want to be seen chewing it. A face that looked to see if you knew what the joke was, and if you didn't, the joke was on you. The happily self-conscious face of a man posing for a portrait between phone calls. A smile that could turn hard in an instant—when he got impatient, he would reach up with his finger and tap one of those front teeth.

He once said: "The press is a very valuable arm of the presidency." He knew where journalists ranked, most of them—on the high end of the lower end of the scale, like tennis pros or warrant officers. Film of one White House press conference shows him dealing with a question about why he has a bandaid on his finger. He smiles the smile. He hesitates, but not because it's none of the reporters' business. Instead, it seems he wants to show them it's none of their business but he'll tell them anyway. He calculates for a microsecond. He knows that even if he tells the truth they'll suspect he lied. He savors this idea—what can they do about it, after all, and besides, maybe an obvious fib would be more charming than the truth.

He says, "I cut it while I was slicing bread—unbelievable as it may sound."

He lifts the hand to show it to them as an afterthought, a conspicuous afterthought, a gift, not an obligation. He knew where the press ranked.

If you liked Kennedy, you could come away from the television feeling as you might have after a Cary Grant movie—as if his grace and quickness had transformed your walk and smile, conferring a heady self-consciousness, like the first whiskey of the day. He once said: "We couldn't survive without television." If you disliked him, was it out of objective analysis or your envy of his charm? Being annoyed by people who were infatuated with Kennedy was easy, but you worried that in arguing with them you became a fogy, a Polonius advising Ophelia to break it off with Hamlet.

Kennedy existed at the point where love and hate converge. Almost everything written about him is touched with infatuation, resentment, or both, from the praise of Arthur Schlesinger and Ted Sorensen to the nastiness, soap opera, and psychoanalysis of books like Nancy Gager Clinch's *The Kennedy Neurosis* or *The Kennedys: An American Drama* by Peter Collier and David Horowitz.

There were successes: pushing back the U.S. Steel price hike, the Peace Corps, the Cuban missile crisis, the test-ban treaty, the enfranchisement of the intellectuals—he wasn't afraid to be seen with André Malraux or Robert Frost. Also, he looked comfortable in white tie and tails, and he could shake hands with Charles de Gaulle without making us worry that he'd embarrass us. But the failures were big: the Bay of Pigs, the Berlin Wall, the lies about Vietnam. Later would come the scandals: his chronically adolescent sex life, the Castro assassination plan and his tendency to go slumming, politically speaking, with Mafia types. Only the young die good, as it happens in the real world, and he was young, but not that young. We don't forgive his failures as much as we ignore them. They are as irrelevant by now as his successes. Like gods or royalty, the fallen Kennedy wasn't accountable, he just was. As early as 1961, Kenneth Crawford wrote in *Newsweek,* under the title "Royalty USA," that "we don't like to have our symbols making mistakes, so we don't acknowledge that they make them."

Good arguments can still be had on what Kennedy might have done if he'd lived: made peace with the Russians, pulled out of Vietnam, passed the social legislation that Lyndon Johnson passed. No matter. As far as the facts go, the revisionists have been revised and revised again. No likely end will bring him loss or leave us happier than before. We've even forgiven Jackie for marrying Aristotle Onassis, who seemed to possess her with the heavy-lidded desperation of a man flying to Switzerland for monkey-gland injections. At the time, there was a popular rumor that explained it away: Jackie married him, it was said, because Kennedy was still alive, though a vegetable, and Onassis could hide him on his island where Jackie could be with him.

Such are the many little corners of Valhalla.

In a poll on the twenty-fifth anniversary of the assassination, 34 percent of Americans said in a poll that Kennedy had been the "most effective" president since World War II, compared with 17 percent for Truman, 14 for Reagan, and 3 for Lyndon Johnson; 21 percent said Kennedy was the best president ever, with Franklin Roosevelt and Abraham Lincoln running second at 17 percent each.

All Kennedy's infatuees ever needed was an excuse to love him.

They've remembered him since the way a middle-aged woman lies awake remembering a boy who got killed on a motorcycle and her father couldn't figure out why she cried so hard—she'd only gone out with him a couple of times, and he wasn't going to amount to that much anyway.

You watch that gray footage of the casket being unloaded from Air Force One, of Jackie moving with the bewildered clumsiness of grief, and you feel the random, empty quality of things. It feels like now, you think—that's when "now" began. It is plain that before Kennedy was shot, everything was different: The colors were brighter, the world was full of purpose. Snug. Wrapped like a trick knee with the Ace bandage of intention. Or maybe what began with Kennedy's assassination was not the present but the past. Bruce Duffy, author of a novel called *The World as I Found It,* once remarked: "I was home sick when I heard he was shot. My mother had died the year before, and Kennedy's death was especially painful because it had the effect of moving her farther away from me. It put her into a whole different era."

This is not an age of character, but of personality, and Kennedy gave us that. This is also not an age of darkness but of glare, as a poet has said, and Kennedy gave us that too. In the long view, he was a violent man of great charm, ambition, and propensity for getting himself in trouble. We have a psychic niche for men like that—Alexander, Alcibiades, Charles XII of Sweden, Napoleon. Kennedy promised nothing less when he said of the American people in 1960, "They want to know what is needed—they want to be led by the commander in chief." Who knows where he would have led us?

As Lyndon Johnson said of Bobby Kennedy: "I almost wish he had become president so the country could finally see a flesh-and-blood Kennedy grappling with the daily work of the presidency and all the inevitable disappointments, instead of their storybook image of great heroes who, because they were dead, could make anything anyone wanted happen."

Anything anyone wanted—if Jack Kennedy wasn't that then, he is now.

Ah, fairyland, with a princess and silk ruffles and diamonds and a little dog named Macho running around.

But no Hitler.

"Tito!" says Zsa Zsa Gabor, reclining on a couch in the gauzy light of the morning sun through hotel curtains. "I danced with Tito, but I never danced with Hitler."

She wears a white morning gown with ruffles and a huge pear-shaped piece of chest showing, which picks up the pear-shaped diamond on her left hand, "24 carats—I got a bigger one once, but I gave it back." She wears silver satin slippers with three-inch heels and little mirrors glued to them. And perfectly painted red toenails. She looks good. She fulfills every expectation, which is to say she looks just like Zsa Zsa Gabor, an institution, somehow, a symbol, not entirely unlike her sister Eva (the one who was on *Green Acres*), or Magda, or Mama Jolie, all of them with those Hungarian cheekbones and those smiles that are startled and sly at the same time, smiles in which possibility breeds.

Tito, not Hitler. Somehow, a Yugoslavian communist dictator and a Nazi tyrant occupy the same mental pigeonhole. Think of all the powerful men she could have named. "Nixon!" ("I became his friend after he lost everything.") Or "Kissinger!" (Her publicity handout quotes Kissinger as telling her mother, "She's one of the brightest women I ever met.") Or "Rafael Trujillo!" He was the son of the Dominican strongman, and the lad who gave her a Mercedes and a chinchilla coat, leading former congressman Wayne Hays of Ohio to attack her for wasting the foreign aid we were sending to the Dominican Republic.

"That son of a bitch congressman, I was working my head off in a nightclub here, and he calls me 'the highest-paid courtesan since Madame de Pompadour.' But look what happened to him, I laughed and laughed." And she laughs again to think of the lovely scandal that ensued when it turned out that Hays had a bosomy blond typist named Liz Ray on his staff who couldn't type.

If Zsa Zsa hadn't invented herself, would she have existed anyway? A known blond. One tough lady. The blond that gentlemen prefer. D-a-a-a-ahhling. She would have made a great goddess if only there'd been a third Conan the Barbarian movie where Arnold Schwarzenegger could have made burnt offerings to her. She's not on the Elvis level of American mythology, of course—nobody ever calls the local TV station to say that Zsa Zsa Gabor's face just appeared on his pancake. But she is Zsa Zsa, and nobody else is.

She looks good. Age cannot wither her, nor custom stale her infinite variety. It can add a few pounds, it can have her drawing her lipstick a little outside her lip line, it can put a few freckles on her chest, but there's nothing stale here.

"Green peppers, green bell peppers," she says, explaining her wonderful skin. And she'll quote Mae West, "She said it, I didn't, 'An orgasm a day keeps the doctor away.' "

In point of fact, she is a woman in her late sixties, by most estimates, with an uncertain waist and makeup halfway down her breasts, but she is not so old that you find yourself rooting for her. She is still what she has always been—the epitome of the triumph of shamelessness over hypocrisy, of the feminine ethic of doing what you can with what you've got, a sort of avatar of that Vaseline-lensed heaven you see on the covers of a billion paperback books, and a combination of three personas, the "adventuress," the "glamor girl," and the "woman with a past."

She has the sort of accent that encloses you, like her perfume (Van Cleef & Arpels No. 1), an accent that along with her diamonds gives her the charisma of dispossessed royalty. And, indeed, at the horse show, she is introduced as "Princess Zsa Zsa Gabor," thanks to a marriage—her eighth, if you don't count a three-day misadventure with some count in Mexico—to Prince Frederick von Anhalt, who strides in presently, in his riding clothes, to be introduced.

"I've been riding this morning," he says. He appears to be in his late forties. He has an air of willed forcefulness about him, and the very firm handshake of a little boy brought up to be manly.

"He is wonderful, this is my best marriage," Zsa Zsa says as the prince wanders off. "I just gave him a purple Rolls-Royce. He doesn't give me a hard time like all the other husbands."

Wait a second. Didn't she once say that actor George Sanders was her favorite husband because he treated her so badly?

Zsa Zsa panics, waving her hands as if she's fighting her way through a cloud of talcum powder. She whispers loudly, "Don't mention the name of another man! He's desperately jealous! That's the only tragedy!" She breathes deeply. She subsides once more to her recline on the couch. "Porfirio Rubirosa was the same way." She is referring here to the Latin playboy of the 1950s. "I said to him, 'I can't marry you, I love my husband,' and he gave me a black eye. He was a wonderful man. He really loved women. He hated being a kept man. George Sanders always wanted to be a kept man, but Rubi hated it."

She keeps talking, the music of a scheming but charming player upon the great sousaphone of public expectation, never failing to wave and smile as she huffs and puffs away. It all comes to sound like those records the guy with the English accent advertises on television, seventeen seconds from each of the world's great classical compositions:

"You men are all alike . . . I am from a very rich family . . . I was Miss Hungary at thirteen . . . the Russian ambassador loved to play-bridge with me because of my décolletage . . . fifteen years ago I was in Hungary, my father died and I tried to take out his portrait of me, but the guard stopped me at the border and said, 'That's a national treasure' . . . married a Turkish ambassador when I was sixteen . . . the head of the secret police in Belgrade offered me a white Cadillac if I would stay . . . My mother said you don't have to marry all the men you sleep with . . . men are all the same . . . my father was a huge landowner . . . junior Ping-Pong champion of Hungary . . . green peppers . . . not mink, chinchilla . . . of course Jack Kennedy wanted to sleep with me, he said I was the only blond he never slept with, he was gorgeous but I was married to a gorgeous American at the time and I was also in love with a gorgeous Englishman . . . I drink forty cups of coffee a day, maybe fifty, before I go to bed I have a big cup of coffee . . . Every morning my mother calls up and says, 'How fat are you?' . . . I swim in my swimming pool every day with diamond earrings on and nothing else . . . A woman doesn't want a good man, I want a man who tells you, 'Don't do that' . . . very rich family . . . Eva's a little bitch, she just made a commercial where she calls me her older sister . . . men like young women, they don't know what good lovemaking is when they're young . . ."

She arrived in America in 1941. There was a party for her at the Turkish Embassy, she says, by way of explaining why her picture appeared in the *Washington Post* over a caption in which she said she had danced with Hitler: "Oh yes, I danced wiz him—twice. He is a good dancer. And I danced wiz Anthony Eden, and wiz Churchill's son—I don't know which one."

But not Hitler. Tito.

She was on her way to Hollywood with Eva, the caption said.

Nothing seems to have come of that until 1951, when she appeared on a television advice show called *Bachelor's Haven,* the sort of thing people usually do on their way down, not up. She started as a has-been, in other words, and since then, except for a part in the movie *Moulin Rouge,* and in *40 Carats* on Broadway, she has been famous largely for being Zsa Zsa, as if there had been some success in her past so huge that we will always be grateful for it. What she has been is a talk-show guest, the wife of hotel magnate Conrad Hilton, a star of dinner theater, the honorary lieutenant governor of Ohio, the wife of the toy consultant famous for perfecting the arm and waist movements of the Barbie doll, the goodwill ambassador for the Montgomery Ward Auto Club ("Now there was a good job," she says now), a vice president of Actors and Others for Animals, and an actress in more than forty movies, according to her résumé, which adds that "the above films were all produced in their native languages."

She has houses in Palm Beach and Bel Air.

"I could live without money, I could live without men, but I could not live without animals."

She picks up little Macho, a Shih Tzu terrier who does not seem to want to be picked up, particularly, but a photographer is on the scene, and Macho will add interest.

"Make a noise like a cat," she says to the photographer.

The photographer mews. Macho bristles.

"I have a cat named Momma back in Bel Air," Zsa Zsa says. "Macho hates Momma. Say Momma."

The photographer says "Momma."

Macho looks frantic. Zsa Zsa laughs.

"He hates her, he hates her," she says.

the wyeths

The gloomy Wyeths—N.C., Andrew, and Jamie, grandfather, father, and son —are the painters laureate of American upper-middle-class WASPs and those who take their style from them. This is the class that leftists used to call the American bourgeois, a tribe that sees itself, and rightly so, as a casualty of the twentieth century.

The fact that they have the support of these people is one reason the Wyeths, particularly Andrew and Jamie, get attacked by modernists. These attacks have been going on for decades. In 1953, just as Andrew Wyeth's star was being installed in the firmament, a critic wrote in *Art News* that " 'nice people' can be at ease with his pictures." Critic Jay Jacobs once called Andrew Wyeth "the spiritual leader of Middle America." Carter Ratcliff wrote in *Art in America* that "those committed to modernism hold Wyeth in contempt of art. Others gauge their contempt for modernism by their love of Wyeth."

The Wyeths' audience looks to Britain and a lost rural past for its identity, while the modernists look to cities and the Continent. The Wyeths defend the work ethic—N.C. could crank out his masterful illustrations one a day; Andrew appears to paint each blade of grass; Jamie records every strand of wicker in the antique wheelchair that holds a woman staring out to sea. They've all made lots of money. They arouse emotions that happily require no moral choices—poignance, wistfulness, nostalgia, depression, self-awareness, satisfaction. They meld those emotions with puritanical vigor and stoic spareness. And they defend the sort of nineteenth-century sensibility that found thrilling meaning in death, moral character, the struggles of nature, production, and solitude—as opposed to the modern sensibility that admires nihilism, personality, the benevolence of nature, consumption, and the masses.

The Wyeths stand for their audience's nobility in the face of their quiet decline in the twentieth century—these people have been losing political power and moral sway ever since the tidal waves of turn-of-the-century immigration, the progressive income tax, the stock market crash of 1929, and the egalitarianism and meritocracy that came out of World War II. In John Cheever's "The Day the Pig Fell Into the Well," a mother looks at her family and asks herself: "Where had they lost their competence, their freedom, their greatness? Why should these good and gentle people who surrounded her seem like the figures in a tragedy?"

This decline has been a major theme in twentieth-century American culture, but art has ignored it, except for the Wyeths. F. Scott Fitzgerald turned it into an ur-myth with *The Great Gatsby*. The *New Yorker*'s tone of wistful perseverance, along with all those memoirs of childhood, used to depend on it. The best gods, it seemed, were dying ones. Nostalgia became a virtue. Irony became the preferred tone, as in Ernest Hemingway or J. D. Salinger. To be upper-middle-class in twentieth-century America means not just living with a sense of loss but reveling in it, flaunting it, laying claim to an ancien regime. This nostalgia has been a merchandising bonanza, resonating through everything from the Anglophilia on public television to the hundreds of dollars that people will spend on a duck decoy. (Once the lion was the totem animal of the ruling class; now it's the duck. A duck's head even appears on the front of a limousine in one of Jamie Wyeth's most sentimental paintings, *New Year's Calling*. And is that Jamie himself staring out of the back window?) The WASPs are acquiring the poignance of a lost tribe—college kids of the 1980s wore WASP, or preppy, clothes today the way they wore Navajo beads and Sioux moccasins in the 1960s.

Early in this century, as he was beginning to illustrate muscular Anglo-Saxon adventures such as *Robin Hood* and *Treasure Island,* N. C. Wyeth wrote: "Anything that I appreciate keenly and profoundly is always sad to the point of being tragic. Whether it is a lone tree on a hillside bathed in the fading light of the afternoon sun, or the broad stretch of a green meadow shining and sparkling after a shower . . . it is all so sad, because it is all so beautiful, so hopeless." His son Andrew was born in 1917, just as the Anglo-Saxon adventure was ending in the horrible ironies of the trenches in World War I. Instead of painting knights, pirates, and cowboys murdering each other with jut-jawed abandon, Andrew has given us pictures of dry, mysterious moments in a vanishing rural landscape where hair glitters in the wind and snow blows over the hills with the glamor of some unspoken aftermath. He says: "I prefer winter and fall, when you feel the bone structure in the landscape—the loneliness of it—the dead feeling of winter. Something waits beneath it—the whole story doesn't show." He summers in Maine, which gives "the impression sometimes of crackling skeletons rattling in the attic . . . I feel things are just hanging on the surface and that it's all going to blow away." He likes painting with egg tempera because "it has a cocoon-like feeling of dry lostness—almost a lonely feeling." James, called Jamie, was born in 1946. He evokes his brand of gloom with irony—a preposterously noble ram in the slanting sunlight, himself with a pumpkin on his head, a huge pig (emblematic of the horrible vigor of nature) trotting in one direction while a locomotive (emblematic of the horrible vigor of the twentieth century) steams in the other. As he says of Monhegan Island in Maine: "Fall, you know, that's the great time. There's a wonderful sort of melancholy. Nobody's here. Houses are closed up, sheets are pulled over furniture. I love it."

A catalogue of one Wyeth show begins with a genealogy.

Nicholas Wyeth came from England to Cambridge, Massachusetts, in 1645. Wyeths died in the French and Indian War, and so on. It's hard to imagine a catalogue of, say, Andy Warhol or Helen Frankenthaler paintings beginning with a genealogy, especially of ancestors with no particular distinction, but with the Wyeths it seems appropriate.

N.C. (Newell Convers) was born on a farm in Needham, Massachusetts, in 1882 and studied art near home. In 1902, the golden age of illustration, he went to Wilmington, Delaware, to study with the dean of American illustrators, Howard Pyle, who exemplified the vitalist movement of the time: "We of today are not children, but men, each of us with a man's work to do." He must have loved seeing N.C., the huge farm boy, come through the door. In 1904, having decided to paint "true, solid American subjects—nothing foreign about them," N.C. went out west to study cowboys and Indians, whom he then painted in countless illustrations that began his career. He never settled on a single style—his palette brightened and dimmed, edges hardened and blurred, paint thickened and thinned. But he threw the paint around with masterful gestures. Where his son and grandson seem to tiptoe up to the canvas in dread, N.C. has a fine old time getting horses to gallop wild-eyed at us, Civil War artillerymen to struggle through the mud.

Unlike Andrew and Jamie, who have had to fight off charges that they are illustrators, N.C. had no choice but to embrace illustration, and in so doing seemed to free himself to indulge the range of his skills. In *Robin Hood and His Companions Lend Aid*," the focus of the picture is archers drawing their bows in Sherwood Forest, but the pleasure of it lies in the huge foreground of grass, which N.C. paints not just in greens, but in salmon, blue, yellow and orange. What amazing energy there is in that gout of paint he wallops onto the sunlit shirt in *At the Cards in Cluny's Cage*, and in the blaze of brush strokes that fling a parrot into the cage in *Long John Silver and Hawkins*. Surrounding the figure called "Winter," who stands in a windblown cape, is a battery of rhythmical brush strokes that seem like a splurge of van Gogh.

His paintings have the glow of the toys from our parents' and grandparents' childhoods. In what may be his most famous painting, *Old Pew,* the satanic blind messenger of *Treasure Island* flails his way through the brilliant moonlight outside a Benbow Inn modeled on the house of N.C.'s childhood. It has the power of a monstrous cri de coeur. When he was killed in 1945 by a train in Chadds Ford, Pennsylvania, he was a man who mourned his failure to be more than an illustrator. He wrote in a letter: "All sense of serenity and security has crumbled away and all I can do, when I think about it all, is to gawk stupidly at the retreating pageant of my dreams and hopes."

He had lived in Chadds Ford since early in the century. "This is a country full of restraints," he wrote then. "Everything lies in its subtleties, everything is so gentle and simple, so unaffected." Andrew would turn this gentility into a genre. His landscapes, in the words of Lincoln Kirsten, the ballet promoter and a family friend, have "affirmed a nostalgic Eden of preindustrial stoic innocence." But so did the paintings of Grandma Moses, who seemed to be the Wyeths' only rival as America's Artist in the *Time* and *Life* magazines of a generation ago.

Andrew's knack is showing this Eden just as the storm clouds gather. Unlike eighteenth- and nineteenth-century artists who dwelled on ruins, Andrew loves to paint the moment when the weeds and the wind are just beginning to pull the stones apart. In *Lovers,* one of the Helga nudes, a naked woman sits by an open window while a dead leaf blows past her thigh. Wyeth likes to place an ominous little flick of white at the top of a painting—foam in *Adrift,* snow in *Spring,* and rocks in *Indian Summer.* His tire tracks in *Spring* or *Border Patrol* show that the twentieth century has been here and nothing will ever be the same. Of course, he could have appealed to the same audience either by assuring them, like Norman Rockwell, that the nightmare wasn't happening, or by painting hokey WASPery like the blessing of the hounds. But he went that sort of thing one better—he confirms decay, and then finds nobility in it. He catches a dour northernness and finds beauty in our Protestant fear that we do not deserve our blessings and are doomed by them, somehow.

In *Siri,* a gloriously attractive tempera, the innocence of the young blond girl is so conspicuous that it insists on the inevitability of corruption. Behind her, the spirit of Jonathan Edwards and the Puritans watches from the shadows on the white colonial woodwork. Her hair snags the light—more of those morbid little flicks of white—and the light is fading.

Everything seems like a symbol in an Andrew Wyeth painting. To some people this points to ulterior motive and corniness, but others are grateful that Wyeth puts meaning into the world. It's an odd sort of meaning, though, and it has little to do with the subjects he paints. Charles Burchfield and Thomas Hart Benton were American realists who dealt, like Wyeth, with common and rural subjects. In their paintings shapes whirl and curve with an animal spirit, as if the whole world is alive and has a soul. The spirits in Wyeth's world are ghosts, wistful harpies whirling over the hills in the guise of snow flurries. He says: "I have such a strong, romantic fantasy about things. . . . You look at my pictures . . . there's witchcraft and hidden meaning there. Halloween and all that is strangely tied into them."

Where Andrew paints the spirit of Halloween, his son Jamie paints jack-o'-lanterns and leaves it at that. He doesn't create nostalgia, gloom, or poignance as much as he gives us totems of them and hopes we'll do the rest with our imaginations, the way Ralph Lauren hopes to inspire thoughts of bygone aristocracy by selling us shirts with polo ponies embroidered on them. Like his grandfather, Jamie paints in oil, and he can't seem to find a style that's comfortable for him. Unlike N.C., he can't surrender to his subjects or his material. He shares with his father a need to dominate everything before him, and the urge to play to that most desired of upper-middle-class attributes—self-consciousness. He paints kitsch, as in the blond woman driving two white horses and a buggy into the ferny forest in the ridiculous *And Then Into the Deep Gorge*. He paints animals—black angus, geese, sheep, pigs. For that subset of WASPdom that measures its humanity by the depth of its love for animals, this is gratifying. There's also the irony of a painter with his skills—as in the commissioned portrait of John F. Kennedy—addressing such trivia. He paints the way a young, nervous man might paint to impress his mother's rich friends.

Even if Jamie didn't paint, he'd have stature as a Wyeth, a family credited with keeping the flame of a particular sensibility. If art is a religion, the Wyeths are somewhere between parish priests and druids. And the metaphysical divines of the more cosmopolitan art world will continue to hold them and their admirers in contempt.

Batman, with his parapet-brooding and dime-store-gothic gloom, is like sex or fascism—most ridiculous when most serious, most serious when most ridiculous.

The Caped Crusader, the Nightblooming Naugahyde Neurotic— he has figured in the American imagination since 1939, accompanied by Robin the Boy Wonder, Alfred the butler, the Joker, the Penguin, the Batcave, Batcopter, Batplane, Batarang, Batrope, Commissioner Gordon flashing the Batsignal on the side of a skyscraper, and the Bat-mobile hurling its low, mean heft through the streets of Gotham. Bat-man: a square-jawed fallen angel with the glamour of the tough guys, the hoods who scared you in school with a fetishy acuteness, every-thing raked and dark, glinting and ironic, pure style and knowing it, as in the scene in the first *Batman* movie where Michael Keaton, in his ridiculous rubber Batsuit (fetish!), listens to a punk scream, "Don't kill me," and then says in a near-whisper: "I'm Batman."

He is not a tough guy, a hood. He's Batman, a rich guy named Bruce Wayne, who dresses up like a bat and spooks around the city fighting evildoers. (Note that unlike Dracula, another rich guy with a bat routine, he doesn't actually become a bat, he just wears a bat costume.) Noblesse oblige. He's a crime-fighting rich guy like Zorro, the Shadow, or the Scarlet Pimpernel, and one of a class of dark and quirky heroes in twentieth-century popular culture: Lash LaRue dressed in black and eschewing guns in favor of a whip; the Phantom looking like Mussolini's pet executioner; Richard Boone as TV's black-clad Paladin in the 1950s' *Have Gun Will Travel;* Sly Stallone and Arnold Schwarzenegger with their latissimus dorsi muscles flaring out like wings, a little batlike, actually; Robocop; the Blackhawk squadron flying through comic books of the '50s in Nazi-cut uniforms.

Terror is a force for good in Batman comics and movies. Alienation is a moral position. Here is where the fascist question arises. In 1986 DC Comics brought out a four-part comic book novel called *The Dark Knight Returns,* written by Frank Miller. It showed a middle-aged Batman tortured by memories, loneliness, and near-psychotic cravings for vengeance.

Two television commentators talk about his image.

Says one, "I regard it as a symbolic resurgence of the common man's will to resist, a rebirth of the American fighting spirit."

Says the other, "The only thing he signifies is an aberrant psychotic force, morally bankrupt, politically hazardous, reactionary, paranoid. . . . he knows exactly what he's doing. His kind of social fascist always does."

What a handy word "fascist" has become! It no longer means a supporter of a belligerent one-party state defining racism and militarism as virtues. In 1989 it means an aura of conspicuous masculinity and power fetishes—leather, guns, boots, whips, muscle-building. It has a twilight-of-the-gods feeling about it, and a sexuality that veers off into silliness—bondage, funny underwear, and all that. It's a teeny bit homoerotic, witness the suspicions all these years about Batman and Robin—"A wish dream of two homosexuals living together," a psychiatrist named Frederic Wertham wrote in a 1954 screed called *Seduction of the Innocents.*

The current idea of the fascist harks back past the Nazis to the Nietzschean notion of the Uebermensch, or superman, who is not to be confused with Superman, the goody-two-shoes Man of Steel. Though on the same side of the law as Batman, Superman is a cheerful buckethead from Smallville whereas Batman is the tortured urban recluse. Superman takes off his costume—his Clark Kent clothes—to fight crime, and Batman puts one on. Superman is a tool of the establishment; Batman is ruled only by a personal code of honor. Superman has superpowers. Batman has only wealth and training, along with a hatred for bureaucracy and its namby-pamby refusal to believe in evil, to see the smoking hoofprints of the Fiend himself in our schoolyards, legislatures and slums. In a comic called *The Untold Legend of the Batman,* the young Bruce Wayne sets out to become the world's greatest detective, only to end up standing before his parents' graves in the light of a full moon, saying, "Forgive me, Mom . . . Dad . . . But I can't become a policeman as I'd intended to—they're too often hamstrung by the very laws they're sworn to uphold! No, there has to be another way."

The way shares the existential-vigilante overtones of *The Dirty Dozen* or *The Magnificent Seven,* in which hardened criminals with hearts of gold take on the Nazis or a swarm of Mexican bandits. But Batman is not a criminal. He is not atoning. In his past, by contrast, lurks a wound: the murder of his parents before his eyes when he was nine. He is scarred. He qualifies as one of yet another subset of American heros, the gimped ones: Doc Holliday, the tubercular Western gunfighter at the OK Corral; the limping Hopalong Cassidy; the wheelchair-bound Ironside on TV; the orphaned newsboy Billy Batson, who says "SHAZAM!" and becomes Captain Marvel; and all the angst-ridden superheroes of the Marvel comics pantheon (Spiderman, the Incredible Hulk, etc.).

During the 1950s and '60s, Batman became just another earnest comic book mesomorph, like Superman. In 1966 he became the campy television Batman with Adam West and Burt Ward as the Dynamic Duo, with words like BAM! or POW! appearing on screen during fistfights. In the 1970s, Batman comics revived the gloomy tone that had been set in 1939, though the pieties of social science were observed: The Joker was no longer evil as much as he was mentally ill, say.

Batman has sidekicks and archenemies, he's acquainted with the night, like most fiction detectives, and he's an isolated genius like Captain Nemo or Sherlock Holmes. But none of them partake of the magic of darkness the way Batman does. Hence the fetishism.

Batman is what one merchandiser describes as "toyetic." For months before the release of the first movie, there were hundreds of Batblazoned fetishes for the Batfaithful to collect: a movie poster that kids have smashed bus shelters to get; model Batmobiles and Batwing airplanes; ballpoint pens, beach towels, board games, boxer shorts, yo-yos, auto sunshields, buttons, bubble gum cards, statuettes, bicycle shorts, penlights, playing cards, satin jackets, T-shirts, handcuffs, key chains, magnets, earrings, bumper stickers, cloisonné pins, sweatshirts; watches, alarm clocks, mugs, cassettes, books, plane launcher, pistol, Frisbee, lunch box with thermos; water bottle, visor, can cooler, handbag, sourcebook, role-playing game, lithographs, movie-souvenir magazine—all of them bearing his power, his mana, his Batmana.

And his primal ridiculousness. As the introduction to the *Dark Knight* stories says, Batman "sums up more than any other the essential silliness of the comic book hero." And of latterday American fascism as well.

There were three theoretical physicists and a couple of journalists in a thirteenth-floor office at Rockefeller University, and nobody was moving. It was like a diorama you see at the natural history museum—the prehistoric family around the fire, Alexander Graham Bell inventing the telephone with glazed intensity —something about it that seemed to need dusting, the otherworldly shabbiness of suspended animation. Nobody spoke. The blank light of Manhattan diffused across bookshelves full of physics journals, a blackboard bearing equations.

A physicist named Heinz Pagels had asked a question several minutes earlier: "What are the major problems in cosmology from your viewpoint?" Now, hands folded and pin-stripe-suited, he sat absolutely still, except for an occasional resettling of the thumbs. A young physicist named Seth Lloyd, in jeans and leather jacket, had been coughing and fidgeting, but now he sat still too. They awaited an answer from the third physicist, who was slumped in a wheelchair. This was Stephen Hawking, the British black-hole theorist, hero of science and author of a book titled, with Hawkingesque wit, *A Brief History of Time*. He was in New York for a party in his honor. He appeared to be asleep.

Hawking cannot talk. He struggles to swallow his own spit. He can barely lift his head. Decades ago, when he was a graduate student in physics at Cambridge University, doctors told him he had amyotrophic lateral sclerosis, also known as Lou Gehrig's disease, after the baseball player who died of it in 1941. They said his motor neurons would waste away until he died, probably in two or three years. Now, wheelchair-bound and almost totally paralyzed, a crumpled gargoyle guarded by nurses and speaking through a computer speech synthesizer, he has defied the doctors, won fame, fathered three children, traveled around the world, become Lucasian Professor of Mathematics at Cambridge (the seat Newton held) and gone on the great Grail quest of physics—the search for the Grand Unified Theory that will unite Einstein's relativity to the tiny quarks and gluons of quantum mechanics, thereby explaining everything.

He has said, "My goal is simple. It is a complete understanding of the universe, why it is as it is and why it exists at all." The gulches of science are full of the bones of people who have said things like that—heroes, cranks, saints, geniuses, failures.

The only sound was the clicking that issued from Hawking's right hand, which held a little box that controlled the computer screen mounted in front of him on the wheelchair. Words and letters rolled across the screen. With the squeeze of a finger, Hawking picked out the ones he wanted and added them to the sentences he was assembling, bit by bit, until he could play his whole answer through the synthesizer. "Why . . . is . . . space-time . . . four . . . dimension. Why . . . is . . . the . . . cosmological . . ." Then Hawking saw his mistake. He went back and added the "al" to "dimension" before going on. He didn't have to—Pagels and Lloyd would have understood what he meant—but he rarely abbreviates.

"Why is space-time four-dimensional? Why is the cosmological constant zero?" This was Hawking's response, at last, with the stale lilt of computer speech.

"Aha," said Pagels, who would say "aha" a lot.

Hawking became a physicist at a time when the promise of dis-
coveries early in the century had not been realized despite huge increases in funding and technology after World War II. Physics had
given us atom bombs, transistors, and lasers, but it had been decades
since it had changed our picture of the universe as Einstein and Newton and Galileo had done. Still, the hope persisted. Einstein had described the relationship of large bodies in the universe and particle
physicists such as Max Planck, Werner Heisenberg, and Niels Bohr
had explained the forces inside the atom. You needed both relativity
and quantum mechanics to explain everything, but the two theories
conflicted at important points. This conflict prompted the search for
the Grand Unified Theory. This is what Einstein spent the last decades
of his life failing to find.

Hawking once said that we could find it within twenty years. If
so, he writes, such a theory "should in time be understandable in
broad principle by everyone, not just a few scientists. Then we shall
all, philosophers, scientists, and just ordinary people, be able to take
part in the discussion of the question of why it is that we and the universe exist. If we find the answer to that, it would be the ultimate triumph of human reason—for then we would know the mind of God."

It would also be the end of cosmological physics as we know it.
Hawking takes an odd, even Wagnerian interest in the idea of a twilight of the physicists. At the end of his book, with no explanation, he
includes thumbnail biographies of Galileo, Newton, and Einstein.
This is the company he would like to be in someday, but for now, he
is still risking oblivion. Along with his brilliance, his silences, his disease, and our desire to enshrine physicists, this risk gives Hawking the
charm of the hero.

Hawking is already part of the folklore and hagiography of modern physicists—beliefs that have little to do with the science these people do, but a great deal to do with the importance that we attach to it.
For every person who understands anything of Einstein's relativity
there are a hundred who understand that he wore no socks, played
the violin, and was a pacifist, the kindly old lover of mankind whom

Life magazine all but canonized in the 1950s. We remember less of Robert Oppenheimer's physics than the fact that he worked on the atom bomb, wore a porkpie hat and looked, as someone once said, as if he were "attending a night school for saints."

Though few people comprehend much of their work, many take for granted that physicists have a claim on Ultimate Reality, or Truth, or even God. Once, laymen believed this of artists such as Leonardo and Goethe or philosophers such as Aristotle and Kant—all of whom did science of one kind or another. Now art is a science of the self, and philosophy has largely vanished into linguistics, but physics remains. Countless gurus and self-help salesmen have sought its imprimatur. Werner Erhard, of the est training seminars, has sponsored conferences of physicists, one of which Hawking attended. The Maharishi Mahesh Yogi's Transcendental Meditation claims links to the unified field theory. Theology may have been hidden away like a dotty old aunt in courses of comparative religion, but nobody has proposed teaching comparative physics—physics does not postulate a truth, but the truth. Physics does not bend with politically necessary beliefs. No student radical of the 1960s demanded courses in liberation astronomy or women's quantum theory. Hawking and his world have transcended opportunism.

Like saints, physicists are credited with a knowledge of God. Hawking might be a candidate for latter-day sainthood of this order —he is a living example of the transcendent mind, a human with all the virtues of science-fiction beings in galaxies eons ahead of ours, pure brain, no body, a man mortified beyond carnal temptation. As for mysticism, Hawking once responded to the notion that Eastern techniques can give us greater insights into objective reality by saying to a journalist: "I think it is absolute rubbish. Write it down. It's pure rubbish." And with his book, which he has aimed at a popular audience—he says he wants to see it on sale in airports—he has returned to a nineteenth-century style of proselytizing for science, like T. H. Huxley on lecture tours, urging us toward truth and fighting superstition, a "man of science," as such were known. The problem is, even if he can make physics plain, he can never be other than esoteric himself. People who have known him a long time say they forget about his disease, but it is unsettling. And he is known for his bluntness. At one point in the conversation, Lloyd, an ambitious twenty-seven, blushed and sweated as he reminded Hawking, forty-six, of a paper he had sent him. Finally, Hawking said: "The paper was good in parts."

In parts! What did he mean, "in parts"? Because of Hawking's prestige, and the huge silences, everything he said had a gnomic quality. It was unsettling, too, to talk with someone whose mood is impossible to judge. At a guess, he seemed happy, cranky, egotistical, preoccupied, and wary, but who knew for sure? He has no gestures except a labored smile. He cannot glue a conversation together with frowns, shrugs, winces, and catchings of breath.

Pagels and Lloyd dodged these dilemmas by sitting absolutely still, a diorama of physics. They listened to the tiny clicking from Hawking's right hand. They had questions about string theory, which attempts to unite relativity and quantum mechanics, and about the black holes that occur, theory has it, when stars collapse to points of no dimension but infinite density—Hawking's work on black holes may be his major contribution to physics so far—and about the anthropic principle, which means, Hawking has written, that "we see the universe the way it is because if it were different, we would not be here to observe it."

Although Hawking rarely abbreviates his answers, he cut off Pagels' and Lloyd's questions as soon as he got the sense of them.

"Would an anthropic explanation of the near-vanishing of the cosmological constant be acceptable?" Pagels began. "Steve Weinberg has . . ."

"Yes."

"Steve Weinberg [a physicist] has written a paper saying . . ."

"Maybe," said Hawking.

"Does the imprecision of anthropic arguments disturb you when one is dealing with . . ."

"Yes."

Pagels got into the principles underlying string theory. "One would have hoped for some deeper principle," he began.

On the screen Hawking wrote: "maybe . . . I . . . better . . . get . . ."

"Even the space-time of the string theory . . .," Pagels continued.

Hawking wrote: "ready for . . ."

"Maybe I better get ready for the party. I have to write a speech," the computer voice said.

"Okay," Pagels said.

Lloyd laughed.

Pagels smiled, a huge delighted smile. It seemed to be a smile of both relief and wild intimacy, as if the truth that no one could admit while talking with Hawking was that his disease makes him closer, not farther; that it amplifies his brilliance rather than obscuring it; and that there's an intensity to talking with Hawking of the sort that maybe only children can bear. Something about Hawking seems happy, too, and it makes other people happy.

"I know it's frustrating for you to speak slowly," Lloyd said, like a man who's waited a long time to say something. "But when I was at Cambridge you were the best lecturer. Maybe because the other guys were so dry."

Hawking searched his computer screen and clicked his control box.

"Thanks," he said.

dennis hopper

Dennis Hopper still talks very hip, a grieved, sidelong way of speaking that's full of italics and drawl. He still looks sad, too—the chevron mouth and the slanting eyes and eyebrows. Everything about him is exaggerated: the wide shoulders, the little hips, the gentle gestures— he puts out cigarettes like somebody killing a mosquito very slowly. He's so plaintive he's nearly grotesque.

A long time ago, back in the '50s and '60s, he kept wobbling up into fame like a bad skyrocket, shedding flaming chunks and threatening to turn and head straight for the crowd. It was all part of being a genius. That's what sensitive young men wanted to be back then, even in Hollywood. It was like being a Puritan, and trying to figure out whether you were among the elect. Am I a genius? Is he a genius? People had a lot of ways of finding out, and it took Hopper a few decades to run through most of them—illegal ways, dangerous ways, crazy ways while he made movies and built a reputation as a madman—*Rebel Without a Cause* and *Giant* with James Dean and *Easy Rider,* among others.

He was a legend. He was said to travel with a painting of a cruci-
fied Christ that looked just like himself, though he denies this now.
He was married to Brooke Hayward, daughter of actress Margaret
Sullivan and producer Leland Hayward, one of the first families of
show business. When he moved to Taos, New Mexico, he lived in the
house that D. H. Lawrence had lived in. He played the outlaw back
when we thought you had to be an outlaw to be pure and a genius.
His drug use was famous. He was quoted as claiming that he'd
stopped the Taos locals from beating up hippies by going on stage at a
high school assembly and threatening the students with a machine
gun. He was married to Michelle Phillips of the Mamas and the Papas
for eight days. He was said to never read books; to have pulled a
knife on a Mafia don; to have sculpted something called "the perpet-
ual erection machine." He was married to Daria Halprin, who starred
in Antonioni's *Zabriskie Point*. He was said to have gone berserk in
seven hours of footage that never made it into *Easy Rider*. Somebody
made a documentary film about him, called *"The American Dreamer,*
in which he did nude scenes that demonstrated honesty back then. He
would later tell interviewers that he did half an ounce of cocaine every
three days and drank half a gallon of rum every day.

This was part of his appeal from the beginning, when Hopper
was a kid trying to tag along with a whole generation of grieved, tor-
mented geniuses: Jack Kerouac, Jackson Pollock, Lenny Bruce, and
Charlie Parker, for instance. In Hollywood alone there were Marlon
Brando, Montgomery Clift, and James Dean, struggling up the beach-
head of 1950s America like turtles with their shells torn off, pure
nerve endings, pathologically authentic. Now, the age of the geniuses
is long gone. Dennis Hopper is a middle-aged guy who plays golf,
drives a Cadillac, and smokes a lot of cigarettes. He is making more
movies than he ever did back when he was ricocheting around Hollywood, New York, and Taos believing that he was a genius, too.

Was genius worth going after? Does it kill you?

"I like the concept of it," he says, sitting in a hotel suite late one
afternoon. "I think everything kills you. This cigarette's gonna kill me
if I don't stop smoking, I'll tell you that. You know, I've stopped

everything else but this. My last friend is my enemy."

It's all over. He is no longer an advance man for the Revolution, as he was after he made *Easy Rider*. Instead, he is working. "This is, like, 'Don't stop working!' " he says. Then he laughs his big Dennis Hopper laugh, which makes a sound like fat hands clapping. "Take a day off. . . . No! Better work!"

In the old days, too, people believed in genius.

"Suddenly I saw James Dean, and I realized, man, I was way out of my league," Hopper says. "I thought I was the best actor, man, you know, going. And I suddenly saw Dean, and I knew, man, I was in another league. I had no concept of what he was doing or how he was working or anything. Because he wasn't giving line readings. He wasn't doing the same thing every time. He was, like, fully creating out of his imagination and improvising and it was way over my head. And that's when he started telling me to do things. Telling me, he'd say, 'Look, just do it, don't show it. You know, if you're smoking a cigarette, just smoke the cigarette, don't act like you're smoking a cigarette.' "

The idea was to be real up there on the screen. Art was supposed to strip away self-delusion and hypocrisy. In a story he told *Life* magazine, Hopper said:

> When I was little, I lived on a farm near Dodge City, Kansas. Wheat fields all around, as far as you could see. No neighbors, no other kids. Just a train that came through once a day. I used to spend hours wondering where it came from and where it went to. Then when I was about 5 my grandmother put some eggs in her apron and we walked five miles to town and she sold the eggs and took me to my first movie. And right away it hit me—the places I was seeing on the screen were the places the train came from and went to! The world on the screen was the real world, and I felt as if my heart would explode I wanted so much to be a part of it.

Hopper started acting at thirteen, after his family moved to San Diego and he got to do Shakespeare in the Old Globe Theater there. When he was eighteen, he played an epileptic on a television show, and got a contract with Warner Brothers. He has played the berserker both on and off screen ever since. He worked with Dean, and then an argument over a scene in *From Hell to Texas* ended up with the director shooting the scene eighty-six times.

He went to New York. He took photographs for *Vogue* and other magazines. He studied acting with Lee Strasberg—method acting, real emotion, the gospel that Dean, Brando, and Clift had taken to Hollywood. Except Dean had driven his Porsche into an oncoming car by this time, and Clift's career was tailing off, and it was getting harder to be a genius, as opposed to someone who just did the work. One of the big shocks came from Brando. Hopper says: "Marlon Brando said it was a craft. Try to follow that one. Marlon Brando said, 'It's only a craft.' I remember this moment, though, when he came out in Life magazine all the actors in New York freaked out, because Brando said there's nothing to it. It's only a craft. I remember that. I remember him also saying, 'I want to grow up now so I may give up acting because acting is for children' . . . the actors freaking out and saying, 'What is he talking about?' But in point of fact it is. It's a lot of work to have a childlike kind of belief, huh?"

Then he directed and costarred in a biker-drug movie, *Easy Rider*, which became a cinematic anthem for the disaffected middle-class youth of the late '60s. It cost $340,000 to make and it has grossed over $50 million. It also punched his genius ticket with the money people. He made *The Last Movie*, a film-within-a-film thing that won the Venice Film Festival. Hollywood hated it, and it died. He moved to Taos, the New Age omphalos, and he worked on becoming a mad saint of the counterculture, a legend. It turned out that this was what he was a genius at.

He waited for Hollywood to come to him.

I said, "Well, they should be bringing me movies, I mean I'm, you know, a genius." So, stories, partly fiction, some truth, grew, and I'd get crazier and crazier and crazier because I wasn't working. Saying, "They've got it against me." And it was all bull, because it was me. It wasn't Hollywood. Okay? It was me. It was me. And what happened? You know, you wake up fifteen years later, and you're living up in the mountains, you're a hippie. You go into the cities, where are the hippies? Where are they? The people that you knew are the executives behind the desk and the major stars in the industry, and yeah, they're still your friends—"Where you been?"

He'd been in what his first wife called "the abyss." He'd also been the crazed photographer in *Apocalypse Now* and a murderer in Wim Wenders' *The American Friend*, among other roles. But mostly he'd been Dennis Hopper, the legend. It culminated with press reports of him going nuts in Mexico while making a movie called *Jungle Fever*—wandering around Cuernavaca naked, trying to escape from the airplane that was hauling him back to the States, and ending up in a couple of mental wards, and then Alcoholics Anonymous.

"I'm out of Taos. I'll never live in Taos again. I'm gonna live in Los Angeles the rest of my life. The Revolution never happened, man."

He works. He plays a lot of losers and maniacs—the town drunk in *Hoosiers*, a bellowing psychopathic murderer in *Blue Velvet*. If Hollywood still believed in geniuses the way it used to, back when it made all the movies about Edison, Freud, Liszt, and so on, maybe it would have him play a genius, too.

hoover

For half the twentieth century, whispers followed along behind J. Edgar Hoover like the little dust clouds behind cartoon characters. The rumors of homosexuality. The Kennedy-bugging. The Nixon-blackmailing. The communist witch hunts. The smearing of Martin Luther King Jr. The self-promotion that transformed a file clerk who lived with his mother into a gangbusting bulwark against all enemies, foreign and domestic.

But the whispers stayed whispers. There were secrets we didn't want to know. It was a matter of national security, really. Or insecurity. America wanted Hoover-as-hero, not Hoover-as-villain.

Then, more than two decades after his death, his villainy swelled like a carbuncular growth: a scandalous best-selling book, a tell-all TV show, and endless wisecracks describing transvestite orgies, graft, treason, endless crimes.

O fickle public.

In his heyday, Hoover belonged to a lost age of American heroes: Lindbergh, Henry Ford, Babe Ruth, Douglas MacArthur, Amelia

Earhart, Einstein, Douglas Fairbanks, Joe Louis. The Lone Ranger gave Hoover a silver bullet. Shirley Temple gave him a hug. He understood that in an era when no one knew the difference between personality and character, he didn't have to seize power, he could just let the people give it to him in the form of stardom.

During his lifetime (1895–1972), most of it spent holding absolute sway over the Federal Bureau of Investigation (1924–1972), few Americans would have paid attention to a book in which a woman provided the following description of Hoover, at sixty-two or sixty-three, in a suite at the Plaza hotel:

> He was wearing a fluffy black dress, very fluffy, with flounces, and lace stockings and high heels, and a black curly wig. He had makeup on, and false eyelashes. It was a very short skirt, and he was sitting there in the living room of the suite with his legs crossed. Roy Cohn introduced him to me as "Mary" and he replied, "Good evening," brusque, like the first time I'd met him. It was obvious he wasn't a woman, you could see where he shaved. It was Hoover. You've never seen anything like it. I couldn't believe it that I should see the head of the FBI dressed up as a woman.

This is a scene from *Official and Confidential—The Secret Life of J. Edgar Hoover,* a book by Anthony Summers. The woman is Susan Rosenstiel. She was the wife of Lewis Rosenstiel, a bisexual who owned the Schenley distilleries and hung around with both Hoover and Mafiosi, Summers says. The book was published in 1993, and made the bestseller list. A *Frontline* television show covered the same ground and got big ratings. The *New Yorker* called the newly revealed Hoover a "G-man in a G-string" and ran two cartoons. One showed a doorway bearing the words: "THE JAYE EDGAR HOOVER BUILDING." The other showed one disconsolate FBI agent saying to another, "Has anyone considered that maybe his dress was a disguise?" In a mock ceremony on *The Tonight Show,* Jay Leno described the age of Senator Strom Thurmond by saying: "When Strom Thurmond first went to Washington, J. Edgar Hoover was still walking around in a training bra." The people who used to call him

"Jedgar Hoover" now called him "Gay Edgar Hoover."

A model for American manhood—he once wrote a piece called "What Makes Men Strong" for *This Week* magazine—was charged with being a hypocritical drag queen (with bad taste in clothes, too— I mean, flounces at his age). It's not so much that a hero was being torn down as a villain was being built. The man who became a legend for solving the crimes of the century was accused now of committing them.

In his book Summers claimed: Hoover could have stopped the attack on Pearl Harbor. He went easy on the Mafia because Meyer Lansky threatened to reveal pictures of him having sex with a man. He may have been behind the shooting of John Kennedy. He promoted Clyde Tolson, an agent with three years on the job, to number two man in the bureau because they were lovers. He tried to hound Martin Luther King into killing himself, and spent the day at the racetrack when James Earl Ray killed King in Memphis. He kept Supreme Court justices under surveillance. He spied on political conventions. He committed character assassination and rewrote history, and did them both on a Soviet scale.

The strange thing is that we've had a lot of heroes with ugly sides—Lindbergh the fascist, John Kennedy the sexual obsessive, and so on—but we've pitied or forgiven their nastiness, or forgotten it. Why this fury toward Hoover—these yelps of resentment, this frantic sifting of the fossil bed for coprolite?

A personal recollection:

It was 1968, the late spring of a bad year. The FBI guy led us through the halls. He was all good manners, with the apologetic cheer of a seasoned gofer. He'd talked us—maybe half a dozen reporters— into putting down the newspapers we were reading in the Senate press gallery, and following him through Senate hallways without knowing why.

It was a particularly bad year for J. Edgar Hoover and everything he represented—the earnest, red-blooded, white-skinned God-bless-America folks who worked hard, always got the right tools for the job, and put the tools back when they were through. Now the country was full of dopers and rioters—criminals who refused to admit they were criminals. Things were getting ugly—the smog of Vietnam shrinking moral horizons, and tear gas lingering in the back of America's throat after the assassination of Martin Luther King. Everybody knew how Hoover had persecuted King—bugging him, redbaiting him, giving tapes of his love life to the media. Then, when King was killed in Memphis in April, Hoover refused to hunt for the killer, on grounds that the killing wasn't a federal offense. The attorney general had overruled him. Now, in late spring, weeks and weeks had gone by and with thousands of agents on the case, Hoover still hadn't caught James Earl Ray. People were saying he didn't want to.

The gofer led us to a big wooden door. He opened it with courtly edginess.

Sitting on a table, one shoe touching the floor, was Hoover. Clearly, he was waiting for us, posed on the table with the coy informality of those old *Daily News* shots of chorus girls arriving in New York on ocean liners. There was a sense of old, oiled machinery at work. His face looked as if it might have just risen out of his collar like a meat periscope. It was the face of the grandmother you were always afraid of, with oddly dark, luxuriant eyes. There were bright round red spots on each cheekbone, very precise, like painted spots on a puppet's cheeks. His mouth was a thin little business that wandered across his chin on a diagonal, like the chart of a bad stock market.

"C'mon in, boys," he said.

Boys? Who was the last person to call reporters boys? Jimmy Cagney? Was this rehearsed, or was it just old-fashioned? He was a regular museum of forgotten Big Guy moves.

"I want to give you the lowdown on this James Earl Ray business," he said. "But don't take out the notebooks, this is all strictly on the Q.T."

Lowdown. Q.T.

He told us he was going to catch Ray. He took no questions. He left by a rear door. I thought: Time stopped for this guy in 1938.

Hard to imagine now what he meant to America in 1938.

In the despair of the Depression the public needed a hero who could whip the evil that was abroad in the land. Hoover did the job by having his men gun down gangsters like John Dillinger. Gangbusting made the FBI the heroes in countless radio shows, comic strips, movies, trading cards, Junior G-Man clubs, and Junior G-Man detective kits. In a detective magazine called *The Feds,* Hoover, the popularizer of "Public Enemy Number One," was "Public Hero Number One."

At a hearing in 1936, Sen. Kenneth McKellar attacked Hoover for running a publicity mill at the FBI, then asked him: "Did you ever make an arrest?"

"No, sir," Hoover said.

A bad moment.

In fact, Hoover had no desire to be thought of as an action detective. He wanted the public to love the bureau as a team of scientific, disciplined civil servants solving crimes through the sifting of records and the laboratory study of tire treads and fiber samples. But the public wanted G-man action detectives. And Hoover knew what the public wanted. A few weeks after McKellar embarrassed him, he flew to New Orleans for his first arrest: Alvin "Creepy" Karpis, the last member of Ma Barker's gang. He couldn't put the cuffs on Karpis because he didn't have any, nor did any of the other agents on the scene.

Somebody took off a necktie and tied his hands. More arrests followed as Hoover yielded to the public's need to make him into a tough guy who liked a scrap.

"HOOVER SAYS STICK 'EM UP," said the *New York Journal.*

The idea of the FBI action detective had its ultimate apotheosis at the start of World War II when a comic book showed the FBI creating not just another brave agent, but Captain America, "the first of a corps of super-agents whose mental and physical ability will make them a terror to spies and saboteurs." Along with Dillinger's death mask and Creepy Karpis's guns, people taking the FBI tour get to see a huge wall painting of a macromuscular superheroic Captain America with red, white, and blue superhero tights and a shield.

During the war, Hoover was our shield while the country lay awake imagining Nazi spies paddling ashore from darkened submarines.

"We know that our protection against some of the most dangerous of them has been, and is, in the hands of Director J. Edgar
Hoover," said *Liberty* magazine.

"The iron-jawed Chief," said *G-Men* magazine.

> Public Enemies One-on-down
> Shudder as he goes to town.
> Saboteurs and other rats
> Reach in panic for their hats.
>
> *Saturday Evening Post*, 1943

In the 1950s he could "make water run uphill," as Jimmy Stew-
art said in *The FBI Story*. It was Cold War time. Hoover stood up for
God and family against the atom spies, and drove stakes through the
hearts of "the vampires of international communism," as he called
them in a book entitled *Masters of Deceit,* which went through more
than twenty printings. More and more, he pronounced on faith and
morals and the virtues of church and family.

He was also a celebrity who vacationed in Palm Beach and drank
at the Stork Club with Walter Winchell. He had once thought seriously
about running for president against Franklin D. Roosevelt. A press release from the FBI in 1944 borrowed the style of Time magazine to
say: "Tough, and looks it, is MR. J. EDGAR HOOVER, Director of the
Federal Bureau of Investigation of America has a sensational record
for bringing public enemies of all kinds, including the notorious kid-
napping gangs, to justice is the hero of all American schoolboys."

Almost all.

> Dear Mr. Hoover,
>   There is a boy I know named Red Hopkins. . . . He took
> your picture and put it on a poster and wrote WANTED below the
> picture. I am not a squealer, but I think you should know about
> Red Hopkins.
>   Sincerely,
>   Mark K.
>   Birmingham, Michigan
>
> —*Kids' Letters to the FBI*, 1966

"A star in his own right," said a Hollywood producer about meeting him. "I felt much as I did when I met Cary Grant."

In *G-Men*, Richard Gid Powers writes: "Once Hoover's stardom had been conferred, no one who depended on the public's good will (and by definition that included presidents and attorneys general) could afford to cross Hoover within his field of acknowledged supremacy. Hoover's power was given to him by the public, not by his superiors, and only the public could take it away."

In 1972, as Hoover lay in state in the Capitol Rotunda, Nixon gave a eulogy that showed how well he understood the half-century dance Hoover had done with the public: "He became a living legend while still a young man, and he lived up to his legend as the decades passed. . . . the invincible and incorruptible defender of every American's precious right to be free from fear."

Six months later, Nixon said to his aide John Dean: "He's got files on everybody, goddamn it." And a month after that:

Dean: "I'm convinced the FBI isn't everything the public thinks it is."
Nixon: "No."
Dean: "I know quite well it isn't."

In 1937 the *New Yorker* described Hoover as being "almost six feet tall." In 1972, after he died, a niece named Margaret Fennell was reported as looking down at him and thinking that he looked "smaller than I remembered." In 1991 Curt Gentry wrote in *J. Edgar Hoover: The Man and the Secrets* that Hoover compensated for his "shortness" by putting a raised dais under his desk, avoiding tall people at parties and keeping tall agents out of headquarters positions. And in 1993 Summers wrote in *Official and Confidential* that "under their breath, agents would come to call Edgar 'Kid Napoleon.' He was dictatorial and diminutive in stature—estimates of his height vary between five feet seven inches and five feet ten inches, the higher figure being the one he had entered in his personnel record."

When did the public start wanting Hoover as villain the way they had wanted him as hero?

In 1951 a writer named Max Lowenthal attacked Hoover in a

book called *The Federal Bureau of Investigation*. But he was preaching only to the left-wing choir. The public didn't want to hear it. By the '60s, the CIA had stolen the FBI's glamour, with spymasters taking over from gangbusters. The FBI had nothing to compare with the charm of James Bond. The case has been made that the general public first got interested in the dark side of Hoover in 1964, after he met with eighteen female journalists in Washington and told them that Martin Luther King was "the most notorious liar in the country."

Did he think he was safe because they were women? His public relations man, Cartha DeLoach, kept passing him notes telling him to put the statement off the record. Hoover told the reporters he wanted it on the record. In the ruckus that followed, Hoover refused to back down. He said King was "one of the lowest characters in the country. . . . I haven't even begun to say all I could on this subject."

By the time I ran into him in 1968, the dope culture, the New Left, the communards, the hip young university teachers, the freaks, crazies, and professional paranoids of bohemia were creating a new Hoover—the iron chancellor of the country club fascists, the Gestapoid shredder of civil rights, the doomed and bogus totalitarian. He was the perfect enemy and bête noire. The same year, the first of a string of books by angry ex-agents appeared: *Inside the FBI* by Norman Ollestad. In 1970 *Hoover's FBI* by William Turner bore a cover picture of Hoover glancing upward with a tired sneer as if he heard the artillery getting closer to the bunker.

In 1972 *Time* magazine eulogized Hoover as "one of the greats." By 1975, after Nixon's Watergate resignation had shaken faith in government, *Time* ran a picture of a nasty, pathetic Hoover.

"The legend is crumbling," the story began.

Senility. Homosexuality. Racism. PR hooey about the gangster cases. Thin evidence in the commie spy cases. The media had known this stuff for years. Why hadn't they printed it? Fear of Hoover would be the obvious answer, but fear of the American people is probably a better one. In any case, to dwell on the facts was to miss the point. He was a legend, and we all—media and the public—had chosen to believe it rather than attack it.

Of course, if he was our Hoover, we could do whatever we wanted with him. We've spent the last fifteen years turning him into a villain. In 1978 a six-hour television docudrama called *King* described Hoover as "a harassing racist psychopath fighting the specter of black insurrection," and it implicated him in the assassination. In 1979 David Levine caricatured Hoover as a sort of crazed, melting chancre with wall eyes.

G. Gordon Liddy, talk show host, felon, and former FBI agent, wrote in a recent *Forbes* "FYI": "It is curious that, at a time when the Left is marshaling all the forces of political correctness in an effort to win for homosexuality equivalency of place with heterosexuality, both culturally and legally, it nevertheless hurls the accusation of homosexuality (upon no evidence whatsoever) at its enemy, the late director of the FBI."

Thus does politics make hypocrites of us all.

Maybe if he'd been a man of action we could forgive him more. Then again, he wouldn't have offered us the Walter Mitty spectacle of file clerk as hero. Maybe if he hadn't been such a preacher in the 1950s, there wouldn't be such joy in defrocking him. If he hadn't been so frightening, we wouldn't be laughing so hard.

As a new Kennedy generation of technocrats, journalists, and academics gained power, Hoover held to his old loyalties to Mr. and Mrs. Front Porch U.S.A. As for protecting himself, Hoover may have had files on everyone, but after forty years in office, the media and the universities were acquiring quite a file on him. And Hoover was a hypocrite, that favorite leper of the new class, which shuns calling someone a sinner, but learned in college that the root of all evil is a contradiction.

Nazi hunter/Nazi, gangbuster/gangster, gay basher/closet queen, action detective/file clerk: He is the picture of Dorian Gray melting into depravity, he is Gregor Samsa—Kafka's bureaucrat who turns into a cockroach. It's as if Toto had pulled away the curtain, and the Wizard of Oz turned out to be a little toad of a man, flapping his arms and hissing: "Public enemy! Public enemy!"

part four

commoner redeemers

America doesn't have a problem with guns, it has a problem with the mystique of guns. Why doesn't anybody talk about this? Gun mystique is right up there with racism as a problem that isn't going away anytime soon, but the amount of serious writing about it wouldn't fill a lunch box. American intellectuals have probably written more about the sword culture of Japan.

The only famous historian to take it on was Richard Hofstadter. In 1970, in an essay called "America as a Gun Culture," he wrote:

> What began as a necessity of agriculture and the frontier took hold as a sport and as an ingredient in the American imagination. . . . For millions of American boys, learning to shoot and above all graduating from toy guns and receiving the first real rifle of their own were milestones of life, veritable rites of passage that certified their arrival at manhood. (It is still argued by some defenders of our gun culture, and indeed conceded by some of its critics, that the gun cannot and will not be given up because it is a basic symbol of

masculinity. But the trouble with all such glib Freudian generalities is that they do not explain cultural variations: they do not tell us why men elsewhere have not found the gun essential to their masculinity.)

To most of the Freudian class, guns are a proletarian anachronism, a vulgarity like some ludicrous sex fetish. The horror of them needs no explaining, the pleasure of them is incomprehensible. So the antigun forces end up buying into the flip side of the same sort of gun mystique that enthralls the lower classes they dread.

There is the mystique, for instance, of the gun that will destroy America and maybe civilization as we know it. It was Thompson submachine guns in the gangster '20s, sawed-off shotguns, zip guns when we started talking about "juvenile delinquency" in the '50s (oh, innocent era), imported military surplus rifles like the one that shot John Kennedy, and the guns that Patty Hearst posed with in front of a Symbionese Liberation Army flag. Saturday Night Specials—cheap pistols for poor (hence dangerous) people—are a myth all their own. They scarcely exist. A rich kid like John Hinckley may shoot Ronald Reagan with one, but down on the street, the kids carry 9mm brushed chrome top-of-the line equipment. It has more mystique. People both pro- and antigun credit guns with powers that verge on the supernatural. It's said a .45 can knock you down even with a close miss; that a .357 magnum can penetrate the length of a car, including the entire engine block.

In recent years, assault rifles have become "high-tech killing machines" of "incredible destructiveness," according to the media. The focus is the AK-47, a low-powered stamped-metal Soviet rifle whose stock looks like it was carved from an orange crate. It is almost half a century old. It hit thirty-fivepeople in the Stockton, California, schoolyard massacre in 1989 and left thirty of them alive. Only four of eleven people survived in 1988 when they were hit with an ordinary 12-gauge shotgun in Sunnyvale, California. But it's the AK-47 that has the mystique.

There's the mystique of guns as pure pleasure—the radiant heft of a loaded gun, a pistol, say, the first time you carry one, feverishly huge on your hip and you can't stop thinking about it, like when you've got a very big roll of bills in your pocket. Push this feeling hard enough, and it can get dangerous. How many people are killed every year by a gun that was bought the same day?

In *Billy Bathgate*, E. L. Doctorow's title character says:

> I will never forget how it felt to hold a loaded gun for the first time and lift it and fire it, the scare of its animate kick up the bone of your arm, you are empowered there is no question about it, it is an investiture, like knighthood, and even though you didn't invent it or design it or tool it the credit is yours because it is in your hand, you don't even have to know how it works, the credit is all yours, with the slightest squeeze of your finger a hole appears in a piece of paper sixty feet away, and how can you not be impressed with yourself, how can you not love this coiled and sprung causation, I was awed, I was thrilled, the thing is guns come alive when you fire them, they move, I hadn't realized that.

Guns are very nice things to have, to play with: a Winchester Model 70 bolt-action closing with the snug ease of a bank vault; blued barrels with an odd depth to them, like an opaque mirror; the monolithic density of a Luger pistol when you pull back the toggle, as if it were one block of steel whose atoms were merely rearranging themselves with the ease of a thought; an Aya .28 gauge side-by-side double-barreled shotgun, a good dove gun that floats to your shoulder with the ghostly self-volition that's like when you were a kid, and you pushed your arm outward against a wall for a while and then stepped back, and the arm rose all by itself; the tenor crack of an M1 carbine; the dark, round boom of a muzzleloader; or the three distinct clicks of an old single-action Army Colt being cocked, an echo of the dark, water-driven, leather-strapped mills of nineteenth-century manufacture, and a sound much like the one that was the last that Jesse James ever heard, as he dusted a picture hanging on the wall.

"He heard the hammer click as I cocked it with my thumb and started to turn as I pulled the trigger," said Bob Ford. "The ball struck him just behind the ear and he fell like a log, dead." Ten years later, Ford was shotgunned to death in Colorado by a James admirer.

The problem for the gun controllers is that guns are so locked into the mystique of American freedom that controlling them becomes a contradiction in terms. Names of gun companies have the sound of a national anthem: Winchester, Remington, Colt, Sharps, Savage, Springfield, Smith & Wesson. An American flintlock fired the shot heard round the world. In recent years a T-shirt has appeared with a picture of a Thompson submachine gun under the motto: "The Last Great American Freedom Machine."

By the time of the revolution, American sharpshooters already had so much mystique that George Washington encouraged "the use of Hunting Shirts, with long Breeches made of the same Cloth . . . it is a dress justly supposed to carry no small terror to the enemy, who think every such person a complete marksman." In his first draft of the Virginia constitution, Thomas Jefferson provided that "no free-man shall ever be debarred the use of arms." Hofstadter argues that he did it in the "anti-militaristic traditions of radical English Whiggery," in which evil was the sort of standing armies that the American revolutionaries fought against, and virtue lay with the yeoman farmers. Guns are "equalizers." God created man and Samuel Colt made him equal, as the saying went. Guns linked the romance of mass production to the romance of individual freedom: the gold-rush madam with her derringer, the mountain man with his rifle. Eli Whitney is said to have demonstrated the marvel of mass production for Jefferson by assembling guns out of heaps of interchangeable parts.

There are a lot of guns in America. Half of American households have guns, somewhere between 150 and 200 million guns in all, according to educated guesses, with 50 or 60 million handguns alone. We add 4 or 5 million new ones a year, not counting imports like the AK-47. The antigun forces seem to think they'll control them, as they say, with prudery, statistics, economic analysis, attacks on the National Rifle Association, and class warfare between gun foes and gun owners.

The class warfare is an old story. Around the turn of the century, people who ran things feared "a number of forces they associated with the handgun," according to Don B. Kates Jr., a criminologist and former civil rights lawyer. Among them: "Blacks who wouldn't keep their place; radicals, labor agitators, assassins, robbers, and by a process of further association, the foreign-born." Kates writes that it was white supremacists in the Tennessee legislature who passed the first "Saturday night special" law banning cheap pistols. In 1941 the Florida Supreme Court ruled that a gun control law had been "passed for the purpose of disarming the Negro laborers and the statute was never intended to be applied to the white population."

This was just another form of gun control that failed.

You can't fight the mystique. Americans crave guns because guns give meaning to their lives and deaths. No other country makes movies and television shows where the guns have such life in themselves. It's an esthetic tradition, a genre: *Winchester '73, Have Gun Will Travel, Gunsmoke, The Left-Handed Gun, Gunfight at the O.K. Corral, The Rifleman....* We've named both a movie and a malt liquor after a gun: "Colt 45." The only comparison to the gun in American movies is the sword in samurai movies. Sylvester Stallone and Arnold Schwarzenegger wander through a smorgasbord of apocalypses with plastic and black-metal machine guns and rocket launchers that have all the grace of something you'd use to spray rust-proofing on the bottom of a car. But this is a mystique in itself, the romance of the brutally functional in a world empty of meaning.

"Guns are always used at pivotal points in films," says Harris Bierman, a Hollywood armorer.

> This goes all the way back. There was the 1921 Thompson in *Little Caesar* and the Webley-Fosberry .455 revolver that knocked off Sam Spade's partner in *The Maltese Falcon*. There were the 1873 trapdoor Springfields in *Birth of a Nation* and the Gatling gun in *Vera Cruz*. You need this stuff. Look at *For Whom the Bell Tolls*, the kid saying the rosary with the Lewis gun on his shoulder, defending against the fascist hordes. Or *Bataan*, with that close-up of

the machine-gun muzzle blasting away at the end—directors always like to come in on them. For Rambo III, they went to Israel because they couldn't get the weapons they wanted here.

The more we see them at pivotal points, the more they get a sacramental glow about them. Detective novels had their gats and heaters. Ian Fleming's James Bond books gave 007's Walther PPK pistol a fetishy charm. By 1984, after sixty-two books in Don Pendleton's Executioner series, the publishers came out with a special "combat catalogue" with thirty-five illustrated pages listing all the guns that had been used in the series, from the Armbrust Disposable Anti-Tank Weapon to the XM174 Automatic Grenade Launcher. We also have postapocalyptic fiction, set in a future after a nuclear war, when the world is one big frontier. Number 6 in Jerry Ahern's Survivalist series begins:

> John Rourke pulled up the zipper on the fly of his Levis with his right hand, his left moving across his body plane to the Detonics stainless under his right armpit in the double Alessi rig, his fingers knotting around the black checkered rubber Pachmayr grips, his left thumb poised to cock the .45 as soon as it cleared the leather. . . . He already had the target—a man about six-foot four, unshaven, his black leather jacket mud-stained, a riot shotgun in his hands, the pump tromboning as the 12-gauge, roughly .70 caliber muzzle swung on line. Rourke's trigger finger twitched . . .

Mystique—that's the problem.

We like our artists disturbed but not disturbing, messianic but not pugnacious, confessional but not vulgar.

"We" is the weight of established opinion—big-media and little-review heaviosity. A century after his birth, Thomas Hart Benton is still getting it dropped on his foot. *Time* magazine's Robert Hughes, reviewing a huge Whitney Museum show in 1990, called Benton "the Michelangelo of Neosho, Mo. . . . flat-out, lapel-grabbing vulgar, incapable of touching a pictorial sensation without pumping and tarting it up to the point where the eye wants to cry uncle."

Hilton Kramer, editor of the *New Criterion,* has written: "The sad tale of Tom Benton has long been a familiar one in American art history. After a brave start in Paris and New York, as a votary of the avant-garde, Benton lost his nerve, abandoned the modernist ideas that allowed him to produce a handful of serious paintings and settled into a long and successful career as a Regional mediocrity."

Still, he lingers in museums all over the country, his easel paintings and murals exalting American arts and industries and the common man. He said he wanted people to look at his paintings the way they looked at the funnies. He also liked to say his stuff should be hung in bars, and when *Persephone* caused a scandal, man-about-town Billy Rose hung it for a month in his New York bar, the Diamond Horseshoe. He acted as if he were trying to convert the energy of America into the mass of culture in a sort of nuclear reaction: Culture = Art x Publicity. He liked to paint in front of audiences. He cultivated the press. *Life* photographed him painting the great, huge nude *Persephone*. He bragged about the authenticity of his research, saying that the fingers of his guitarists and violinists were placed to be in tune (but in *The Suntreader* he shows a piano with a bottom note of E, not A.) Like his art, he came on strong, and became one of those American heroes who by their works or their very presence leave you feeling that the circus is in town; a public figure in the American tradition of Mohammed Ali, Buffalo Bill, Walt Whitman, and Frank Lloyd Wright.

He painted big and fast. After doing the drawings and clay models for a mural commissioned in Indiana, he painted the whole thing in sixty-three days—it was 14 feet high and 230 feet long. He said: "The very thought of large spaces puts me in an exalted state of mind, strings up my energies and heightens the color of the world. . . . I get cocksure of mind and temperamentally youthful. I run easily into childish egomania or adolescent emotionalism." The mural appalled people by showing a state where slaves got whipped and babies' bottoms got wiped, where Abraham Lincoln leaned on an ax in his grotesque homeliness, and the Ku Klux Klan burned crosses, all of it writhing and glowing with Benton's dizzying line, palette, and scattershot vanishing points. Benton showed these people as moral beings, not the muscular economic entities of socialist propaganda or the bogeymen of the upper middle class. The energy of his Missouri state house mural moved a state senator to say: "They looked like they was jumpin' out at me." A newspaper said: "Shame on you, Thomas Hart Benton [for] declaring that Missouri's social history is one of utter depravity."

Benton was born in 1889. He was named for his great uncle, the Missouri western expansionist and duelist who was a senator from

1821 to 1851. Benton's father was a Confederate veteran who made a lot of money as a lawyer and spent four terms in the House of Representatives. His mother, 19 years younger, was a culture-climber from Waxahachie, Texas. It was not a happy family. His father was a crude little populist, 5-foot-3 and 200 pounds. His mother kept a carriage and socialized when the family lived in Washington. Benton would always remember her screams and protests when his father would take his crudeness into her bedroom at night.

He grew up to be a 5-foot-3 picker of fistfights and a Bohemian poseur. Then he cartooned for a newspaper in Joplin, Missouri. He went to the Art Institute of Chicago, where he decided he was meant for art, not illustration. He talked his parents into sending him to Paris. He got hauled back to Neosho when his mother learned he was keeping a mistress in his Left Bank studio.

While serving in the Navy as an architectural draftsman during World War I he had an epiphany. He later recalled:

> My interests became, in a flash, of an objective nature. The mechanical contrivances of building, the new airplanes, the blimps, the dredges, the ships of the base, because they were so interesting in themselves, tore me away from all my grooved habits, from my play with colored cubes and classic attenuations, from my aesthetic drivelings and morbid self-concerns. I . . . opened thereby a way to a world which, though always around me, I had not seen. That was the world of America.

He began spending summers in Martha's Vineyard, where he used the natives as models, like the couple portrayed in the 1926 dinner-table scene called *The Lord Is My Shepherd*. It is modern but it is mostly Benton: the cartoony hugeness of the hands, the Cubist foreshortening of the table and the hint of de Chirico surrealism in the self-conscious artificiality of the jarful of spoons. The drapery has the simplified massiness that would mark social realism between the world wars, and then revive with all its doughy, tonal roundings when commercial artists such as Robert Grossman took up their airbrushes in the '60s and '70s.

Self-Portrait with Rita, a Vineyard scene from 1922, has a touch of the surreal in the handless wristwatch and the otherworldly face of his wife, an Italian immigrant. It unleashes the sinuous, rhythmic line that would blazon everything Benton painted. It warms and enlivens, but it also writhes and alarms. There's an obsessive quality to it, like the doodles on high-school notebook covers, with odd fetishy exaggerations of feet and hands in the manner of cartoonist Bill Davis in the EC horror comics of the 1950s. Locomotives lean forward like the Little Engine That Could. Clouds curl around like a combination of a snake and an unmade bed. It's the world the way it looks when you're very, very young and everything's alive, the world that makes movie cartoons so charming, with their grinning trees and dancing brooms.

From 1925 to 1928, Benton spent each summer on the road, sketching cotton pickers, fiddlers, mules, cowboys, holy rollers, oilmen in boom towns. Meanwhile, the house of modernism was making a temporary loan of its guest bedroom to social realism and regionalism. The movement appealed to the right with its patriotism and the left with its exaltation of the common man—this being an age when both communism and fascism appealed to the culture-bearing elite.

Time magazine put a Benton self-portrait on its cover in 1934. In 1940 a book called *Modern American Painting,* published in part by Time-Life, said: "America today is developing a School of Painting which promises to be the most important movement in the world of art since the days of the Italian Renaissance. . . . Under the banner of Henry Luce [publisher of *Time* and *Life*] and his associates and assistants, the work of carrying appreciation and knowledge of art to the far corners of the land has been wisely guided." The book made much of Benton. It put him next to other artists who exemplified the American and regional spirit as defined by Luce: Raphael Soyer, Charles Sheeler, Georgia O'Keeffe, Peter Hurd, Doris Lee, Edward Hopper, Charles Burchfield, Paul Cadmus. By this time, though, Benton had begun to lose favor with the intellectuals and the Left.

In 1935 Lewis Mumford had looked at Benton's murals at the New School and the Whitney museum, and written in the *New*

Yorker: "In order to do a big canvas, it is not enough to have big figures. One must also embody significant ideas. . . . Afraid of being highbrow, he takes refuge in puerility. . . . The fact is that much of Benton's larger studies of the American scene . . . belong to the level of journalism."

At the same time, Benton was exhausting the capital of his fame on endless, needless fights with the art establishment. He bullied. He red-baited. He gay-baited, stating that "precious fairies get into positions of power and judge, buy, and exhibit American pictures on a base of nervous whim." Back in Kansas City, teaching at the Art Institute, he claimed Eastern decadence had infected Missouri: "Our museums are full of ballet dancers, retired businessmen and boys from the Fogg Institute at Harvard. . . . They hate my pictures and talk against them." He ended up getting fired at the beginning of World War II.

By the end of the war, Benton was a relic. He had no place in the high culture of an America that discovered it was running the world—abstract expressionism, the metaphysics of be-bop, the *Partisan Review*, Jackson Pollock, Charlie Parker, aesthetics as theology. Benton had been Pollock's teacher and mentor for years, and they ended up railing at each other. Social realism vanished like running boards on cars. It was an art form that sought to sing America in the tradition of Whitman. But postwar art was about decontextualization and alienation—architecture's vast empty plazas, Jasper Johns's gloomy, stolid, ironic paintings of the American flag.

Benton's colors got soft, his figures got sentimental, but he kept painting. He did a mural for the Truman Library in Independence, Missouri, between 1959 and 1962, and Truman called him "the best damned painter in America." He lived on in Kansas City. For all his homophobia, he was a fan of Allen Ginsberg's epic *Howl*. In 1975 he finished a mural for the Country Music Hall of Fame in Nashville. On January 18, he went out to his studio to chew tobacco and look at his work. He told his wife Rita that if he liked it, he'd sign it. He died with a paintbrush in his hand, and the mural unsigned. He was eighty-five.

the '80s

Here is the secret history of America in the 1980s. It's what really happened, as opposed to the pseudo-Churchillian, neo-Weberian, proto-Dickensian stuff about best of times, worst of times, greatness and ethos and so on. History is a nightmare from which we are trying to awake, as James Joyce would have put it.

In the 1980s:

We, the people, cried at weddings, resented the guy at the supermarket who carried nine items into the eight-items-or-fewer line, worried that our sex lives weren't quite what they were supposed to be, turned out the lights after we'd decorated the Christmas tree and just looked at it for a while, felt guilty for rejoicing when the neighbor's dog died (the one that barked all night for years), and took pictures of beautiful sunsets on our vacations and wondered why they never looked like much when the pictures came back.

Life went on. The world had been crazy for as long as anyone could remember. The new thing was, we began to suspect none of it made that much difference to us personally, at home, riding our lawn tractors, painting our toenails. It's not that we denied there were crises. In fact, it was depravity if you publicly denied a national crisis when an ozone hole widened over the South Pole, or seven people died from Tylenol laced with cyanide, or international terrorism caused people to cancel European holidays. Denying the importance of crises was like denying Satan in Salem, Massachusetts, three hundred years ago (or in California day-care centers in the '80s). But more and more, this was public show. Privately, we had better things to think about, we had our Voltairean gardens to tend.

After the Iran hostages came home early in the decade, and the inflation and recession ebbed in the early '80s, and yet another panic over nuclear holocaust—caused by the TV show *The Day After*—calmed down, and the price of a gallon of gasoline went back to normal (a little less than the price of a pack of cigarettes), we, the people, began to suspect that life had every chance of going on. This belief provoked a pleasant feeling, a self-conscious stability, like the feeling you have when you walk toward baggage claim after a bad plane trip.

America was back, it was morning again, as the Reagan campaign people put it. Not dawn's early light, but sort of a placid midmorning, 10:30 or so, with Doc down at the drugstore thinking about pulling the skin books off the magazine rack, the 55-mile-an-hour speed limit a thing of Jimmy Carter's age-of-limits past, the school kids back to basics, and most people back to work.

Did medical waste stop washing up on beaches, or did we stop paying attention to it? Why did we stop worrying about pit bulls? The media-political complex furrowed its brow and warned of global warming, American decline and fall, racism on the rampage, banks collapsing, plague, bastardy, homelessness, drug addiction, and a White House ruled by astrology, ignorance, and greed while the president took his afternoon nap. Was it all too overwhelming? Or was it an onslaught of peace, prosperity, and presidential popularity that told us, "don't worry, be happy."

In 1984 the press reported up to 50,000 missing children in America, and sure enough there was a national panic. Supermarkets put photographs of them on paper bags and milk cartons. Remember

Johnny Gosch? He was missing then, and he's missing now. But by 1989, most of us had forgotten about missing children, almost all of whom turned out to have run away, or gone to live with an estranged parent. And supermarkets were putting pictures of the American flag on their paper bags, after a national panic over flag desecration.

AIDS settled into the headlines, starting with the first reports of deaths in 1981, but even after 60,000 people had died of it, most people figured it wouldn't happen to them. The press told us AIDS had ended the sexual revolution. Wasn't that what they'd said about herpes, which we'd forgotten by the end of the decade? Or was that chlamydia? What was chlamydia, anyway? In any case, the revolution's Lenin, or maybe its Daniel Ortega, which is to say Hugh Hefner, the Playboy himself, got married.

Meanwhile, we, the people, worked. We drove aging cars to ugly places to work for bright types who got promoted because we were making them look good by driving forklifts, punching data, listening to customers whine, and then coming home with the smell of truck exhaust and Big Macs all over us. The bright types understood a lot about our work's costs, and not as much about its moral worth. We were used to that. The hell with them. We, the people, watched television. Households had their TV sets on an average of 7 hours and 2 minutes a day in the 1988–89 broadcast year, compared with 6 hours and 26 minutes ten years before. But we had new power over it. Television's unblinking eye no longer made us whimper like a stared-at puppy. Networks—and their advertisers—lost viewers to scores of cable channels and countless antenna dishes and videocassette recorders, all of them ruled by remote control from the couches where the couch potatoes sat.

By the end of the decade television journalists were so desperate for enough drama to compete with professional wrestling, evangelists, and *Gilligan's Island* reruns that they actually hired actors to perform the news in docu-dramas. Was it a real change or merely a difference of degree from the performances of the past? Of Walter Cronkite's performance as America's Uncle, for instance. Cronkite left the anchor chair in 1981, and even Dan Rather's V-neck sweater couldn't give him the same warmth. There was something single-minded and ambitious about him, just as there was about big actors of the '80s: Sigourney Weaver, Michael Douglas, Meryl Streep. Meanwhile, the great Hollywood stars, the ones who used to show us how to walk, talk, dress, and smoke cigarettes, kept dying: Cary Grant, Bette Davis, Fred Astaire.

And we, the people, kept meaning to plant the daffodil bulbs in the fall. We felt guilty for staying away from nursing homes where our parents didn't recognize us. We felt guilty for arriving at day-care centers where our children didn't recognize us, and thinking they'd be better off if we hadn't gotten divorced. We got our hair done especially to go see Wayne Newton in Las Vegas. We knew that our private lack of public concern worried people. It worried the media-political complex, which decried low voter turnouts. It worried the people who got christened "the knowledge class," or "the new class." They were to be found at dinner parties using the word "redneck," the last ethnic slur permitted in polite company. The rednecks called them "liberals." There was also the ascendancy of conservative intellectuals or "neo-conservatives," who called the new class liberals too, and also did it at dinner parties. In Washington, they each accused the other of having an "inside-the-Beltway mentality." All their world was a teapot, and there were many tempests in it.

It was Reagan's decade, particularly after a crazy rich kid named John Hinckley shot him in 1981, thus conferring on him a double dose of *People* magazine psychobabble: He was not only "victim" but "survivor. Reagan took advantage of a shift in public morality. In the nineteenth century, private life (home, hearth, women on pedestals) was the bastion of virtue in a world where public life (bribery, booze, women in bordellos) was corrupt. By the 1980s, it was private life where corruption lurked—child abuse, patriarchy, addictions. And Reagan had no private life and so the media-politicos couldn't hound him the way they hounded John Tower or Gary Hart, and howled after the memories of Lyndon Johnson and Martin Luther King. He drove intellectuals crazy. Here was a man who had the populist appeal of Andrew Jackson but hung a picture of Calvin Coolidge on the

White House wall. He combined free trade and nationalism. He defied all the laws of political science. The knowledge class concluded that Reagan was stupid. Well, fine. If Reagan wasn't outsmarting them, he was outdumbing them. He left the jittery mandarins of the national press corps frantic and grimacing, like the Diane Arbus photograph of the boy holding the toy hand grenade. Reagan was blessed, in particular, with the presence of ABC correspondent Sam Donaldson. He used Donaldson's coy on-camera petulance to persuade the nation what a nice guy he was, by comparison.

His magic seemed to fade when the Challenger space shuttle blew up in 1986, killing a black-white-Asian-male-female crew whose symbolic value, like Reagan's, was enormous. It also turned out Reagan's staffers had been selling arms to the Iranians, in hopes of getting back some hostages we didn't get back. But Reagan survived it all, even survived being upstaged by Mikhail Gorbachev.

The national debt rose and rose like a tidal wave in a nightmare, but it kept not breaking, unless you count the tsunami of foreign money that bought up factories, farmland, Hollywood studios, and 51 percent of Rockefeller Center. The stock market fell 508 points in one day in 1987, and took two years to recover. A bunch of dirtball bankers and mall sleaze looted America's banks of hundreds of billions of dollars, and the press paid no attention. In our retreat from public life, we, the people, didn't care. It was very mysterious. The top fifth of the American population saw its income rise 16 percent from 1979 to 1987, and the bottom fifth lost 8 percent. Why didn't the poor get angrier? Why didn't the upper fifth raise hell when it saw its 16 percent raise devoured by a 50 percent increase in college costs, along with housing prices that doubled, tripled, and quadrupled in the sort of neighborhoods where the upper fifth wanted to raise its college-bound children? Norman Mailer once said that you either had to change or pay more to stay the same. The upper fifth paid more. And the lower fifth had less to spend, so it borrowed to stay the same. More and more households needed more and more people working to make the money that Dad had once made all by himself. No one seemed to see this as a swindle, and feminists called it liberation.

Where would all of this psycho-statistico-economics end? It ended with Donald Trump being called "The People's Billionaire" by the *New York Daily News*. He wore white shoes and looked like he was moving his mouth around to hide a dental problem. He named everything after himself: his casino, his apartment building, his castle, and his yacht, whose captain described Trump as "the epitome of the American dream." Trump himself said of his fans: "They're my people. For whatever reason they love me." For one thing, he acted the way Mr. and Mrs. Front Porch U.S.A. thought rich guys should act. Unlike lawyers, Wall Streeters, and the media-political complex, he actually built stuff—the casinos, the apartment buildings, and so on. Actually he made money by creating hysteria, turning himself into a one-man tulip madness. If Trump's name was on it, invest. Then he lost a lot of the money and the name was never the same.

The idea was to be something, not do something. Be rich, be famous, be a success. In Los Angeles, a curator named Mary Jane Jacob wrote a catalogue essay called "Art in the Age of Reagan: 1980–1988." She could have been talking about a lot of people in public life—businessmen, politicians, actors, journalists, professors, or athletes—when she said: "The goal of the artists is now to build a career, not just to make their art." Critic Alfred Kazin wrote, "Our literary period may yet be remembered as one in which the book business replaced the literary world, in which literary theory replaced literature and in which, as Irving Howe has said, Marxism came to its end—in the English department."

We, the people, began to worry when we looked at *People* magazine or the Oprah or Donahue shows and realized there were now so many famous people in America we hadn't heard of half of them.

Things did not fall apart, they congealed. They calcified like public life in Tokugawa-era Japan. Vintage rock-and-roll became elevator music. Postmodernist buildings made hip and ironic gestures out of the past: Greek columns that supported nothing, endless Palladian windows. Fashion and leisure were hypnotized by a moral quality called "authenticity." We ordered it from catalogues that offered mock–World War II bomber jackets, wistful WASPery in tweed and flannel, and decorator duck decoys, which were collectible. Everything was collectible. Preservation societies fought to save old building facades, behind which builders built new office buildings. The idea was to make real Main Streets look like the fake one at Disneyland, which wasn't so much fake as it was "hyperreal," to use the coinage of Jean Baudrillard. More and more people lived, worked, and shopped around shopping malls, which had the desirable hyperreal quality. The favorite ritual of the decade was the anniversary: the Statue of Liberty's 100th, Elvis's death's 10th, the end of the '80s. Congress turned into a sort of polyester House of Lords, with almost 99 percent of incumbents getting reelected, election after election. The Vietnam memorial became the most popular monument in Washington. Models of it were collectible.

Meanwhile, we, the people, had a tired feeling that wouldn't go away and doctors who gave us blood tests that didn't tell us why. We dreamed that we had a biology exam the next day, and not only hadn't we studied, we'd never even been to class. Then we went to a high school reunion and were astonished to discover that when we added it all up, we were one of the most successful members of our class (though still not the best looking).

We are the world, we are the children. What charity was that song sung for? There was the "we" that *USA Today,* America's generic newspaper, kept putting in its headlines over stories based on endless statistics: We're Eating Less Fat, We're Sick of Dirty Politics.

Meanwhile, we, the people, got paper cuts and headaches. We bought lottery tickets and had all the money spent before we even got home. We peacefully accepted the biggest wave of immigrants since the turn of the century, as they slipped quietly out of the frying pans of Central America, Vietnam, and Russia and into the melting pot of America. We bought pistols and after two trips to the shooting range never fired them again—hated the noise and couldn't hit anything. We told our children what fall had smelled like before the environmentalists said we weren't allowed to burn the leaves we raked off our lawns.

We knew there were big problems, but we didn't see them in our neighborhood. By the end of the decade, only six out of ten Americans said things were going well in the country, but nine out of ten said things were going well in their personal affairs, according to a *Time* magazine–CNN poll. Nine out of ten said we had a drug crisis, but only half said it was where they lived. Our leaders yelled louder and louder about illegal drug use but it fell 37 percent between 1985 and 1988, according to government figures.

As the modal, metaphorical disease of the time, addiction was to the '80s what tuberculosis had been to the nineteenth century. It was a disease of repetition, stasis, appetite, and economics. There was Narcotics Anonymous, Gamblers Anonymous, and Sexaholics Anonymous. Alcoholics Anonymous branched out into meetings for spouses and children of alcoholics. We heard the words "workaholics," "foodaholics," "jogaholics," "chocoholics," and "rageaholics." Much as we look on obsessions of medieval nuns, the future may look back on an addiction to weight loss that led young women to starve and vomit themselves into thinness. This actually killed some of them, such as singer Karen Carpenter.

Meanwhile, we, the people, were sure we had brain tumors, never paid retail for anything, figured we could have married better, applauded madly at boring school plays, felt a little foolish about singing "The Star-Spangled Banner" at the start of ballgames, and, on calm reflection, felt guilty, ridiculous, or just bored with our occasional flashes of hatred of Asians, Jews, kids, rich people, blacks, immigrants, and that ethnic entity described in stately tones by a subway drunk or two as "the white man."

Among the poets laureate of public probity, some sang of a resurgence of racism. They blamed the election of George Bush on the Republicans making a bogeyman of Willie Horton, a black murderer who raped a woman in Maryland after being furloughed from prison in what Republicans never tired of calling "the People's Republic of Massachusetts." One of the few people to make a difference in public discussion of race was Tom Wolfe, in a novel called *The Bonfire of the Vanities*. By making all of his characters equally repellent, black and white alike, Wolfe got away with talking honestly about opportunism

and hatred in racial politics. Let mention be made of black dema-
gogues such as the Rev. Al Sharpton or Louis Farrakhan (who called
Judaism a "gutter religion") and someone would say: "Have you read
Bonfire of the Vanities?"

A black middle class arose. In Nassau and Suffolk counties on
Long Island, 49 percent of black families had higher incomes than the
typical white family in America. In the Miami metropolitan area it
was 24 percent. In Oakland it was 36 percent. Nobody cared. "Successful blacks are the most forgotten group of Americans there are,"
said George Sternlieb, director of the Center for Urban Policy Research at Rutgers University. Bill Cosby did his best to remember
them by creating the Huxtable family on his television show.

Meanwhile, we, the people, looked at ourselves on videotape and
said, "Am I really that fat?" We tried to figure out if we were in love
enough with the person three desks down that we could make love in
a car and it wouldn't make any difference.

The closest we got to a rebellion came from white males—who
had lost all moral claim to public stature after so many years of being
attacked for racism and chauvinism. The press paid next to no attention to them, either. Harry McPherson concluded his memoir of a life
in the Democratic Party with a postscript saying that

> Democratic primaries and conventions often rocked with the lan-
> guage of rebuke. Very like, it has occurred to me, the language
> many wives use in speaking to their husbands, particularly toward
> the end of marriages. You never think of the children, or of my
> mother, or of me; only of yourself. Substitute the ignored disadvan-
> taged, the homeless, people trapped downtown. The reaction
> among husbands, for whom read "white male voters," is what is
> normally provoked by attempts to burden people with a sense of
> guilt.

In other words, white males did the political equivalent of utter-
ing the great American male exit line, "Honey, I'm going out for a
pack of cigarettes." They stopped by the polls to vote for Reagan and
didn't call home to say when they'd be back. The press fell in love

with "the gender gap," which described a women's vote so powerful that it would defeat both Reagan and Bush. *Newsweek* scandalized the feminist community by saying that single career women in their thirties had about as much chance of getting married as being killed by a terrorist. Meanwhile, men were edgy—a marriage had only a 50 percent chance of lasting. "Why get married?" they said. "Why not just find a woman you hate and give her your house?"

Meanwhile, we, the people, dreamed we were smoking cigarettes again and they tasted wonderful. We showed each other baby pictures. We worried about that clunk when we shifted out of reverse. We cried at weddings, we resented the guy at the supermarket who carried nine items into the eight-items-or-fewer line . . .

the daily news

In the late 1960s, when I worked there, the newsroom at the *New York Daily News* was like a museum of lost air—a smell of paste pots, Aqua Velva, and cigarettes stamped out on the floor, the essence of a 1948 that lived on and on, a slice of twilight where reporters hoped for the murder story that would make them famous and fifty photographers waited for the Hindenburg to blow up again.

Editors shouted "Boy! Copy!" and sat at the city desk playing a card game with cards so old they were soft. Slap, slap, went the cards, and then you heard the doughy flutter of another shuffle. Who were these guys? What was the name of the game? I knew better than to ask. I was a trainee, one of the college graduates the top editors brought in as fresh blood, an intruder from a terrible present. Even they knew that they couldn't stay stuck in 1948 forever. I felt as if I were walking through the Museum of Natural History, looking at dioramas, the Plains Indians in their tepees, that sort of thing, a gone world. Why did the sportswriters shout obscenities at each other all the time? And those women who sat at the desks in the vast hush of the women's section, some wearing hats—what exactly did they do? Was it true the big old Speed Graphics were still sitting on shelves in the photo department stockroom? I didn't ask. To the card players and photographers, the trainees were candy-ass college kids, the shock troops of the very 1960s they hated.

They suspected we wanted to write for the *News* without paying our dues, without spending years sitting on the copy boys' bench, hoping to get lucky and haul some french fries and coffee for quarter tips. They knew that when we looked out the dirty windows we didn't see the same New York they saw. They were right.

We saw Black Panthers, riots, antiwar demonstrations, gay rebellion, marijuana, and the Grateful Dead at the Fillmore East. They saw New York, New York, a fabulous town where the Bronx was up and the Battery down, with Friday night fights and a Sunday kind of love, heat waves and crime waves, ferryboats and café society, a city of 8 million working stiffs, tycoons, coeds, hubbies, moms, starlets, shylocks, heiresses, bookies, and socialites who were oh-so-snooty, all watched over by Irish cops who had big hearts and French headwaiters who had none.

Jews were a powerful but benevolent mystery, Puerto Ricans didn't exist, and there were hardly any blacks at all except for the boxers on the back page, their faces turned to rubber by a knockout punch and the flash-frozen spray leaping off the backs of their heads. A cub reporter was coming in from Brooklyn one day and saw a gigantic fire, people jumping, mothers tossing babies out of windows, the works. He called the city desk, which had one question: "Black or white?"

"Black," said the reporter.

"Give it to the Brooklyn page," said the desk, and went back to the card game.

The paper was full of men: con men, hit men, bag men who delivered hush money and then got caught by G-men after FBI wiretaps were ordered by J. Edgar Hoover, who was god. And the girls: B-girls, call girls, showgirls, girls Friday. Leggy lovelies and glamour pusses were curvaceous and statuesque.

Once the editorial policy had been liberal, but founder Joseph Medill Patterson had broken with Franklin Roosevelt. The result was editorials about pinkos, spy rings, and the United Nations, which was called "the glass cigar box on the East River." The readers responded with letters that Steve Allen used to shout on his television show, for laughs. Reds! Weirdos! Send 'em back where they came from!

The editorials were written by Reuben Maury, a bent old man with a vest, a shaved head, and his shoulders up around his ears. Every afternoon when he'd finished savaging the pinkos and State Department cookie pushers, he went into the men's room with a towel, a bar of soap in a soap dish, and a scrub brush. He rolled up his sleeves and gave his hands a surgical scrub-down. It was as good to watch as the city desk card game. *News* old-timers liked to boast that he had once written liberal editorials for *Colliers* magazine—it was all in a day's work for a pro like him.

Such strange creatures. Mornings the press agents (known in the newsroom as the United Jewish Appeal) would line up to pitch their clients to the columnists, Bob Sylvester and whoever was writing Ed Sullivan's stuff. The idea was to get "a mention," turn their clients into "an item." It helped if the press agents had snappy lines: "Watch out for the new drink at Joey Vitale's Kit Kat Klub—they call it the Bowling Ball because two of them and you're in the gutter."

Afternoons, a bookie known as The Ear came through to pick up bets. They called him The Ear because he was missing an ear. He'd been born that way, with a question-mark patch of flat skin where his ear should have been, just a lobe sticking out. He worked the newsroom like a Good Humor man.

"Hey, Ear," somebody would say. "Gimme Tuesday's Child in the fifth at Hialeah and if he wins put it all on Getaway in the seventh."

"I don't take if-money," The Ear would say.

A guy from outside the paper had us place bets with The Ear. All fall, the guy kept winning. We followed his money. We won too. At Christmas, The Ear bought us a bottle of whiskey. How strange, I thought, until I saw too late that The Ear knew something we didn't—that time was on his side. Our luck ended before the year was out and it never came back. Where is The Ear now?

Where is the copy editor who used to get so drunk that his jaws locked and he could only grunt? Where are all the old headline writers who were forgotten novelists living in West Side hotels and spending dinner hours on the phone to children who lived far away? I was privileged to be present one night when they debated the precise difference between calling someone a "Mafia Big" and a "Mafia Biggie." I think "biggie" was held to be more colloquial.

What I'd hoped was that the *News* would someday shed its hokey resentment and return to its founding dream of working-class heroism, the sort of thing that was enshrined on the front of the building in 1930 by a social-realist mural showing the rays of the sun, the blessings of Heaven itself, reaching down past skyscrapers to the heroic masses—a man carrying a sack, a kid with a dog, a cop, a businessman, a woman in a shawl, the men in hats, all of them toiling away beneath the words: "He Made So Many of Them." Which is from a line attributed to Lincoln: "God must have loved common-looking people—He made so many of them."

This sort of sentiment wasn't fashionable in the '60s or the '70s. In the '80s, Reagan made it safe for Mr. and Mrs. Front Porch U.S.A. to feel proud of themselves again, and I thought it might come back. The problem was, it had no place to come back to. Its New York had vanished.

A *Daily News* headline had already said it when President Ford blocked a loan to the city: FORD TO CITY—DROP DEAD. The Irish and Italians had left, the cops lived on Long Island, and Manhattan was being fought over by monstrosities—the homeless on one side and yuppie millionaires on the other, a bonfire of many vanities indeed.

mice

The mouse is the all-American animal, a mascot for democratic man. Everyman Mickey, gallant Mighty, and so on. Brazen Ignatz in the old "Krazy Kat" comic strip. Speedy Gonzales and his cousin Rodriguez. (Arriba! Arriba!) Fievel Mouskewitz, the immigrant in *An American Tail*. E. B. White's Stuart Little. Cute Jerry outsmarting Tom. Blabbermouse. Dangermouse. Pixie and Dixie.

It's hard to imagine another animal holding the mouse's place in American mythology. Bugs Bunny as Everyman? Donald Duck? Rocky the Flying Squirrel? Felix the Cat? It takes a mouse. Mice seem to have a moral claim, even a heroic claim, but it's hard to say what or why, except that there is something thrilling about Mighty Mouse rising into the sky with that determined little fist stuck out in front of him.

In 1928 Mickey Mouse appeared in his first animated cartoon, which was called *Steamboat Willie*. Four years later, a movie historian named Terry Ramsaye wrote that Mickey "is at one with the Great Common Denominator of the great common art of the commonality in terms of expression. . . . The triumph of the boob, the cosmic victory of the underdog, the might of the meek." Psychologist Erich Fromm wrote that "the extent to which the average person in America is filled with the same sense of fear and insignificance seems to find a telling expression in the fact and popularity of the Mickey Mouse pictures. . . . the spectator lives through all of his own fears and feelings of smallness and at the end gets the comforting feeling that, in spite of it all, he will be saved and will even conquer the strong one."

On the other hand, a kid can watch cartoons about heroic mice and then go upstairs and toss a real mouse to a pet snake. Nobody cares about pet mice the way they care about parakeets, cats, or horses. Mice are throwaway mammals, the nonreturnable bottles of the totem-animal world. Unlike pet snakes or pet birds, pet mice don't provoke worries that they might be happier in a state of nature. Nor do people care about wild mice the way they care about eagles, lions, or wolves. This is partly because so many wild mice aren't really wild—they live in houses and are vermin. And mice don't symbolize virtues like pride, bravery, loftiness, obedience, or tenacity. Mice carry salmonella, typhus, and plague. They gnaw wires that cause fires. They inspire a mental condition called "musophobia," which is represented by cartoons of women standing on chairs while quizzical mice stare up at them. Mice are anonymous and bland. They are consumers. Mythically, they fit right into an era of bureaucracy and shopping.

They have a unique claim on the American psyche, as you can see by comparing them to rats. So many things that are true of mice are true of rats, technically speaking. In fact, "mouse" is an imprecise term that includes some small rats and voles. But: Mice are timid and rats are sneaky. Drab women are mousy and the men who break their hearts are rats. It's rats, not mice, that are spoken of as being the size of cats, of ice chests, of UPS trucks. It wasn't mice that the weirdo in the Dracula movies liked to eat, it was rats. It wasn't rats that the hero of *Never Cry Wolf* liked to eat, it was mice. In a movie called *The Great Mouse Detective,*" the archenemy is the evil Professor Rattigan.

When we walk our fingers up a baby's stomach, we say, "Creepy,

creepy, little mouse, come to live in baby's house." We do not say, "Creepy, creepy little rat, come to live in baby's hat." When our cats catch mice, we're sorry. When they catch rats, we're proud. And no rat ever comes along to save the day, but Mighty Mouse is on the way.

John Canemaker, a historian and animator, says it was around 1915 when "animators began to fill the movie screens with tiny, round rodents. All of them were anonymous, except Ignatz the Mouse, who stood out because he was based on a character in the famous George Herriman comic strip." They were popular with animators because they're easy to draw—a couple of circles, a triangle, a few dots.

Ignatz threw bricks at Offisah Pup and Mickey made music by squeezing farm animals' teats and tongues in *Steamboat Willie*. Mice were pranksters, cruel and irresponsible. Was this what we wanted to encourage among the common folk? Mickey the sadistic became Mickey the mischievous of *The Sorcerer's Apprentice*, and finally evolved into the Mr. Front Porch U.S.A. of the last cartoons. Now he's a greeter at Disneyland, like the docile old boxers who stand around Las Vegas casinos shaking hands. His name is a synonym for bureaucratic trivia, as in: Why do we have to put up with all this mickeymouse nonsense? The taming of the mouse image in the 1930s and afterward fit an age in which government became more parental and popular, and cranky individualism, as an admired American character trait, vanished in the team play of World War II and what critics called the "conformity" of the 1950s.

As Mickey matured into a solid citizen, though, he grew more childlike in looks. The Mickey of *Steamboat Willie* had smaller eyes and a narrower snout than the genial host of the Mickey Mouse Club. In an essay called "Homage to Mickey Mouse," Harvard biologist/geologist Stephen Jay Gould argues that the Disney studio sought to make Mickey more babylike, therefore more lovable. He says that "children, compared with adults, have larger heads and eyes, smaller jaws, a more prominent, bulging cranium, and smaller, pudgier legs and feet."

That was how the Disney artists drew him, the epitome of cheery go-along-to-get-alongism, a grateful child of the welfare state. Perhaps it was this image that had angered James Michener so when he attacked Mickey in 1968, saying in the *New York Times* that "one of the most disastrous cultural influences ever to hit America was Walt Disney's Mickey Mouse. That idiot optimist. . . . I suppose the damage done to the American psyche by this foolish mouse will not be specified for another 50 years but even now I place much of the blame for Vietnam on the bland attitudes sponsored by our cartoons."

House mice evolved on the steppes of central Asia. They weigh from about half an ounce to an ounce, are two-and-a-half to three-and-three-quarters inches long from nose to rump, and produce litters of four to seven young five or more times a year. In captivity, they can live to be six years old. They have consorted with man at least since the late Pleistocene period—the evidence is house-mouse remains in Crimean caves. Later, Babylonians and Greeks built mousetraps, to judge from excavations. Mice spread to the New World on the ships of European explorers.

Leviticus 11:29: "These also shall be unclean unto you among the creeping things that creep upon the earth; the weasel, and the mouse, and the tortoise after his kind." But a woman in Chaucer could feel sorry for them.

> She wolde wepe, if that she sawe a mous
> Caught in a trappe, if it were deed or bledde.

An illustration of I Samuel executed about 1250 in Paris shows "the mice that mar the land."

The *Dictionary of Subjects and Symbols in Art* defines mice in western art as "a symbol of decay, hence of the passing of time." In the eighteenth century, folklore had it that mice were born of dirty laundry, the way frogs were born of mud. At the same time, Robert Burns could write "To a Mouse" in 1785, and give a sympathetic picture of a "wee, sleekit, cow'rin', tim'rous beastie" whose nest had been overturned with a plough—with overtones of the common man turned out of house and home by the ruling class, industrialization, whatever.

In nineteenth-century Russia, Tchaikovsky's aristocratic audiences were given a villain in the form of the Mouse King, in *The Nutcracker*. In *Four Quartets*, T. S. Eliot, who was no friend of modern democracy, returned to the theme of decay when he described our age as:

> A time for the wind to break the loosened pane
> And to shake the wainscot where the field-mouse trots.

Hitler said that Mickey Mouse was "the most miserable ideal ever revealed . . . mice are dirty." Otto Messmer, creator of Felix the Cat, said: "To me, a mouse is a repulsive thing." When cartoonist Art Spiegelman put out *Maus,* a book about his father's journey through the Holocaust, he chose cats for the Nazis, pigs for the Poles, and mice for the Jews.

In 1984 *Pravda* attacked a prosperous sixteen-year-old girl named Alisa for having antidemocratic tendencies when she and her friends, looking down on their less-fortunate schoolmates, said, "All those little gray mice simply can't understand our conversations." This arrogance, said *Pravda,* is "a far cry from the ideal toward which we all are striving."

To ruling classes, mice have seemed like the horrible masses, the mob trotting after the tumbrels in revolutionary France, the lower orders whom the English landowners drove from their cottages in Ireland, the turn-of-the-century populist hordes who heard William Jennings Bryan attack—what else?—fat cats.

It was the genius of cartoonists early in this century that turned this ruling-class opprobrium on its head. If mice were like the masses, they seemed to say, shouldn't we like them, even admire them? However, this does not explain how we can have a mythical hero whose live counterpart inspires phobias; whose sufferings arouse apathy; and whose slaughter has become a synonym for progress and good business: "If a man write a better book, preach a better sermon, or make a better mouse-trap than his neighbour, tho' he build his house in the woods, the world will make a beaten path to his door," said Emerson in a lecture, according to Mrs. Sara S. B. Yule, who said she heard him. (One Elbert Hubbard claimed he'd said it first.)

You can't eat them. You can't pet them. They are vermin. But you'd hate to think of them all being exterminated. Though sometimes, you hear them running through the walls, a phantasmic scuttling that sounds like what you'd hear if you were starting to go crazy, and so you set a trap. You lie awake all night in panic that it will snap. It does. You feel guilt. Then dread. In the morning you will have to get rid of the mouse, pull it out of the trap by its tail, the feeling of which will linger on your skin like a gruesome great-aunt kiss.

America, what have you done with your hipsters? Who still journeys with Céline to the end of the night in bare-lightbulb apartments? Who never watches television, except for *Attack of the Giant Leeches,* which they say is the greatest movie ever made, though they only watch it for the carpet warehouse ads? What sexual revolutionaries and sidewalk existentialists lope around in those thick-soled Thom McAn shoes? Who rants about conspiracies over breakfasts of cigarettes and hot dog rolls? Who steals Allen Ginsberg's diction?

Harvey Pekar, in middle age, is one of the last hipsters, a cosmic shrug-meister, the kind of guy you'd see slouching around city downtowns twenty or thirty years ago, picking through the jazz bins at record stores, his pockets full of bus transfers and library cards and his peripheries blurred by a smog of willful poverty, street wisdom, and egomania. Not hippies, Maoists, or sweethearts of the cocaine rodeo. We're talking about a subtler breed: underground men and saints of self-consciousness with the collective face of a Baltimore Harbor Tunnel guard.

Anyway, Harvey Pekar (pronounced PEE-kar) is a balding GS-4 file clerk in a Veterans Administration hospital in Cleveland—a "flunky file clerk," he calls himself in the comics, an "alienated schlep" and paranoid sniveler.

He has holes in his undershirts. His nose runs. He steals his neighbor's newspaper. He freeloads doughnuts, whines about loneliness and screams at women he calls "rotten bitches" and then shows himself doing it all in comic books entitled: *From Off the Streets of Cleveland Comes AMERICAN SPLENDOR—The Life and Times of Harvey Pekar.*

All the time, he knew there had to be more, that his day would come. Sure enough, David Letterman had him on *Late Night,* and he's been telling people that Fox Broadcasting even wanted him to audition as a talk show host.

He said no. He loves telling about how he said no.

"Would you want a talk show? No? Why? I don't want one either, so you and me are on the same wavelength," he says in the frantic tenor of a man whose life involves fighting his way out of corners or getting other people into them. "I say how can you question me if you don't want a talk show yourself?"

He is in a seafood restaurant sitting next to his third wife.

"He's got no shame, he's got no pride," she says. Her name is Joyce Brabner. She's thirty-three, with thin bangs and huge glasses. Something about her makes you think of used-book stores and bad arguments.

"I'm certainly not the kind of guy who's . . ."

"He hasn't grabbed the brass ring, which a lot of those guys would've. I mean, he gets offered a talk show on Fox."

"I don't have salable skills, I can't even type," Pekar says, as if he has said it to a hundred employment counselors, a thousand girlfriends.

"I'm teaching him how to type."

"She will never do it, she will never . . ."

"Well, okay."

"I do it to humor her."

"He does it to humor me. He's getting better at it. The truth of the matter is that I think that Harvey has got some kind of learning disability because . . ."

"She has no way of saying that, no way."

"Do I get to say this?"

"I don't know that I have no shame," Pekar says. His upper lip lifts and the corners of his mouth turn down so you see a plaintive trapezoid of teeth. "I just don't think it's any big deal if I stole something when I was a kid and I write about it, or, you know, I was manipulative. Misery loves company. I know the people identify with my work a lot, they say it means a lot to 'em when they write me letters."

Pekar is a hair-in-the-sink realist who shows us a world of iffy morals and petty pleasures amid meaninglessness bordered by oblivion. The rent is due, the news is bad, the view is phone wires, old cars and people walking with their shoulders hunched against the cold. The stories have titles such as "An Argument at Work," "In the Parking Lot," or "Standing Behind Old Jewish Ladies in Supermarket Lines." He writes the words and gets the pictures drawn by artist friends, including R. Crumb, who was the biggest star of the underground comics scene in the late '60s. The effect is one of cartoon monologues about Harvey Pekar skulking around Cleveland and hating his job; pushing his girlfriend's car out of the snow; eating hot dogs and potato chips for dinner; buying used shoes; bitching at editors, bosses and coworkers; trying to get to sleep; masturbating; stealing records from a radio station's library; yelling at an ex-wife; and generally coming on like the 5 o'clock shadow on the face of American life.

"Awaking to the Terror of the Same Old Day" begins on a Sunday night with Pekar walking down the street over a word panel that says: "It's been a bummer weekend. All he's done is hang out on the corner and watch TV." He thinks about how he broke up with his girlfriend a week ago. He thinks about how another woman he knows is a "rotten little flake." He thinks: "The weekends are lousy and the weekdays are lousy. It's just a different kind of lousy." He goes home to his apartment. He decides not to watch an Abbott and

Costello movie on television. He brushes his teeth. He goes to bed. He gets up, shaves, goes to work, schmoozes with the guys on the loading dock about the football game and hangs around the office. By afternoon, he says: "I only feel normally lousy. I hate t'admit it, but workin' sort of helps me keep from goin' nuts. When yer alone alla time, like I am some weekends, y' start concentratin' on yer problems an' thinkin' yer the only person in the world." He concludes: "Sometimes things seem so heavy, other times everything seems like a joke."

That's it, another slice of American life that Harvey Pekar sits atop like a fly on a piece of processed cheese.

Why does anyone care? Most important, this relentless pursuit of the mundane begins to seem like an enormous gag, like the late Andy Kaufman standing up onstage and lip-syncing to a record of the Mighty Mouse song, or Andy Warhol putting on an endless movie consisting of a single view of the Empire State Building. These stories are a tour de force of schlemieldom. People go on TV talk shows to confess they like to watch their wives make love to the vacuum cleaner, but who goes public with stinginess, chasing women because they're easy to get, and shouting pointless obscenities at coworkers? Finally, Harvey Pekar and his comic books seem authentic—and in an age when people learn how to raise children by reading books, there's an audience, however small, for authentic.

Pekar puts himself in the realist tradition.

"I started writing comic books when I was thirty-two," he says. "Which is kind of old, and by that time I had a hell of a lot of influences, like novelists and short-story writers and comedians like Lenny Bruce and movies like *The Bicycle Thief,* stuff like that. But I think probably that Dostoevsky, I remember reading that *Notes From Underground* and being real impressed with it, but I was also impressed with, you know, anything like George Orwell's *Down and Out in Paris and London,* I don't know if you're familiar with it."

Pekar's books certainly seem real. They confirm our worst suspicions about low-rent, near-ghetto, polyester-collar, lumpen-treadmill urban life. Existence is a self-deluding struggle to get through the day. The characters are trapped in a swamp of typicalities. Pekar is fascinated with invidious stereotypes: Jews are stingy, bosses are jerks, women are snooty, everybody hates his job. In a strip called "Pickled Okra," a black office worker says: "ah ain' nevah ate no pickled okry befo'." Pekar even shows himself speaking in dialect—most people only notice it in others, but Pekar is the eternal spectator, especially of himself.

The problem is, Pekar's stories show not so much the world of the lower classes, but that world as a lot of people in the upper classes see it. Hence authenticity. To be authentic, all you have to do is seem real, not be real, like a genuine imitation World War II bomber jacket in a catalogue. Why doesn't Pekar show us the richness in the lives of the lower classes, who have their myths to protect them from despair just as the upper classes do: Elvis, personal honor, religion, the lottery, cancer cures, patriotism?

"I'm not into myths," he says. "I'm not into legends, I'm anti-ceremony, I'm antinationalistic, I mean, you know, I'm sorry that people have to get through that way."

"Put it this way," his wife says. "You put him in a beautiful environment, he'd see bleak. It's true, Harvey, the knee-jerk pessimist, the Jewish tragedy, what's the difference?"

"Joyce, I believe the question was directed to me."

"Let's see if he writes down your answer."

"I used to live in a real bleak grim neighborhood where there was a lot of bitterness around me."

"We don't live in the gritty city," Brabner says. "There's a lot of things you need to know about Cleveland, including it's nicknamed the Forest City because they have this terrific urban forestry, so where we live we have more goddam trees than most people have out in the country."

Pekar says: "One of the reasons I write is to push people's face into life rather than to have them try to escape it. If people started to face up to their responsibility as citizens and started to read the goddam paper and find out what the hell was going wrong with the goddam country and worry as much about politics as they know about pro football . . . and I know something about pro football too, you know, I'm a sports fan, I think if they did that they wouldn't, like, elect some guy to be president, some guy who's mediocre, and they choose him, they'll pick people for political office who are, you know, who are like them."

Wait a second. Who is he to be condescending—this childless, middle-aged college dropout with twenty-two years in the same job, this shameless flunky whose wife made a doll of him with an "anatomically correct bald spot" and carried it around a booksellers' convention?

"Yeah, I'm kind of a klutzy guy, like a screw-up. I don't feel like I'm a loser but at a lot of things I'm inept, as Joyce has so eloquently testified. I mean, you know, starting with my mother always yelling and screaming at me for screwing up things, you know, I've had that image of myself pounded into myself."

So now he has the right to yell at everybody else?

"Well, first of all . . ."

"Who yells at them otherwise?" Brabner demands.

Back and forth: You said, I said, what I meant was, don't tell me what I meant.

Brabner says: "We had a way of solving arguments that maybe we ought to start getting back to—that he could pick me up in the air and I could scream and yell at him as long as I could keep a straight face, and he could yell at me as long as he could hold me up in the air. Then it became insufferably close to Spencer Tracy and Katharine Hepburn cute crap."

"I don't hold her over my head, I just pick her up, I don't know," Pekar says.

"He just holds me up in the air . . ."

"You wouldn't be impressed."

"You'd be impressed," Brabner says.

"I'm strong for my size, I can do one-handed push-ups, okay? Like, you know, I'll do some out in the parking lot and prove it to you. It's a matter of public record, it's on tape . . ."

"If you don't watch out you're gonna become like Norman Mailer," Brabner says.

"All I can tell you is that on the second David Letterman show I did some one-handed push-ups. I'll do them for you outside."

Outside, in the parking lot, in his lumberjack shirt and corduroy pants, Pekar lies on his stomach. He puts one hand behind his back. He gets his balance, and he pushes himself up on one hand. He does this four times. It's quite a feat, especially in a restaurant parking lot. It says something.

Brabner checks to see if anybody's looking, and doesn't say a word.

On the last day at the bus station there were fingerprints all over the glass doors and no air conditioning. There was a man with a radio in his hat arguing with a policeman named M. E. Lapsley.

The man said: "Too hot."

Lapsley said: "Relax, Max."

"Too hot."

"Relax, Max."

There was an old man who wore a cap that said: "I'm No. 3—I Don't Try at All." He kept losing money in the pay phone.

It was August 5, 1987. The bus station in Washington, D.C., was closing. It was hard to imagine it gone: all that timeless monoxide haze of cigarette smoke, diesel exhaust, and bad diapers dissipating into the night, the last hustler being rousted from the men's room. No more Christmas Eve soldiers or worried children sitting next to sleeping mothers, wishing they knew how to operate the vending machines themselves. It was the end of an era.

Admittedly, it is not pleasant to contemplate people who have sold a pint of their blood to buy a bus ticket, or old guys with no shoelaces or teeth, down in the restroom trying to save themselves from entropy by shaving with a bare razor blade; and so on through the long list of the tenuously enfranchised Americans who ride the bus or wait for those who do, or just hang out in the bus station: Bible salesmen, maniacs, the Amish, college girls who have found the answer in Kahlil Gibran and then lost it somehow, job hunters, job losers, grandmothers with wigs, and the restroom commandos with too-small eyes and minds like Army-Navy store windows . . . They were being consigned to another bus station next to a warehouse, where no one would ever see them.

It began with such excitement. More than 25,000 people toured the bus station on opening day, March 25, 1940. The *Washington Post* printed six pages of ads and stories about it. Back then, the station was a testament to the New Deal–era vision of a planned and streamlined future for all Americans, with Mr. Bus Driver exuding the twinkle of progress itself as he welcomed us on board with a knowing and congratulatory air. The spirit was that of machine-age pioneers— the history of the Greyhound company, said the *Post*, was "one of the most romantic of all sagas of transportation." It was a time when intellectuals exalted the common man, in the style of Walker Evans with his sharecropper photographs, or the social-realist sculptures and murals scattered across the country.

The *Post* wrote: "The walls of the main waiting room have been finished in walnut, as have the waiting room benches, and trimmed with burnished copper. . . . The dome-shaped ceiling of the waiting room has been finished in coral buff green and tan and here too, burnished copper has been used to add to the appearance."

On closing day there was no coral buff green dome at the Greyhound station. There was acoustical tile the color of an erased pencil drawing, and it hung over twenty-four plastic chairs, twelve with pay televisions bolted to them. Nobody was watching the televisions. Sitting in one of the seats was a woman with a baby whose skin had turned gray in the heat. The woman was twenty-six and she was

going to Cleveland to fight her ex-husband in court for custody of
two sons. She said: "The price is right. That's why I'm riding the bus."

Somehow, in the national psyche, buses and bus stations have
been assigned the role of lowest common denominator. Our romance
with them, along with our romance with the common man, has vanished, a victim of prosperity after World War II, of the shift of the
American population from the country to the cities, of the culture of
the car, and of the rise of do-your-own-thing individualism, a laissez-
faire and lone-cowboy attitude that goes against the communalism of
the bus. There was no first-class seating on the bus—it was the great
leveler. Even before the war, buses never had the glory of railroad
trains. Buying a train ticket was like buying your own piece of industrial might. Buying a bus ticket was like enlisting in the Army—a sort
of anxious resignation about it. Buses became a mere necessity, like a
change of socks or a vaccination. Unlike airplanes, buses had excitement of change—no leap from piston to jet engines, no doubling or
tripling of size and speed. For fifty years, buses stayed basically the
same. The biggest innovation was the Scenicruiser, a double-decker
that gave the illusion of a railroad observation car. This came along in
the 1950s, an age of curiously useless inventions, such as the Princess
phone or the wraparound windshield—novelties that imitated techno-
logical progress but were only a matter of style.

Buses' share of intercity travel fell from 8.8 percent in World War
II, back when the Greyhound terminal was at its height, to 1.3 percent in 1987. Greyhound had 4,000 buses in 1979. It had 2,700 in
1987, only 500 more than in 1940, when the Washington terminal
was opened. And the neighborhood around the station moldered into
a lumpen-panorama of pornography arcades and sex bars, gay and
straight. Male prostitutes started hanging around the little park
across the street. In 1976 Greyhound decided to hide the old streamlined building under a boxy façade. Rising crime, along with liberal-
ized attitudes toward bizarre behavior in public, made the station
seem strange and dangerous. Lunatics bellowed at the ticket sellers.
Hustlers and pickpockets followed people to the restrooms.

In 1940 it might not have been too different, except that the floors were swept and people still found romance or authenticity or charm in the lower classes. "If you wish to find out what kind of people come in and out of Washington, drop in at the Bus Terminal at Twelfth Street and New York Avenue," said the *Washington Times-Herald* in a piece by a reporter named Wilson L. Scott in 1943. In the style of the day, Scott celebrated the variety of American life at the Greyhound station—the tough waitresses, the kindhearted cop, the dishwashers shooting craps, and, of course, the wry newspaper reporter joining other students of American humanity who make it "a regular practice to slip in and out of the depot whenever they are in its neighborhood. I, like many others, do it because I know there is never a dull moment there day or night." Scott saw the same cavalcade of humanity you see today, including the crime. "Black Marias and military patrol wagons roll around regularly to report or to pick up occasionally irregular patrons. Anybody who will sit for an hour or so in the depot will have the opportunity of witnessing at least one minor drama."

He writes with the sort of populist flair that has dwindled—the tradition of Walt Whitman in "Song of the Open Road":

> Here the profound lesson of reception, nor preference nor denial,
> The black with his woolly head, the felon, the diseas'd, the
>   illiterate person, are not denied;
> The birth, the hasting after the physician, the beggar's tramp,
>   the drunkard's stagger, the laughing party of mechanics,
> The escaped youth, the rich person's carriage, the fop,
>   the eloping couple . . .
> None but are accepted, none but shall be dear to me.

This is the tradition that the Beat generation—Kerouac, Ginsberg, et al.—sought to continue in the 1950s. But there was a difference. The Edenic acceptance became a Hellish fascination. Here are some lines from "In the Baggage Room at Greyhound," in which Allen Ginsberg describes how he chooses to occupy his thoughts with God and time, and not:

the millions of weeping relatives surrounding the buses waving
    goodbye,
nor other millions of the poor rushing around from city to city
    to see their loved ones,
nor an indian dead with fright talking to a huge cop by the
    Coke machine,
nor this trembling old lady with a cane taking the last trip of
    her life,
nor the red capped cynical porter collecting his quarters over the
    smashed baggage,
nor me looking around at the horrible dream.

The same shift happened in movies. Bus travel had a charm back
when the Greyhound station was being built—as in the 1934 Frank
Capra comedy *It Happened One Night,* starring Clark Gable and
Claudette Colbert, and set on a bus. In the last twenty years, Hollywood has set movie scenes in buses or bus stations when it wanted to
show us the seedy, the deviate, and the disenfranchised, as in *Midnight Cowboy* or *The Last Detail.*

As the bus station decayed, people started to say what a pity it
was that people had to arrive in Washington in the middle of such
grittiness. The irony was that the station was being closed just as the
neighborhood improved. But it was real estate developers who were
improving it, and in their downtown there is less and less room for
bus station people. The property had gotten too valuable to house the
nuns and sailors, the weight lifters with cowboy hats and stuffed animals, the old folks with matching leisure suits and brand-new lug-
gage, the sort of ordinary people who always cover the toilet seat with
toilet paper when they're in the big city.

A historical preservation movement has since preserved the station, cleaning and restoring it to make a sort of lobby for the office
buildings around it. It looks now like model of itself, long on perfection but short on humanity.

On that last day in 1987, Herbert Ewing, eighty-nine, was there
to observe humanity. He'd lived in the neighborhood all his life.

"Same kind of folks ride the bus as used to," said Ewing, who used to stop in at the bus station every day to check things out—he remembers when it was built, and the station before that over near 14th Street. He's seen it all, the soldiers in World War II, the tenant farmers heading north in the '50s, the gamblers going to Atlantic City. "Most all kinds come here."

No more.

They were the Young Fogies, and they were part of the history of our time, if only as a codicil to the National Will.

You saw them in downtowns all over the country. You saw them at law firms, Republican party conventions, fundraisers for public television—baby fat in horn-rim glasses, white bread in black wingtip shoes, twenty-four-year-old staff assistants whose conversations resonated with words like "escrow" and "breakfront," twenty-nine-year-old lawyers doing the Burberry Shuffle through financial districts, their raincoats belted right under their armpits as they moved along with a kind of anxious bustle, as if their snap-front boxer shorts were riding up. For a moment or two in fin de siècle America, they were modal personalities, epitomes with Mont Blanc pens.

You saw them at night in restaurants, both sexes checking their watches when the waiter asked if they wanted coffee. You saw them in newsrooms, frowning with bewilderment at jokes about the latest massacre or bus plunge story. You saw them eating yogurt lunches in law firms and looking forward to careers in trusts and estates—

"they're most comfortable working with the dead," as a Washington lawyer named James "Komodo" Spears once said. They were not trend-setters, culture heroes, role models, neo-liberals, proto-fascists, preppies, or the sort of people who appeared on leaders-of-tomorrow covers of news magazines. They saw themselves not so much as architects of the future as its caretakers. They hoped to be the cruise control for the aging four-door sedan of state. We knew so little about them, and that's just the way they wanted it. They knew that invisibility is the key to their sort of success, that quiet resentment can be a way of life.

In an America of irredeemable national debt and the constant rattle of gunfire, the Young Fogies may have been the younger generation the country needed. There was a primness about them, an odd way of being wary and presumptuous at the same time. They were the children who identified with the coyote in the Road Runner cartoons, who asked for combination-lock briefcases for graduation presents.

The women were proud of having a certain mousiness. They borrowed cocktail dresses and Kenneth J. Lane door-knocker earrings from their mothers. They bought garden party hats, but they were afraid to wear them, though sometimes on house tours you'd see them carrying them at their sides. The men got their shirts boxed at the cleaners instead of putting them on hangers. They cultivated a fussy domesticity, and could own a pair of gardening kneepads from Brookstone. They had uncertain handshakes. They had that odd quality of looking much older than you even when they were younger, sort of like your parents in their high school yearbook pictures. This observation would not have troubled them. Young Fogies loved hanging out with their parents, their grandparents, their parents-in-law, and their friends' parents, with whom they went to brunches and restaurants. Their idea of a great restaurant was the kind their parents used to take them to, with popovers and a little waterfall out back. Parents would be a favorite subject of conversation. They'd tell each other: "Your parents are such neat people."

They took a custodial position toward all of reality. They worried about taste more than style, about doing things right more than doing them well. They liked things packaged, listed, tidy—classic rock, prix fixe dinners, season symphony tickets, extended warranties. They bought a lot of life insurance. They bought picture frames and then found pictures to fit—botanical prints were popular.

"Okay, we'll buy it," the Fogy husband would say to the Fogy wife as they studied a wingback chair in a furniture store. "But promise me—we're not going to sit in it till we've Scotchgarded it."

They liked antique hunting, which they called " 'tiquing." They would have liked to collect something but could never decide what. They owned a huge number of umbrellas—at home, in the car, the briefcase, the office, in case they ever lost one, which they never did. They read lots of memoirs and biographies, preferably of Winston Churchill—they did imitations of him at their dinner parties. "We will nevah surrendah." They liked giving dinner parties so they could worry about the seating arrangements and silver. They shopped by catalogue whenever possible—the women bought bathing suits from Lands' End, for instance. They had a blackboard next to the kitchen phone, and they left messages in color-coded chalk. They kept a Christmas card list. They took it with them when they went to Europe and used it for addressing postcards that began "Hi Guys" in tiny handwriting.

They watched a lot of public television—*Mystery, Masterpiece Theatre,* the Fred Astaire movies. What they really loved, though, were the fund-raisers where nervous upper-middle-class people stood in front of phone banks offering prizes to viewers who supported quality television—umbrellas and tote bags filled Young Fogy closets. They hoped someday to sit on the phone banks themselves.

They were the first generation of American youth to dislike cars. They had a hard time with parallel parking, for one thing, and they could never learn to drive standard shift. They may have owned Volvos or Toyotas, but their favorite car was the old Buick Electra their grandparents gave them after the move to Florida. If it got dented, the Young Fogies said, "Grampa would be heartbroken."

They bought nice houses in nice neighborhoods with no black people, a lack they rued loudly to prove their liberality, even their sophistication. They liked working fireplaces, but they had a hard time making them work. This caused arguments that had a sudden, inexplicable and ferocious quality, sort of like their sex lives.

"Did you open the flue?"

"Yes, I opened the goddam flue, do you think I'm a complete idiot?"

"I was just . . ."

"Do you? Do you? I want an answer."

It is not true that they were sexless. Eros entered their lives in college, usually—the men recognized it as a sort of required course, and the women may have had flings with a professor or two. And passion would get renewed with the arrival of the Victoria's Secret catalogue or a new canopy bed. They planned to have children—they pictured having sons who looked like miniature versions of George Will.

They didn't exercise with much gusto. Sometimes a Young Fogy couple went out and bought a badminton set. They played in the back yard, all by themselves.

Their parents and their grandparents were disappointed in them.

"Do you think it's normal for people that young to go to Bermuda on vacation?" they'd ask. "Shouldn't they be having more fun?"

I was a Marine in Vietnam.

Every time there's a big new movie about Vietnam, people tell me I should go see it. They tell me I should read novels, memoirs and magazine articles about Vietnam, too, and see the documentaries and television shows, and tell them what I think. They've been telling me this for years, ever since I got back.

"You really should read what he *Times* had to say about the Tet offensive last Sunday."

"You should see *The Deer Hunter*."

"You should be watching this Vietnam series on ABC. I'd be curious to know what you think of it."

Why?

My father was in World War II, but I don't remember anybody telling him that he really should see *The Sands of Iwo Jima* or read *Catch-22*. He was interested in the war—he loved *Mr. Roberts* and *Victory at Sea*—but I don't think anybody was giving him suggested-reading lists the way they've given them to me for half a lifetime.

It's often men who missed the war who do this. They aren't looking for catharsis, tribute, or memorial, like Vietnam veterans; they seem to be looking for reality, the war itself. Do they think they can find it in a movie? Male or female, I'm talking about the crowd that got important from the middle 1960s to the middle 1970s—lawyers, college kids, journalists, academics, dinner-party hustlers. They had enough clout to stay at one remove from both reality and the draft board, and enough money to protect their naïveté, which is a major asset of any ruling class. They believed life is what you think and feel. They wanted to be hip, and they thought irony would get them there. They smoked marijuana even if it made them anxious. They saw a lot of movies and believed in the media. They were the people who come to mind when somebody says that art is the religion of the upper middle class.

Since I was among the first men back from Vietnam, I assumed these people would have a lot of questions for me. They didn't. They'd squint at me for a while, like physicists studying a stray decimal point that wandered into an equation, and decide I was irrelevant. After a while, they'd tell me about Vietnam—the books they'd read, the columnists they favored, the movies they'd seen.

"I was there in 1966," I'd say.

"Have you read *Going After Cacciato*?" they'd say. "I'd be interested to know what you think of it."

Clearly, I was no expert on Vietnam. I'd been a corporal on a pacification team in Chu Lai for three or four months before my enlistment ran out. Days, we won the hearts and minds of the Vietnamese people. Nights, we'd catch a little carbine fire and the occasional grenade. I supported the war because the best and the brightest said they thought we could win it. Later on, I changed my mind when I saw they'd been lying.

For the war or against it, people meant well. Right after I got back home to Connecticut, the curate from my parents' church stopped by. He was fresh out of Yale Divinity School and very concerned about the war. He wanted to know how the guys in Vietnam "felt" about it.

"I don't understand," I said.

"You know, when they talk about the war, what do they say?"

"I don't understand."

It turned out he wanted to know our moral positions on the war. I told him we'd been too busy to have any, where I was. He couldn't grasp this. He seemed to have a picture of us debating ethics and geopolitics under the mortar flares. Maybe he'd gotten that idea from a book, like *The Naked and the Dead*.

There was the future lawyer who told me I wasn't on a pacification team in Vietnam.

"Why not?"

"Because it's a contradiction in terms."

They meant well. I've wondered if it was like this for blacks back when white liberals would start talking about reading James Baldwin or going on a poverty-agency bus tour of Bedford Stuyvesant; back before the black power movement told them to sit down and shut up. It's worth noting that "they meant well" is one of the worst things you can say about anybody. The media coverage of Vietnam meant a lot to these people. They were concerned citizens. They told me that television was "bringing the war into America's living rooms." These were people who wouldn't go to a foreign movie dubbed into English—it wasn't authentic—but they thought they could know what a war was like by watching television. They told me I should read the stories in this or that newspaper. They talked as if they made a huge difference. So I read them. These were stories about how the ambassador contradicted himself in a press conference or Navy jets screamed north for the ninth straight day. They weren't about the war, they were about officers and politicians keeping their jobs, as far as I could see. This was sad. If ever there was an enlisted man's war, it was Vietnam, but the media—with exceptions like Michael Herr and Jimmy Breslin—kept hanging around the officers. You get better quotes from officers, and mixed drinks with ice. And the higher the officers get, the more their war is like something you can discuss at a dinner party—a theory, a movie of sorts.

Then the movies started coming out, such as *Apocalypse Now*,

Coming Home, and *The Deer Hunter*. People said I should go see them. They wanted to know what I thought. I'd tell them.

"But it's such a good movie," they'd say. "How isn't it like Vietnam?"

I'd try to explain that it was just a movie, it was colored light moving around on a screen. It wasn't that these folks couldn't tell the difference between a war and a movie; they didn't want to. They were going to movies the way some people might go to church. When they liked what they saw, they wanted me to tell them that art's truths were The Truth, The Word, the war itself. In their way, I think, they wanted to be veterans, too. They had their field jackets, their marches. One movement slogan said: Bring the War Home.

Maybe they figured it would make a hell of a movie.

part five

inalienable rites

Best of all was the cigarette afterward.

You blew out the match with a thick, authoritative exhale. You lay back in the dark, maybe put the ashtray on your belly, and smoked in silence so profound that you could hear the tiny whistle and crack of the tobacco burning. It was an offering. It was communion. It was said to be as indispensable to lovemaking as the smashed bottle of champagne was to the launching of an aircraft carrier.

"Ah," you said.

After a while, you might tell the old joke:

Do you smoke after sex?

I don't know, I never looked.

This was back before you quit smoking, or wanted to. Back when smoking was like a haircut or a new pair of shoes—it showed the world who you were, or wanted to be. Back when it was an art you practiced in front of the bathroom mirror when your parents were out for the evening, an art you copied from the masters— Bogart, Bacall, Edward R. Murrow, Franklin D. Roosevelt with his cigarette holder pointing skyward at an angle always described as "jaunty." Or Bette Davis, for whom cigarette smoking appeared to be a noble burden she had cheerfully, even extravagantly, shouldered. And all those novelists with their dust jacket cigarettes and their novels full of people who kept lighting another one, or stubbing it out angrily (or "dinching" it, as John O'Hara might put it). And the baseball players with bats on their shoulders and cigarettes in their mouths in ads that told of how kind Camels were to your "T-zone," which was your mouth and throat. And the actors, bandleaders (this was back when there were "bandleaders") and celebrities—including Ronald Reagan smiling behind a burning Chesterfield.

Everybody smoked cigarettes. Lucky Strike. Old Gold. Call for Philip Morris. Willy the Penguin says, "Smoke Kool." Actually, in 1949, the peak year for it, only 44 percent of adult Americans smoked cigarettes, but it seemed like everybody. Now nobody smokes. Actually, 26.5 percent of Americans still smoke, but smoking has lost its glamour and its meaning. It is no longer a ritual of fraternity or powder room (remember when there were "powder rooms"?), nor is it a private ceremony performed in honor of one's own style and personality. Like hats and gloves, it marked boundaries and defined class. It was a necessity, like clothing and food (the government put cigarettes in C-rations, right next to good old ham and limas). Now it's another kind of necessity—an addiction, according to a recent surgeon general's report.

Once, the idea was to advertise your smoking, to luxuriate in it, to exhale cigarette smoke so it unfolded in front of you like an old map, with the slow acrobatics of cream when you pour it into iced coffee. Smoke was an all-purpose word-balloon you could hang above your head, cartoon-style, and even if there were no particular words in it, it told of a desirably intense self-consciousness. Now, cigarette smoke is the furtive vapor that people vent off behind their hands. Who is proud to smoke anymore? When's the last time you saw anyone do it well—with the panache of Rita Hayworth releasing clouds of metaphysical eros from her cigarette holder, or the worldliness of Murrow on *See It Now,* peering at us past a column of smoke that rose like a pillar of Truth itself?

Lost, all lost. Murrow died of lung cancer. Humphrey Bogart died of throat cancer. In the movies of the past twenty years, smoking has become a sign of gimped psyches—Glenn Close in *Fatal Attraction*—or a token of a bygone era—*Chinatown* or the remake of *D.O.A.* It never looks as good in color as it did in black and white, either. It has become lower class, like lawn flamingos and leisure suits. Smoking has been harried out of fashion by the specter of drowning in the tumorous sump of your own lungs, by the sort of people who do things for your own good, and by prudes who flaunt their puzzlement over your reluctance to value health and statistics above the ambiguities and etiquette that smoking stood for. It invites harassment by police and nagging by your own children, rather like the practice of religion under a totalitarian regime. It is so déclassé that it has a raffish appeal when you see John Kennedy Jr. doing it in a society photograph in the *New York Daily News.* It has been demystified. Nothing has replaced it. We're forgetting that cigarette smoking, for all its lethal filthiness, meant something. Even more important to its universal significance was that it meant anything, whatever you wanted it to. (Or, in the slang of the Cigarette Age, it meant anything—but absolutely anything.) It made you manly, womanly, an insider, an outsider, happy, sad, an intellectual, a common man.

"Got a match?" said Lauren Bacall to Bogart in a terse evocation of possibility in *To Have and Have Not.*

"My father sits alone with no lights on / His cigarette glows in the dark," Carly Simon sang in a terse evocation of despair and generation gap.

"He took one last drag on his cigarette and snapped it away. Then, with that faint, fleeting smile playing about his lips, he faced the firing squad; erect and motionless, proud and disdainful, Walter Mitty the Undefeated, inscrutable to the last."—James Thurber in *The Secret Life of Walter Mitty.*

"He took a cigarette from a pack on the table and lit it with fingers that bumped gently and incessantly against one another. He sat back a trifle in his chair and smoked without any sense of taste. He had been chainsmoking for weeks."—J. D. Salinger, describing the unstrung Sgt. X in "For Esmé, With Love and Squalor."

"Shall we just have a cigarette on it?"—Paul Henreid urging Bette Davis to commemorate the nobility of their undying love at the end of *Now, Voyager,* in which Henreid made what may be the most romantic move in the history of cigarette smoking—lighting two at once and giving one to Davis.

Smoking was a personal ritual you performed in living rooms, hospital rooms, restaurants, offices, newsrooms, railroad cars and movie theaters. A haze hung over America like visible proof of a national soul. Nobody gagged and fanned their hands at a lit cigarette in an elevator. (Why not? Didn't they have allergies then, too?) You smoked everywhere that a more important ritual was not taking place, a wedding, or a funeral, say. (Veterans will recall that you could not salute a superior officer with a hand that held a cigarette.) It was a rite of passage. It was something to do with your hands when you got nervous at parties. It established your turf, your membership, your claim on life.

Consider a sailor strolling into a railroad station, in 1954, for instance. A guy with a duffel bag and a sailor hat that seems to be cocked over both eyes at once. Just back from Korea. He stops in front of a wooden bench and rolls the bag off his shoulder. He sits, puts one black shoe up on the bag and extracts a pack of Pall Malls from his sock. He raps the pack on the back of his thumb. Three or four cigarettes appear, staggered like organ pipes. He installs one in the corner of his mouth. He takes a book of matches from inside the cellophane wrapper on the cigarette pack. He strikes a match toward himself, precisely the way his mother taught him not to, and cups the flame inside his palms, sailor-style.

With the wince of a man who has made a decision, and still without touching the cigarette (as if to demonstrate not only that he knows how to light one in a high wind, but that he can smoke it while coiling a rope), he blows a thin, carbureted stream of smoke through the benevolent snarl at the side of his mouth.

There is a young woman standing near him, with a daughter of no more than seven. They both wear hat and gloves. The little girl watches the sailor light his cigarette. He winks at her and, pointing to the mother with a lift of the cigarette, he says: "Zatcher big sister?"

He gets no answer. The mother drifts off with her daughter in the manner of women moving away from sailors in railroad stations everywhere, inexorable but somehow motiveless. The little girl wonders if her mother will go to the ladies' room to smoke a cigarette herself. She doesn't wonder why her mother can't smoke in the waiting room but the sailor can. She just knows. It's one of those things that even seven-year-old girls know. The sailor gathers his mouth in a large, fleshy O and sends a smoke ring chasing after them.

Cigars were the symbol of gangsters and Wall Street plutocrats. Pipes were the province of Maine hunting guides, old square-rig sailors, and ivory-tower professors, a relic of the nineteenth century, the age of achievement and character. Cigarettes were pure twentieth century, the age of gesture and personality. As early as World War I, they were also a symbol of the Forces of Right, as in this account from the *New York Globe* in 1915 of the sinking of a British battleship: "Captain Loxley of the Formidable went down with his ship, standing on the bridge calmly smoking a cigarette. . . . We often hear also of other heroes who go to their doom lipping a cigarette between their teeth. It never is a cigar or pipe, but always a cigarette."

They were actual war materiel. "You ask me what we need to win this war," said General John Pershing. "I answer tobacco, as much as bullets."

They revealed the new world order. George Orwell wrote of anarchist troops in the Spanish Civil War: "If you wanted to slap the general commanding the division on the back and ask him for a cigarette, you could do so, and no one thought it curious."

They were something to do, as in the Statler Brothers singing, in 1965: "Countin' flowers on the wall / that don't bother me at all /

playin' solitaire till dawn / with a deck of 51 / smokin' cigarettes and watchin' Captain Kangaroo / now don't tell me I got nothin' to do."

They were entertainment, as in the barroom conundrums involving a Camels pack: the riddle about where the camel would hide in a sandstorm (in the city on the other side of the pack) and something about counting the E's on the pack, and you always came up one short if you didn't know the trick.

They were a Times Square landmark, as in the Camels billboard where the guy blew huge smoke rings that were always disappointing, something grimly obvious and mechanical about them.

They were beloved. "What lovelier sight is there than that double row of white cigarettes, lined up like soldiers on parade and wrapped in silver paper? . . . I love to touch the pack in my pocket, open it, savor the feel of the cigarette between my fingers, the paper on my lips, the taste of tobacco on my tongue. I love to watch the flame spurt up, love to watch it come closer and closer, filling me with its warmth."— Film director Luis Buñuel in his autobiography, *My Last Sigh.*

Above all, smoking gave you those all-important virtues of the Hemingway era: experience and authenticity. It made you a private eye with a bottle of rye in the drawer or an intellectual like André Malraux. If you could put a cigarette in your mouth and smoke the whole thing down without touching it, it made you an existential psychopath like Jean-Paul Belmondo in *Breathless,* or two of Faulkner's greatest characters: Joe Christmas in *Light in August* and Popeye in *Sanctuary.* If you were a college-kid folk singer in the late '50s, you acquired the romance of a Depression working stiff by tucking a lit cigarette under the strings of your guitar, up by the tuning pegs. Even Fred Astaire smoked in his movies, although he never seemed sincere about it—he smoked like a magician about to perform a trick with the cigarette: a puff or two and then he was dancing again. Astaire wasn't world-weary, or at least believably so, and cigarettes seemed best on people who were striving for a hint of world-weariness, irony, or tough-old-damedom (Lillian Hellman, Janet Flanner).

In *Grand Hotel,* John Barrymore—a roguish baron with a cigarette in his hand—sidles over to Joan Crawford, who leans on the railing of the atrium. She smokes too. (She is both smoking and leaning, and these cast doubt on her moral rectitude. Why?)

"You know," says Barrymore, "I've often wondered about what would happen to that old porter if someone jumped on him from here."

"I'm sure I don't know," says Crawford. "Why don't you try it and find out?"

"Thank you very much."

"Not at all."

Barrymore glides away. Crawford turns—twists, really, with her whole body—and aims a huge, dense cloud of smoke at him—it's as if she were releasing a feather boa from her mouth. If she had turned and Barrymore had blown smoke at her, it would have been an insult. But when she does it to him, it's an invitation. We know this. How do we know this? Cigarettes were used like ladies' fans as signalling devices.

In December 1952, *Reader's Digest* published a story called "Cancer by the Carton," and the end began. Over the next thirty years, the tobacco companies gussied up cigarettes with filters, colored paper, and new sizes and slogans, but cigarette smoking was wandering away from the center of our lives. The surgeon general's report of 1964, along with bans on television advertising and health warnings on cigarette packs, brought on the twilight of the Cigarette Era.

In another generation or two will anyone remember that tough guys hold a cigarette between thumb and first two fingers, that aristocrats hold it between the first joints of their first two fingers, unless they're sadistic monocled German counts, in which case they hold it like tough guys but with the lit end up? How about knowing that "French inhaling" means letting a little smoke leak out of your mouth and then drawing it back through your nose; that ladies don't smoke on the street; that it's bad luck to light three cigarettes with one match; and that a woman touching a man's hand and looking in his eyes as he lights her cigarette is tantamount to a contractual arrangement?

Someday, museums of natural history will display artifacts of the Cigarette Age—ashtrays, cases, Raleigh coupons—but something will be lost. They can exhibit all the Zippo lighters they want, for instance—brushed chrome Zippos, matte black combat Zippos, Zippos with lanyards and yacht club burgees on them, the name alone evoking a peppy, futuristic America—but they can't reproduce the sweet, simple smell of the lighter fluid as you dripped it into the cotton, or the fat flame that left your cigarette stinking of hydrocarbons but endowed with a dividend of male magic.

Gone, all gone. Butts, fags, smokes, death sticks, coffin nails, spuds . . . Mike Hammer tearing open a "deck of Luckies" (a fresh pack of cigarettes had the same tight heft as a fresh deck of cards), a cigarette behind your ear, a pack of them rolled up in your T-shirt sleeve, tamping one against your thumbnail, scrubbing the yellow off your fingers, the first one of the day and how it made your skin feel as if it were dizzy, cooling and tightening as the nicotine shrank your capillaries . . . running out of cigarettes at 3 o'clock in the morning and picking through ashtrays for the longest butt in the house . . . "Smoke Gets in Your Eyes" . . . watching the wind tug the smoke out the wing window of your coupe . . . it went on and on.

What does it say about our position in the world that we're quitting? Is it leadership? Isolationism? Imperialism? Let us not assume that the decline is permanent. Mankind has the knack of outwitting reason and progress. Norway had an advertising ban, an antismoking campaign, and a decline in smoking, and then, in 1984, smoking started to increase again.

For now, the bulldozers of American highmindedness are clearing the forest that the smoking tribe lived in. And a good thing, too. Smoking is a rotten habit.

Ah, but what it meant.

Think of a droplet of sweat arising from your forehead. Think of the tiniest waterlily of worry blossoming on your brow, or arriving like a kindly postcard from the Mother Ocean inside us all, perhaps a freckling of sweat, sweat scattered across your face like a sort of Protestant work-ethic confetti, like thrown rice at a wedding of Animal and Heat, sprouting, burgeoning, gathering into dank little mule trains that skid down the mountainsides of your face, your neck, collapsing down your thorax like the rain on a movie windowpane just before the flashback, starting and stopping, rappelling down your rib cage while an outraged mob streams through the fever ports of your armpits—flooding, leaking, turning the hair on your arms into low-tide seaweed, turning your bellybutton into a jolly little hot tub, igniting your mosquito bites, turning your shirt into something that feels like chain mail made out of fresh pasta, making your clothes soggy and stiff, your skin slippery and sticky at the same time, making you feel both befouled and cleansed, as it happens, an odd combination, part of the moral ambiguity of sweat, a frantic and pathetic quality about it all, like an overcooked duck falling apart in its own grease.

"She liked the sweat, liked the way it felt, slick as oil, in all the joints of her body, her bones, in the firm sliding muscles, tensed and locked now, ready to spring—to strike—when the band behind her fired up the school song: "Fight On Dead Rattlers of Old Mystic High."—Harry Crews, in *Feast of Snakes*

People do like to sweat. Admittedly, some don't, particularly women, but there are those who like it, who think that a big sweat is a good sweat, that sweat means power, health, authenticity, and saintliness. A good, big sweat may not make you feel ready for a speech or a job interview, but it does set you up for whatever primal challenges life might throw at you—boxers like to come into the ring in a full sweat before the fight has even started. If you pay the big money for ringside seats, you can get it on you too. Maybe that's why people buy those seats.

In 1882 one F. Blumentritt reported in a German-language journal that "In Tud, or Warrior Island, in the Torres Straits, men would drink the sweat of renowned warriors . . . in order to make themselves 'strong like stone, no afraid.'" The rest of us only have to watch Sly Stallone and Arnold Schwarzenegger movies to get our fill of warrior sweat.

As air conditioning becomes standard in stores, buses, cars, houses, and offices, and as more and more people work indoors in service jobs, good sweats are getting harder to find. They are becoming a discretionary luxury, like horses after the invention of the automobile, like wood stoves after the triumph of central heating. Sweat is becoming quaint and reassuringly authentic. Maybe you'll be able to order it from the L.L. Bean catalogue soon.

You jog, you row, you play at physical work in order to sweat. Once you got paid to grunt and lather over rows of dark machines in factories—now you pay to grunt and lather over dark machines in Nautilus rooms. A good sweat makes you feel purged, prepared, virtuous. It is the true altar wine of Calvinism. On the other hand, you tend to associate it with the lower classes, with brutality, with a failure to be "feminine," a semimystical advertising concept that gets linked with other semimystical concepts such as "freshness." They all preclude sweating.

A good sweat can make you feel healthy, make you feel you've lost weight, and you have—Brooklyn Dodgers pitching great Don Newcombe once claimed he lost twenty pounds in one game. In the seventeenth century, according to a history of sweat in *Sports Illustrated,* an Italian physician named Sanctorius "built a large metal arm balanced on a fulcrum. He placed weights equal to his body weight on one end of the arm and sat on a platform on the other end for hours at a time—his slow ascension proving beyond doubt that his body was losing weight through so-called 'insensible perspiration.' "

Just about everybody in America thinks there are times when it's healthy to sweat, according to a Research & Forecasts Inc. report on stress for Mitchum antiperspirant and deodorant. Seven out of ten find it pleasurable to sweat when they're doing hard work or sitting in a sauna. And eight out of ten Americans think it's "very acceptable" to sweat when exercising. Also on the "very acceptable" list: "on a hot day" at 70 percent, "at the beach" at 57 percent, "when dancing at parties" at 32 percent, and "in romantic situations" at 18 percent.

It depends on what you mean by "romantic situations."

You might be thinking of a verse by Aldous Huxley:

But when the wearied band
Swoons to a waltz, I take her hand,
And then we sit in peaceful calm,
Quietly sweating, palm to palm.

You might also be thinking of "Fish, Chips and Sweat," by the Funkadelics:

Sweat was dropping off of my face,
Fish and chips were all over the place.
You should've seen my baby move.
Hey, hey, hey, we got us a groove.

Black music seems to have more references to sweat than white music. Think of: James Brown's great "Cold Sweat" (1967), "Sweat

(Til You Get Wet)" by Brick (1981), and Aretha Franklin's album, "What You See Is What You Sweat" (1991).

White music has the band Blood, Sweat and Tears, a name taken from a speech by Winston Churchill. It's hard to think of other references. In 1945 Stan Kenton's big band did "Easy Street," with June Christy singing: "If the sun makes you perspire / There's a man that you can hire / To plant trees so you can have some shade / On Easy Street."

"Perspire" is a euphemism for "sweat," as in the old saw: "Animals sweat, men perspire, ladies glow." This euphemism is a tradition. So is complaining about it. In 1791 a British magazine complained that "it is well known that for some time past, neither man, woman nor child . . . has been subject to that gross kind of exudation which was formerly known by the name of sweat; . . . now every mortal, except carters, coal-heavers and Irish chairmen . . . merely perspires."

Men like to sweat more than women do. Women worry more than men that they're going to sweat, and they get more embarrassed when they do, according to the Mitchum survey. Men take such pride in all their fluid output, though—the spitting and writing of initials in the snow and so on. Maybe it's a case of fluid envy—their production is so tiny when you compare it with women's feeding and breeding of the human race.

Why aren't women proud of it?

Some aerobics instructors tell their women clients that they're sweating out toxins. This is part of the lore of steam baths, saunas, and Indian sweat lodges too. And there's an odd sense of peace that comes with waking up after a night sweat—the fever has broken, you feel released. Sweat researchers tell us that this is hooey, that sweat bears off little in the way of impurities. It's mostly water with a few salts in it. Still, you feel cleansed. Even blessed. During the day of her appealing religious crisis in the ladies' room of Sickler's restaurant, J. D. Salinger's Franny Glass does a lot of sweating.

Her date, the awful Lane Coutell, says to her: "You're sweating. Not sweating, but I mean your forehead's perspiring quite a bit."

"It is? How horrible! I'm sorry."

But we readers are proud of her. Her sweat proves her authenticity in a world of phonies.

On the other hand, it proves fraud beneath the eyes of judgment. Wasn't that Richard "I am not a crook" Nixon sweating away on television, back in the old days? Then he stopped. Word went around that he was putting antiperspirants on his face.

People who are physically fit sweat more, and sooner, than couch potatoes. People who worry sweat more than those who don't. We sweat for two reasons—heat and emotion. The emotional sweat gives us clammy palms, wet feet, and wet armpits. It gives us the cold sweats referred to by poets from Sappho to James Brown. An absence of sweat can be a sign that something is wrong, evil wrong. Sweat has a morality to it. In *The Big Sleep,* Raymond Chandler describes the ancient, half-dead, and all-rotten General Sternwood sitting in an overheated greenhouse, surrounded by dripping orchids and wrapped in a traveling rug, hardly warm, reminiscing about a son-in-law of wonderful vitality, a man capable of "sweating like a pig." Actually, animals don't come close to our capacity for sweat. "The development of sweat glands and of the associated nervous apparatus has been most highly attained in man," according to Yas Kuno, who published the benchmark *Human Perspiration* in 1956. It's a human thing. Hence its association with Original Sin, work, worry, and truth-telling—sweat is one of the things that lie detectors measure.

The climax of *The Great Gatsby,* with its terrible truth-telling, happens on a hot day, everyone sweating except Gatsby, that gorgeous fraud. Daisy says to him: "You always look so cool." In *On the Road,* Jack Kerouac's Dean Moriarty never stops sweating. Sweat is water from the rock of hipness. Dean goes to hear George Shearing play the piano, "innumerable choruses with amazing chords that mounted higher and higher till the sweat splashed all over the piano and everybody listened in awe and fright."

We like to watch performers sweat. It means they're working and they care. The American public can even rank movies by how much sweating goes on in them. Given a list of *Rocky, Body Heat, Fatal At-*

traction, Sea of Love, Broadcast News, and *Who Framed Roger Rabbit,* they will rank them in precisely that order for containing "the most memorable sweaty scene," according to the Mitchum report.

Work up a sweat. Sweat it out. Sweat bullets. Sweat blood. Ride 'em till they sweat. On the other hand: No sweat. Don't sweat it. Thoreau, the great cosmic wise guy of the nineteenth century, said: "It is not necessary that a man should earn his living by the sweat of his brow unless he sweats easier than I do."

If you don't like to sweat, imagine what life would be like if you couldn't. Imagine those high-tension occasions when you dread sweating, and think of the alternatives—giving a speech, say, and having to periodically pick up the pitcher of ice water and pour it over your head, like an elephant. Or doing a job interview while slavering like a Saint Bernard.

Better to sweat.

The Festival of of American Folklife is self-conscious and soothing at the same time, like National Public Radio without the upper-middle-class accents. It leaves you feeling as though you've just attended a service at the First Church of the Great American Idea. It happens every summer on the Mall in Washington, between the Capitol and the Washington monument—it has become a sort of monument in itself.

The last time I went, American farmers, rhythm and blues musicians, North and South American Indians and Indonesians were drumming, threshing, carving, singing, storytelling, canning, dancing, weaving, cooking, explaining, costuming, trumpeting, irrigating, building, and generally going through the yearly ritual of proving that yes, indeed, we are a nation of nations, a family of man, one world, E Pluribus Unum, hands across the water, black and white together.

"I like the smell of that wood fire," a woman said while she watched a Bolivian Indian blow through a tube at a little cook fire.

Down the Mall you could hear the the electric guitars stretching notes taut, the sound of Delta blues. Up toward the Washington monument a 1920s Advance Rumely Ideal threshing machine turned bundles of oats into sacks of grain with a dry, lackadaisical clatter, the loose-socketed circling of old shafts driven by a sagging belt connected to a kerosene tractor.

"Now, when we were twelve, thirteen, or so, they'd put us out in the field to pitch the bundles, and they'd have the bigger boys to carry the sacks," said Phil Brueggen, a dairy farmer from Cashton, Wisconsin. "My father would be building the straw pile. You had to know how to do it so it would shed the rain."

He tied up a sack of oats with a miller's knot—a half-hitch twice around. "I think you'll see the small farm fade away," he said. "I can see it happening in front of my eyes and I feel so bad."

The whole notion of folklife came out of a nineteenth-century despair over the state of man's soul after revolutions from French to industrial. So much was fading away. The romantics brooded about the national soul, and later both Nazis and Communists would use the idea of folklife to legitimize their power. Ein reich, ein volk . . . In this country, the idea was taken up by most shades of the left, and during the New Deal we saw it in social realist murals on post office walls and heard it in recordings of folk music commissioned by the Library of Congress. When the big, bad wolf of McCarthyism ended up in the kettle in the late '50s, folklife resurged with the Weavers, Pete Seeger's cult heroism among college kids, and the sexy purity of the young Joan Baez. There was weaving and potting. The voice of the autoharp was heard in the land. One big appeal was authenticity. In the middle of plastic America, of Norman Mailer's cancer gulch, of tail-fin conformity and Ozzie and Harriet families, folklife seemed real, somehow. Even pure.

Indeed, up and down the Mall there were real Indians carving, real bluesmen playing, real Indonesians sitting cross-legged under a thatched roof making ornaments out of palm leaves. But how a folk purist would have been shocked to learn that the crunching noise under the thatched roof was the stapler the Indonesians use to fasten the palm leaves together. One Delta bluesman wore a New York Mets hat. The farmers had brought handmade wooden weather vanes in the shape of Hollywood cartoon characters, Tweety Bird and Sylvester the cat.

An unpleasantly ironic Tlingit Indian named Nathan Jackson said he had been been working the folklife scene since the New York World's Fair in 1964. He was a carver and he was teaching his son so he could have a career on the folklife circuit too.

"He's got the determination," said Jackson. "I think that the greatest motivation is . . . " He thought about it for a while. Then he said: "Money."

This was troubling. What was the difference between him and your local Chevy dealer? Folklife is supposed to be something you do for your own kind, not for strangers. You do it for friends, family, neighborhood, clan, tribe, state, fellow union members, whatever. Which makes you wonder why they don't have, say, an upper-class wedding some year at the festival, with the men in morning coats, an announcement in the *New York Times,* and so on. One year the festival had lawyers, and in the early '80s they had break dancing. (Remember break dancing?)

Doing it for your own kind: but if you're doing it at a folklife festival you aren't doing it for your own kind anymore. Then again, folklife festivals don't usually happen in places where there's a lot of folklife, which is just why people are interested in them. Folklife festivals are a sort of folklife themselves, a preposterous, earnest ritual like Morris dancing. They put quotes around reality, take the menace out of it, make it quaint. They may not be authentic, but they are "authentic." In any case, one of the pleasures of the Smithsonian's Folklife Festival is that it turns everybody there into your own kind.

crayons

You can still buy the original eight Crayola crayon colors introduced in 1903. They come in boxes that say "different, brilliant colors": red, blue, green, yellow, orange, brown, violet, and black, double-wrapped in that soft, grippable paper and smelling of rainy days and car trips, a smell of paraffin so memorable it's one of the twenty most recognizable smells among American adults, according to Binney & Smith (the first two being peanut butter and coffee), though it's strange that something that smells as distinct as a crayon has almost no taste, just the feel of those waxy crumbs in your mouth.

We have all crayoned.

Think of this the next time you see some pin-striped executive heavy cruiser gliding down the sidewalk toward you in all his dignity—picture him working away at a spaceship-monster shootout. Know that he felt bad just as you did when he broke one and said to himself he shouldn't have pressed so hard, and tried to pretend it hadn't happened. Finally he had to tear the paper in half and make it two short crayons. These always fell to the bottom of the box when he put them back, which made the other ones stick up too high and so those perfect rows of crayons that were lined up in the fresh box like organ pipes or a choir were ruined.

Ah, the pristinity, the virginity, the infinity offered by a brand-new box of crayons—and then you'd look around the floor of your room at the end of an afternoon of coloring and see the squalid mess of paper and crayons and the stuff your kid brother had scribbled on the wall just as you heard your mother say the three sentences that awoke you from so many reveries:

"Oh.

"My.

"God."

Peter Dunne, a decorated Marine veteran of Vietnam, learned how to color in his cousins' apartment in Brooklyn. He recalls:

> They had a shoe box full of crayon pieces, two girls. Girls color better than boys. It was there that I learned how to outline areas in the same color. As you get older you learn to color in the same direction, instead of like an asterisk. If you had to fill in big areas it was best to color in circles that overlapped. If you colored until there were layers built up, the crayon clicked when you took it off the paper. When you grow up, you can use oil pastels—they're more like lipstick. The color saturation is great but you don't have the edge control. Grease pencils are fun. When you were a kid, remember how you'd always pull that string back one dot too far? I still like to color. If it rains at the beach and you've already bought sandals you go to the Ben Franklin and get crayons and a coloring book, except they call them activity books now. I leave them behind at the house, and the next tenants come in and their kids say, "Wow, a major leaguer was here."

Crayons begin life when you open the box and see that gorgeous chord of color in seventy-two-part harmony, or that perfect octet of the original eight—the truth being that you don't need or really want lots of the colors in the bigger crayon boxes—think of what a disappointment silver and gold always were. They looked great, you figured you could do great ray guns and crowns with them, and then they just came out shiny gray and brown. (Though Binney & Smith says that the "metallics," as it calls them, are often mentioned by adults as their childhood favorites.)

Crayons end up in dusty cacophony under car seats, behind bookcases, under porches. They melt on sidewalks and windowsills, and they are never the same again.

Your mother carried them in her purse, and after you got tired of looking at the tropical fish at the dentist's office, she'd take them out with a coloring book and say: "Color me a picture."

You'd come back and show it to her.

"I went outside the lines," you'd say.

"That's the best part," she'd say. You still thought it looked stupid.

Your parents told you not to sharpen them in the pencil sharpener, they would ruin it, and you did, and they ruined it. You could take a fistful of them and draw a whole bunch of colors all at once, and it would look like when the fighters go over at the air show and let out the different-colored streams of smoke. When they got small enough, you peeled the paper off and pushed them sideways across the page, but without the label you couldn't be sure what color they were anymore.

"I need crayons," you'd say, knowing your mother believed crayons were educational, were maybe even a child's right.

"I just got you some."

"I used them when Grandma was sick and we had to be quiet."

"I'm not getting that huge box. You never use half the colors in it."

That's fine. The worst you could do is the package of the original eight, all of them "different, brilliant colors" and all them with that smell.

Washington has close-order drill the way New York has theater. Troops go through "the usual maneuvers in a masterly manner," in the words of a newspaper describing the Marines parading past Thomas Jefferson on July 4, 1801. The ritual at the Tomb of the Unknowns will end only when America ends. Dress-blues platoons slide through the winter twilights of inaugural parades like Kodachrome ghosts with their red ears and white gloves, the same white gloves that fold flags over coffins at Arlington National Cemetery.

Some years ago, the Army decided that flag details were folding flags too quickly at the ends of funerals.

"We used to do it in sixty seconds. It was too showboaty," Staff Sergeant Kenneth Moomey told me. "We shoot for ninety seconds on the flag fold. We're averaging eighty-eight seconds."

Drill once moved troops across battlefields. Now it teaches discipline and generates beauty. It has become art by virtue of its uselessness. It is performed all over America: by Girl Scouts in berets doing the endless, earnest shuffle of dress right, dress; by color guards marching out at the start of banquets, bridge dedications, and playoff games to do that slow, wheeling high-step reminiscent of pistons working inside some old ship's engine room; by ROTC types in chromed helmet liners and sunglasses, and by old American Legion guys who fire a ragged salute on Memorial Day while little kids crawl around their feet, grabbing the ejected brass shells.

In Washington, the Navy, the Air Force, and the Coast Guard have their color guards and drill teams, but the serious drill is done by the Army and the Marines. They hold each other in contempt.

"If you want to know about drill, there's two places you ask," says Gunnery Sergeant D. L. Hall. "The Marines of Eighth and I, and Black & Decker."

Says Army Sergeant 1st Class James P. Savage, at Fort Myer: "I can show you Marines when we have joint-service ceremonies, you got to beat it into them with a baseball bat."

"In the winter, they wear earmuffs," says a Marine sergeant.

"The Marines have done a good job of advertising themselves," says Army Major Tom Askins.

The Marines favor a severely classical drill, a style that impresses you with its modesty, not its difficulties. It values clarity and directness. It is Apollonian to the point of being forbidding, of turning into Blake's "fearful symmetry." To the Army, it may well look mechanical to the point of arrogance.

Army ceremonial drill has more texture. Rifle butts ease to the ground. There's a tendency to add a subliminal curve here, a hint of a pause there, until the simplest of gestures, such as a salute by the corporal of the guard at the Tomb of the Unknowns, acquires a mysterious gravity. In facing movements, heels may flare out a little more than necessary—a mannerist touch that comes from the same instinct that leads boys to customize cars. The slide and glide of the Tomb sentries can have a catlike delicacy. To Marine purists, it may look cute.

Drill is art in its working out of meaningful forms. It is ritual in the way that it means to change not just the people who do it but the people who see it. (General George Patton said: "Ceremonies are important as a means of impressing our enemies, our allies and our own troops.") Drill is also what anthropologist John M. Roberts calls "judged display," like figure skating, the Miss America pageant, or jams and jellies at the state fair. Imagine the doctoral dissertations that would fill libraries if close-order drill were done by the Eskimos or nineteenth-century slum dwellers or the insane. We take it for granted, maybe because it has been part of Western thinking at least since the ancient Greeks.

It is founded on the ideal of perfection, a classical aesthetic that got buried in the landfill of nineteenth-century romanticism and twentieth-century modernism. The idea is to get all the heads floating evenly, to get men and rifles moving together with an evenness that looks lethally self-conscious. It's an aesthetic of infinite detail, delicate and implacable at the same time, a balancing of rigidity and ease. You see and hear perfection when drill has a quality that gets described with words like "tight" or "locked on" or "crispy" or "snap." The fourteenth revised edition of the *Guidebook for Marines* defines "snap" as: "In commands or signals, the quality that inspires immediate response. In drill, the immediate and smart execution of movement." Snap is to drill as swing is to jazz, an unmeasurable but conspicuous precision that gives you a rush you have to feel to understand. It can happen toward the end of basic training, when your platoon is out drilling for the millionth time and suddenly it comes together, it feels like the moment when your airplane lifts off the ground, a smoothness, a sense of possibility and infinite vista, oddly enough, given the fact that all you can see is the head of the man in front of you, the stubbled phrenology of the military world view. Nothing can stop you, and you can't do anything wrong. Power and virtue, together at last, rifles cracking from shoulder to shoulder. The men in front of you wheel into a column left, the platoon curling 90 degrees with the deft tidiness of a Slinky going downstairs. You know that when you hit the pivot point you'll turn with the same bite. It has a satisfaction that verges on the smug.

Snap comes from attention to detail: the thumbtacks holding the cloth tight on a dress cap; the corsets that the Army wears—for back support, they say, but it's hard to imagine they haven't noticed the look that they create; the safety pins at the waists of trousers to get the bottoms just touching the shoes, but never breaking; the blacking on the bottoms of shoes; white gloves in a perfect row down a rank standing at parade rest; the men on burial details lifting weights six hours a day and drilling with empty caskets so that the full ones float from church to hearse to grave with the rectilinear ease of a cursor moving across a computer screen. Snap is conspicuous simplicity. Every mistake shows. Members of ceremonial drill units usually stand within an inch of six feet tall. Even those differences are hidden by lining men up by height, front to back and right to left. If a man lowers his head too far when looking down to fix bayonets, he is taught not to correct himself even a fraction of inch, lest there be a visible shift in the crescent of light reflecting from the visor of his dress cap. Drill has no gray areas or forgiveness. It is an art of contrasts: between motion and absolute stillness, sound and silence, hard and soft. The trick is to heighten the contrasts. Marine rifle butts crash and then the drum major drifts down the lawn in front of the drum and bugle corps, spinning his mace in exquisitely slow circles. Soldiers pop rifles to port arms, then lower them softly to order arms.

Heels crack—Army heels, at least, with the metal clickers on them. The Marines don't do that. They bang rifle butts, however. When done very well, on the concrete troop walk at the Marine Barracks, they make a single wet snap, like the sound of a bone breaking. The command for this is "order arms."

HHhhO . . . Oooorrderrr . . . Then, theoretically, the word "arms" but actually, it is a throaty blast driven upward by the officer's diaphragm with such pneumatic force that you expect to see a wisp of vapor trailing from his mouth like the mist from a pop-top soda can. The butts come down. The Friday night audience at the Marine Barracks twilight parade goes: "Ahh."

"The Greeks believed they were morally superior because of the way they fought," says Victor Hanson, author of *The Western Way of War: Infantry Battle in Classical Greece*. Drill was a practical matter of teaching troops to fight in the tight formations called phalanxes, which drove over their enemies by sheer pushing power and discipline. The phalanxes were manned by small landowners. Their style of warfare had replaced the aristocratic combat of the Homeric age, when individual warriors such as Achilles would do battle with each other. The new style symbolized the virtue of a community of citizen-soldiers protecting each other through discipline. In the fifth century B.C., a Spartan general named Brasidas lectured his troops about the contemptible Macedonians: "Since they do not have any formation, once under duress they have no shame at all in abandoning their position."

After the Roman Empire collapsed, drill declined, and the West had a resurgence of warrior combat in the form of the knights of the Middle Ages, aristocrats in single combat. Drill was revived in the late 1600s, when the musket replaced polearms. Robert Wright, an Army historian, says: "Frederick the Great's army was exquisitely drilled, and it inspired terror in opponents with its robotic movements. They fired. They turned sideways to reload. They brought their weapons back straight up in the ready position. An officer would give them the order to turn. There would be a flash of those blue uniforms, an effect like flipping Venetian blinds. They would level five or six hundred muskets all at once. Imagine looking at them, if you were the enemy. Then they fired."

Like the Greek phalanxes, eighteenth-century armies met on level, open ground in hopes of a quick, decisive, honorable encounter—the sort of encounter that eluded us during all our years in Vietnam. Despite the legends of American sharpshooters, George Washington knew that the war could not be won by farmers hiding behind trees. He asked Baron von Steuben to take Frederick the Great's drill and make it suitable for his volunteers. Von Steuben believed that each country's drill should reflect the "natural genius" of its people, hence the American style with its ordinary gestures and common-man simplicity, as opposed to the German goose step, or the huge swing of the British. When American drill is good it looks ordinary and effortless.

Newly accurate rifled muskets in the Civil War and then machine guns in World War I ended stand-up maneuvering by troops under fire, although British generals thought it suitable for the Battle of the Somme, in which 14,000 troops, ordered to advance at a walk, not a run, were killed in the first ten minutes of the battle.

Still, we do it. We believe in it.

"The importance of close-order drill could not be overestimated," writes Colonel David Hackworth, the most-decorated hero of Vietnam, in his autobiography, *About Face*. He recalls: "I was so proud to be a cog in that finely tuned machine. I loved the discipline: the relentless repetition—basic drills reinforced again and again—that conditioned a soldier to react to orders not only on the parade field but on the battlefield as well."

Late on Friday afternoon during Washington summers, two companies of Marines form up in the dead fluorescence of an underground parking garage. It makes an ugly racket, the commands and the rifle butts bouncing off the gloomy concrete. There's something unpleasantly ancient here. The Greek underworld could have looked like this. Then they march up a ramp in white trousers and blue jackets, rifles suspended in white gloves, sliding and gliding past the burial detail's practice casket, past the sandbags in front of the sentry post, the perfect rhythm of feet in a sound that feels more like silence than noise as they emerge into the the light of day and the twentieth century.

Soon it will be dark, and five thousand spectators will hear the rifle butts snap down at the first "order arms." They will go: "Ahh."

Stare at the monster long enough and you become the monster. Did Nietzsche say that? And did he really have five consonants in a row in the middle of his name?

Anyway, stare at the Miss America pageant long enough and you become, well, not Miss America, surely . . . But what would Nietzsche, prophet of the superman, have made of this madness on the boardwalk, this yearly pageant-rite of our old democracy's furious vulgarity, this winnowing of young womanhood to find the highest possible lowest common American female denominator? Then again, who cares? It's certainly not a question that's ever apt to be asked of any of the ten finalists, who are better prepared to offer their opinions on world peace, the handicapped, and the role of women in "today's modern world," as it's called by pageant people.

It's the press that keeps coming up with the strange questions, a whole Miss America press corps that returns year after year. They love this thing, they handicap all the girls like horseplayers, but they have a tendency to lob the occasional smoke grenade onto the track, just to see what the horses will do in a panic.

Like: What about breast taping?

That is a question asked at a press conference with Mary Ann Mobley, Miss America 1959, and now, decades later, a cohost of the pageant. She is a smidgen of a thing with a red sweater slung over her shoulders and eyes so deep-set that the overhead fluorescent lighting turns them into black holes. She takes Step One of the emergency action Miss Americas are trained to perform, which is to say she smiles, a smile with a conspicuous public vastness reminiscent of the huge flags you see flying over Cadillac dealerships.

Does the press have no shame? It has probed the Firm Grip gunk that the contestants (not girls or women) sprayed on their derrieres (the approved pageant word) to keep their swimsuits (never bathing suits) from riding up as they strolled the runway in front of 15,000 ticket holders and 50 million television viewers. There was the inquisition about Saran-Wrapping of thighs for spot reduction, the hemorrhoid cream to tighten eye bags, and the Vaseline inside the lips to make it possible to smile for minutes on end. The *Atlantic City Press* has discovered that thirty-seven contestants have been arrested for speeding sometime in their lives, and a hairy fanatic from the *Philadelphia Inquirer* has been pointing out that although it's called a "scholarship pageant," some of the contestants don't even know their grade-point averages.

Now breast taping. While Mary Ann Mobley does her Step One smile at the questioner, who is the guy from the *Inquirer,* reporters ask each other what the hell breast taping is. (It involves bending over, letting gravity move the breasts into the correct position, then applying a broad band of tape to keep them that way.)

Step Two: Mobley starts talking through her smile: "I don't mean to denigrate your question but that's an awfully cute beard you have." She keeps on smiling, bravely helpless or humbly triumphant, or maybe even triumphantly helpless.

Step Three: "I wish I had enough problem to worry about it," she says in an echo of the Great American Woman's Chest Obsession, an anxiety that contestant after contestant will voice unasked ("Flat as a board," said Miss Mississippi of herself in her high school years, after winning a preliminary swimsuit competition, going away).

Step Four: She thickens her Southern accent. She puts the backs of her hands on her hips. She pleads for understanding of the horrible dilemma of womanhood.

"With all due respect," she says, "I think we're discussing things that are irrelevant. I mean, all of us, I've gotta tell you, I put on makeup today, I probably should have put on more. Whatever it takes, ladies, for us to get out there and look good." And then a desperate puzzlement to her voice: "Men, don't y'all like it? Don't y'all wear cologne?"

Well, scoff, oh ye cynics, ye marching feminists, ye climbers toward an enclave free of the ironies of middle-class American femininity, but: These fifty-one young women have figured out how to fit in and stand out at the same time; to be famous and anonymous, noble and common, virgins and dynamos, nuns of the religion that has millions of American high school students praying daily: "Dear God, let me be normal." As Miss America 1970 once said: "I am representing the typical girl, not someone who's outstanding at all."

"I never said ten words in high school," says Kaye Lani Rae Rafko, Miss America 1988, who gets interviewed the way retired quarterbacks get interviewed at Superbowl games.

"I never said ten words in high school," says April Fleming, a former Miss Virginia, adding: "It's hard to be a woman. You want to be attractive to men, but to women, too. In school I was in the in-group but not an attention getter, I was real conservative, I was just a skinny little thing, no figure, nothing."

They have learned how never to set off the feminine group ego alarm whose siren goes: "WHO DOES SHE THINK SHE IS? WHO DOES DOES SHE THINK . . ." They tend to come from the America of a million unwritten rules, surrounded, in the world at large, with a billion unknown ones. Like everyone else, they have grown up feeling like fools, with feet in mouth and egg on face, the existential horror of childhood. But instead of blaming the rules for their misery, they have decided not only to play by them but to win. Though more men than women direct state pageants, and a man heads the national pageant, the rules—particularly the unwritten ones—seem to be policed by women, particularly in the swimsuit competition. Miss Virginia says: "Men are, 'Ohh, she looks good, give her a 10.' Women say, 'That doesn't look quite right.' They see you covering your flaws."

Somebody mentions to Kaye Lani Rae Rafko that the past seven Miss Americas have all been swimsuit winners. Flashing a little frown, she says, "Kellye Cash won swimsuit?"

Women also make up the bulk of the pageant haters. It was on the boardwalk here that the legend of the burning bras began after a demonstration by feminists in the late 1960s, back when the bras that Miss America types wore were a symbol of oppression and the body hair they tweezed, shaved, and depilated was a symbol of liberation. Whatever the symbol, and whether the bras were burned or not, the pageant remains, defending the swimsuit competition with preposterous claims that it demonstrates physical fitness, that sort of thing. Still, Miss America glows like an archetype, an anima figure in girlhood psyches.

Night after night, the crowd at the preliminary judging in Convention Hall is shot full of girls who have been Little Misses, Junior Misses, Miss Wallala County Teen, untold crownings in the Miss America locals, the Miss USA system, the Miss Universe system, the Miss Teens Encouraging Excellence Nationwide (T.E.E.N.), and so on in all the minor leagues of pageantry. There are girls as young as thirteen who split the colors on their eye shadow and mascara their lashes until they spread apart with frozen suddenness like the smoke from fireworks shells, who wear utterly public smiles and hair in twists, who sit there watching and never yawn or crack their knuckles, not even during the baton acts or the acrobatic dancing, all of it done in the spirit of small boys taking their baseball gloves along to a baseball game, and done too because they know the rules. Like the contestants, they aren't that great looking, on average. Not knockouts. And it goes without saying that if they had any major talent for singing or dancing or whatever it is they do, they wouldn't be doing pageants.

But they stand out. They fit in. Both at once. They can't get enough of the monster.

"Just by being here I'm more motivated," says Samantha John Fetters, 20, of Fayetteville, North Carolina. She is wearing one of her two Barbara Barbara dresses, along with pendant earrings, and has blond hair and eyes the color of light blue bathroom tile that has a dusting of talcum powder on it. She has wangled a press seat by the runway and she is staring up at the tense sashays of the swimsuit contestants.

She says: "Now that I'm here, I see it can be done, see what I'm saying? I was Miss Fayetteville and Miss Cumberland County High School. I won enough scholarship money to put me through a year of private college, Methodist College in Fayetteville. I couldn't have done it without it. It's a business, it's just like a business. My father is a heavy-equipment mechanic. We're just a middle-class family. I've had a job ever since tenth grade. I kind of envy the girls whose parents have given them everything, you know what I'm saying? Like the Steve Yearick competition gown I got, I worked two jobs to get it. I wanted it, I got it. You want to hear something funny? I drive a 1977 Ford Granada that's worth about $700 but I've got a $3,000 gown hanging in my closet."

There is so much to learn. The runway walk, for instance, is precisely the walk any woman would want to have if she had to walk through a bus terminal at 1:30 in the morning to be greeted by a father she is delighted and relieved to see, but who just might be drunk. It is devoid of sex, this walk, like almost everything else about the contestants.

Winners of ancient beauty contests would be given to the Great Panjandrum for his delectation. Imagine for a moment how we'd reel with horror and fascination if Mary Ann Mobley announced that immediately after traipsing down the runway with the roses, Miss A was going to be delivered to the highest roller of the day at the Atlantic City crap tables, or, yes, helicoptered naked out to the yacht of Mr. Donald Trump himself.

N-O no! That is not the point of the pageant, and stop that. Better instead to marvel at the variety of smiles that must be mastered: the standard happy-surprise flaring of mouth and eyes (with optional blown kiss) when you're pretending you see someone you know in the crowd; the full-bore princess smile, one that makes you think less of orthodontists than piano tuners, for proving that no amount of wolf-whistling from the crowd will challenge your poise as you parade around in your swimsuit; a stately pleasure smile created by dropping the jaw and then baring the lower teeth; a cool and medium smile for still photographs, with face idling in a sort of neutral.

And, if needed, there is the ultimate smile, should you be named the winner—the anguish-of-joy-and-astonishment finale smile, beginning with gasp, supernova eyes, and lifted eyebrows, then closed eyes and the frown of humility with slight twist of jaw to the side in preparation for the tears, then perhaps a lip compression followed by an inverted smile with the corners of the mouth pointing down and eyebrows tenting up toward each other (possibly accompanied by a placing of the hands in a little steeple on either side of the nose), followed by a suitably brief oval of ecstasy converting into a figure-eight that leads to the obligatory sob.

These women will talk about almost anything personal, but is there one who would admit to practicing this look in the mirror? Perhaps there are some things better left secret.

Stare at the monster long enough . . .

good wars

War in the age of the Good War has looked like sex in the age of safe sex—you wondered if it was possible to have it at all. Then in 1991 came the fracas in the Persian Gulf. It turned out that war still had something going for it.

Iraq's Saddam Hussein sent his tanks into Kuwait, whose ruling class fell back weeping to the casinos of Cairo.

"There was no doubt who started it, or what we were fighting for, or who were the good guys and who were the bad guys—it was a war that could have been written by Hollywood," said Van Johnson, who starred in a lot of World War II movies. He said it in a documentary about World War II, which was the last good war, the one all wars are compared to.

President Bush compared Hussein to Hitler. Official Washington made you think of John Wayne standing on the bridge of a World War II destroyer, barking to his engine room, "Gimme everything ya got." The United Nations passed resolutions, different lands banding together like the old World War II movie where the first sergeant asks for volunteers and he gets O'Hara, Koslowski, Jackson, Shapiro. (Was that movie ever made, or was it just a routine for stand-up comics on *The Ed Sullivan Show*?) "It feels like the start of the Second World War," said a happy senior State Department official. In a nation dispirited by a budget crisis, collapsing banks, and recession, the Persian Gulf looked like it had every chance of being the kind of war people mean when they say, "What we need is a good war."

The good war is a national idea, an I-beam holding up the American psyche. It is a ritual, with rules. Some of the rules:

In the good war, the other guy starts it. He isn't just a bad guy, he has to attack us. The Germans and the Japanese had been crushing countries on three continents for years before Pearl Harbor roused Americans to fight. Remember the Tonkin Gulf, Pearl Harbor, the Lusitania, the Maine, the Alamo.

In the good war, we are "innocent, unsuspecting, the underdog, the victim," says Van Johnson. The problem is, this means that we're unready for it, as we were for World War II. In *A Country Made by War*, Geoffrey Perrett writes: "The idea of perennial unreadiness . . . fits the American self-image of a peace-loving people dragged reluctantly into war. Civilians and military men alike find that idea appealing. For another thing, it is the stuff of epic drama—the ultimate triumph, after near defeat, of good over evil, us over them."

The good war is fought with American know-how, ingenuity and industrial might: modern cannon from Yankee factories, the Great White Fleet of the late nineteenth century, the B-17 of World War II, McNamara's electronic wall in Vietnam, the F-111s that attacked Gadhafi in Libya. They will win the war cheaply, efficiently and scientifically. In *Wartime*, culture critic Paul Fussell says that the start of World War II was much like the Persian Gulf buildup: "At first everyone hoped, and many believed, that the war would be fast-moving, mechanized, remote-controlled, and perhaps even rather easy." We have a particular romance with air power. John Updike writes: "America is beyond power, it acts as in a dream, as a face of God. Wherever America is, there is freedom, and wherever America is not, madness rules with chains, darkness strangles millions. Beneath her patient bombers, paradise is possible."

In the good war, as Douglas MacArthur said, "there is no substitute for victory."

The good war is not ambiguous or ironic. There is no colonel saying, "I love the smell of napalm in the morning," as Robert Duvall says in *Apocalypse Now*, looking out over the Vietnamese jungle. There is no real-life colonel saying, as one actually said at Ben Tre, "We had to destroy the village in order to save it." And there are no truckloads of troopers driving past the press shouting, "We're not supposed to be here! This isn't our war! Why are we here?"—which is what happened during Bush's Thanksgiving visit to Saudi Arabia; it was forgotten after the victory, like most of the doubts and anger about the war. History is written by the winners.

We were together during World War II. Intellectual celebrities supported it—Archibald MacLeish, John Steinbeck, and Carl Sandburg helped lead the American propaganda effort, for instance. Instead of being the rednecks of Vietnam, our soldiers were the salt of the earth, Bill Mauldin's Willie and Joe. "I'm no hero, I'm just a guy, I just want to get this thing over and go home," said William Bendix in one movie. This came at the end of more than a decade of social realism and intellectuals' celebration of the common man.

After World War II, the common man faded. American art turned to the international language of abstraction. Dwight MacDonald warned of the tackiness of mid-cult America. Among the policy makers and theorists, war became a tool rather than a crusade, therapy rather than brute violence. It was a precise means of attaining ends with carefully graduated responses, surgical air strikes, systems analysis, and highly trained elite forces such as the Green Berets. The good war no longer required common men or heros. Heroism went the way of John Henry, defeated by the steam-hammer of the machine gun, the tank, the B-52, missiles, nuclear weapons—all of which made survival in combat far more a matter of chance than of skill.

Among the governing classes, war came to be seen as a phenomenon of the lower classes, like tractor pulls or deer hunting. The elite was having it both ways, though. Polling from 1965 to 1971 shows that the college-educated supported the war far more than the high school and grade school-educated. Of course, the upper classes didn't have to fight the war. And they weren't about to take the blame for losing it. The loss was blamed on factory workers and people who live in trailer parks. It looked like Oscar Wilde had been right. He had predicted that "as long as war is regarded as wicked, it will always have its fascination. When it is looked upon as vulgar, it will cease to be popular." Popular with the governing classes, that is. (Wilde was not thinking of the tattooed masses in mirror sunglasses, heading into Army-Navy stores to buy T-shirts bearing slogans like "Join the Army, Travel to Distant Lands, Meet Interesting People and Kill Them.")

The good war came to include pruderies about violence and racism. Both were seen to be flaws of the lower classes, who called the Vietnamese "gooks," and so on. Once the uppers had too, but times had changed. For instance, Paul Douglas, a liberal senator from Illinois, said that he joined the Marines during World War II "to get myself a Jap." The good war precludes this sort of language now. There was little talk about wogs or tentheads during the Persian Gulf war. A cool depersonalization was called for. In World War II, the final training film in Frank Capra's Why We Fight series showed pictures of the Nazi hierarchy while a voice said: "If you ever see one of these men, kill him!" Violence prudery would forbid this now. Despite the demonization of Saddam Hussein, there was no public fantasizing about personally killing him. In the middle '80s, Fred Downs, a decorated Vietnam infantry officer, lectured an infantry class about killing and was told afterward by a high-ranking Army officer that the word "killing" had been replaced by the phrase "servicing the target." Feelings were important. Among Vietnam veterans, post-traumatic stress syndromes moved people more than their missing legs. During the Persian Gulf buildup, a newspaper ad urged support for our troops: "It's not the desert heat. It's not Saddam Hussein. It's wondering if you care."

We forgot all the anger and doomsaying about the war in the Persian Gulf because we won. It was a good war. We remembered it all about Vietnam because we lost. It was a bad war. There was plenty of cynicism about World War II as well. Presidential adviser Robert Sherwood recalled in 1948 that that World War II was "the first war in American history in which the general disillusionment preceded the firing of the first shot." We have forgotten all about that disillusionment. It was redeemed by the good war to end all good wars. As it happened, the disillusionment had come after the previous good war, World War I, which we won. In 1937 disgust with World War I was so great that only 28 percent of Americans said we should have fought in it, but that number doubled as Pearl Harbor made the first war look good again. Then again, months after Pearl Harbor, a Gallup poll showed that only about half of Americans knew why we were at war. All of this is forgotten.

We'll keep believing in the Good War. It offers a redemption that nothing else does, not feeding the hungry or tending the sick. William James was wrong: There is no moral equivalent of war. War is its own morality. That's one of the million reasons people love it so much. As the staff sergeants used to say in Vietnam: "It ain't much of a war, but it's the only war we got." Vietnam did not end up being such a good war, but we've always got our eye out for another one that is.

If you're the anxious type . . .

Which is to say that if the words "California vacation" make you think of earthquakes and glassy-eyed surfers walking around in fingerbone necklaces; if touring America means only a list of horrible illnesses—Lyme disease in New England, AIDS in New York, leprosy in Texas (a remarkably high incidence of leprosy there, as it happens); if you feel intimidated by the sight of fashionable matrons standing on dunes and touching their front teeth together as they survey exactly who's on the beach today; if you ever see a kid standing on a bridge over the turnpike and wonder if he might drop a cinder block through your windshield the way kids do now and then, no denying it; if you're the sort of perfectly normal but perhaps somewhat high-strung personality who worries that all those slightly overdressed weekenders waiting in line at the Martha's Vineyard seafood restaurant might start fistfighting in a spasm of free-floating resentment; if you rarely hear the word "swim" without thinking of "attempts at resuscitation," or you can't hear "Glacier National Park" without thinking of "blood-flecked pieces of sleeping bag"—if you're a worrier, in other words, then perhaps you shouldn't go on vacation at all.

Not that there's anything worth worrying about. Millions of Americans go on vacation every summer without a second thought about rogue waves, brown recluse spiders, tennis court snubs and freeway snipers. Millions of families return from vacations without their daughters having come back from a clambake at 4:30 A.M. on a motorcycle driven by a young man named Jason, who dropped out of college to work year-round as a carpenter out there on Lout Island (he's the one who didn't get the deck built on your house in time for summer). How many travelers to New England broke down on the Cross-Bronx Expressway and vanished last week, leaving behind only a burned-out station wagon resting on milk crates under a bridge? None, probably. You may be worrying about lightning, but how many people actually got killed by lightning last year? A mere hundred or so. Besides, all you have to do is crouch when you smell the telltale ozone that means a lightning strike is imminent. Maintain as little contact with the ground as possible. You may look a little foolish if you're the only one on the miniature golf course who's doing it, but better safe than sorry.

There's nothing phobic about people who are afraid of shark attacks or drive-by shootings, of hypothermia deaths, of poison ivy, oak, or sumac turning people into something that looks like the Michelin Man made out of bacon rinds, of water-skiing into a stump, of the lifeguard looking out at them and not realizing they're in the state described so well by British poet Stevie Smith: "I was not waving, but drowning." What about the vague sense of inadequacy inspired by all those Jeeps and convertibles hurling up and down the roads of the Hamptons with such purposefulness that you spend two weeks out there convinced that you're missing something? If you are a teen-ager, what about All the Other Teen-Agers, whose tans, cars, bodies, and apparent belief that life can go on like this forever provoke a combined dread and craving akin to that brought on by the prospect of using some particularly evil drug (which they all use, as it happens)? There's no reason to feel guilty or neurotic about these fears—they could all come true, though of course they almost certainly won't.

There are no reservations at the hotel, it turns out. You do have reservations at the restaurant, but one of the kids forgot his shoes.

"I'll carry him," you say to the manager.

"Dad," your son says. "I'm fourteen years old."

At the motel down the street, your neighbors are either a couple, one of whom is Jimmy Swaggart, or a bunch of fraternity brothers amassing a pile of empty beer cans the size of a Volkswagen Beetle. Or you keep driving till you get to the campsite, which is full, but the kids make you listen to the campfire lecture by the official U.S. Park Ranger.

"Now this furry little fellow, we call him the marmot," says the ranger in the genial, hearty voice of a talking dog biscuit on television. You hate him. And somehow you sense that he hates you, too.

You leave home as a disciple of Jean-Jacques Rousseau, who preached the perfection of nature and the glory of the noble savage. You return a disciple of Thomas Hobbes, who knew that life away from civilization is nasty, brutish, and short. Your back goes out when you're packing the car. You know the dog is going to jump out the window, which you've opened because the air conditioner broke in the middle of the traffic jam outside Sandusky, Ohio, and you'll spend all night looking for it in a swamp that reminds you of the disappearance of Jimmy Hoffa. You know the children will nag you to stop at Stuckey's for pralines until you turn around with the whites of your eyes showing all the way around and you scream: "CAN ONE PERSON IN THIS CAR EVEN TELL ME WHAT A PRALINE IS?" And the next day you'll be standing in line to get into Splash Land so you can stand in line to buy raw mullet so you can stand in line to feed them to the porpoises, which you try to pet while wondering if they hate you.

If you're the anxious type, you can spend an extraordinary amount of your vacation wondering if you are hated.

The answer is yes. Porpoises, park rangers, praline salesmen, mullet vendors, the guys who pump gas on the Jersey Turnpike, the creepy motel clerk, the guy who rents you the air mattress at the beach, anyone walking around a theme park in the costume of a cartoon animal, the year-rounders, and the other summer people who hate you either because they've been there longer than you have or because you've been there longer than they have. They hate you, unless you're giving them money, or raw mullet, as the case may be. Down South, snake farms are an organized form of hate—they are set up for the sole purpose of mocking and bilking Yankees, who are the only people who ever go to them. This keeps Southerners busy till fall, when they clean the restrooms.

All those people dispensing moccasins, maple syrup, speeding tickets, tetanus shots, last rites, and folk wisdom . . . they hate you, too. They are all Hobbesians. They laugh at your jellyfish stings, your mosquito bites, your rope burns. New Englanders see the first summer people and put up signs on the clam flats warning of the "red tide" that poisons all the shellfish except the ones they sell to you and leaves after Labor Day. Eat a red-tide clam, and you can die a death of indescribable horror, sort of a cross between tetanus and a rainy afternoon buying shoes and towels at factory outlet stores.

"Well, we got some nice towels," you say, and then you go back to practicing your Maine accent until your children tell you that you're embarrassing them.

Rain: Don't measure it in inches, but in Reader's Digest Condensed Books (the Official Literature of Summer Cottages), as in how many you have to read while you sit there next to the fire that won't light. The cloud cover, though, gives the Mafia a chance to dump hospital waste about 11 feet offshore. When the sun comes out, you'll hear the air mattresses bursting as they hit the syringes.

If you want a break from being hated, check out those people who seem born to be summer people, the shaggy insouciant Jasons-on-motorcycles, the sort of women who seem like golden retrievers with good backhands, the boys in perfect pickup trucks, the men who know how to make willow whistles and do the J-stroke in canoes, the waitresses who spend all day on the beach with their endless legs and those little dimples above the backs of their bikini bottoms, the old guys who drive old cars very slowly to the airport to pick up their heirs for the big race weekend, that pretty bicyclist with the slightly chipped front tooth, the surfers, the guys with biceps where veins stand out, the charter members of the Rousseau society, the foster children of silence and slow time. . . . They're like those people who were such wonderful successes in school, merely on the strength of a certain grace and attitude. They don't hate you. They don't even know you exist. You hate them.

But these are the kinds of things that only anxious types worry about. The rest of us, the ones who know how great vacations are, can watch a raccoon trot toward our tent without looking for froth on its little black lips. We can go to Texas and not worry about shaking the scorpions out of our shoes every morning, at least in the better hotels. We can be bitten by a tick without watching for the telltale rash of Lyme disease until somebody tells us that sometimes there is no rash. At that point our faces don't pucker with fear as we ask: "What's Rocky Mountain spotted fever?

Sunburn: Anxious types can't get themselves a good sunburn—the kind that has the kids making fire siren noises whenever you stagger past on your way to doing another one-and-a-half-gainer into a jar of Noxzema—without thinking of skin cancer, especially with the ozone layer melting or evaporating or whatever it does to let in more ultraviolet rays but not let them out, leading to the greenhouse effect and the polar ice caps melting and the oceans rising, which means that beach house you're going to fall in love with and buy will be halfway to Bermuda by next summer.

As it happens, there are some things worth worrying about. Drownings, car crashes and falls, for instance, are the three leading causes of injury deaths in the United States. Drowning is just the kind of thing that natural Rousseauian summer people don't think about at all. College students ranked swimming as the least dangerous of thirty activities listed by a polling group, while experts put it tenth. Between 1978 and 1984 an average of 6,503 persons drowned every year, more than half of them in the summer.

Vacation involves a lot of driving. Driving involves more than 45,000 deaths a year. And so on. On the Connecticut and New York

State turnpikes you can note the bridges that have collapsed in recent years, prompting educational discussions about how to get out of a car that's 23 feet underwater. How long does the air bubble last? Do you lose the bubble if you open the window? Can you open the door without opening the window first? How do they do it in disaster movies?

But why worry? You might have fretted about reindeer gorings all the way over to Lapland for a once-in-a-lifetime look at the midnight sun, and then found yourself dusted with a nasty dose of fallout from the Chernobyl reactor disaster instead. Still, anxious types will keep thinking about shark attacks, rogue waves sweeping children off beaches like bread crumbs off table tops, undertow; about hearing some woman at the island market say, "they just appeared on the beach one day with all these children" and realizing it's you she's describing; about words like "stranded" or "tow truck" or "next of kin"; about the trooper saying, "There's nothing you could have done. There was nothing anyone could have done."

Home: You could have stayed home. If you had, you wouldn't have spent the whole time worrying that it had burned down. Been burglarized. With the cat trapped in the furnace room. So perhaps the best idea is to just stay home. Edge the gardens, organize your slide collection. Watch the tourists come through, asking directions. You see the fear in their eyes, the terror and living hell that is vacation. You realize it wasn't baseless anxiety that kept you home, it was good sense.

"Oh, turn left down about . . . there," you say, in a tone you acquired long ago on vacations yourself, sort of like a park ranger talking in a Maine accent. With a little luck, the vacationers will say it before they're out of earshot: "You can tell, these people take our money but they really hate us."

Then you can catch up on your reading—maybe some of those Condensed Books that have been piling up all winter.

Here is what the space shuttle Discovery sounded like on a bright and quiet September morning at Cape Canaveral, Florida, as it rose in a ritual redemption of Challenger, which had blown up two years before.

Like nothing. Like God's own Velcro ripping apart. Like a piece of wrinkled yard-thick tinfoil the size of Rhode Island being smoothed flat and you're under it. Who can say? It was the noise made by 4,520,276 pounds of shuttle acelerating to a speed of 100 miles an hour in the first 7.6 seconds of liftoff. You heard it on television—a roar that became a rasping anthem of a noise, Louis Armstrong singing the Wernher von Braun Songbook. But you had to be there to know what it was like.

It began with the flag lolling and a lot of birds on the creek. Lots of delays. The countdown hit one. A vapor cloud rose firm as a palmful of shaving cream. Then the shuttle was standing on a wall of clear orange that was bright as a welder's torch, so bright you couldn't see the color of it if you stared right at it, so bright it made everything around it dark. But not a sound. The shuttle cleared the gantry in silence. Then the birds went nuts, panicking up from the water.

A moment later, you knew what drove them berserk—just a muttering at first, an afterthought to this mad, fiery afflatus before you. That was the instant in which you realized not that you were about to be hit hard but that you already had been, a sucker punch, a fist the size of a canned ham hitting you in the chest. A touch of adrenaline prompted a personal systems check—fight, flight? The shuttle cleared the tower and lounged over on its back, reclining with all the brilliant ease of a 1943 movie where Rita Hayworth lounged back on a couch in silk pajamas. A roaring Rita Hayworth? Why not? By this time the sound was breaking up into pieces, first sharp little rappings then big pops, and it was as if your head were getting run through the same machine that puts the dimples in golf balls.

After a while, you could hear the press guys applauding. Old launch hands love to tell new guys about it, couldn't stop telling the new guys about it in 1988, for instance, when Discovery had the mission of redeeming not just the 1986 explosion of space shuttle Challenger, but also postwar America's national idea—the endless frontier meets the triumph of engineering. This was the freight we had loaded onto the Challenger on Jan. 28, 1986, and it blew up after a 73.621-second flight. There had been so many national failures since the glory days of the space program, from Vietnam to Watergate to the oil crisis to the hostages in Lebanon, and here was another, a failure of both technology and image. In the national mourning that followed, it seemed we hadn't even thought that symbolism could have real risks. It was as if nature, the heavens, even God, had turned against us. In an age when heaven was a dream of endless second chances, it was impossible that there was no escape hatch, no parachute for the Challenger crew.

There's nothing like it, but why were we doing it at all?

There has been the argument that mankind was biologically destined to head off into space, as if our DNA's little travel alarm had gone off and the whole species had awakened to go where no man had gone before. Another justification was the experiments the shuttles have carried, but they have had a tinge of make-work about them. There was the argument that space travel would bring peace to the world, along the lines of Carl Sagan's proposals for a joint U.S.-Soviet Mars mission. There was the idea of bleeding off excess population. These arguments weren't new—they had all been made before in support of exploring the American frontier, in one way or another.

As it happened, the space program was sold as science, which itself had been sold as part of the religion of progress. But the real mission was symbolism, right from the beginning when the Russians put up Sputnik in 1957. One of our early satellites had the mission of broadcasting Christmas greetings from President Eisenhower. The Apollo 8 astronauts read Genesis aloud. The Viking lander made it to Mars for July 4. There were questions about whether it was wise to be so self-conscious about imagery in space. Wasn't it a little like the aluminum piano on the Hindenburg, something that didn't really belong there? There was an aesthetic of space, too. Not the old Buck Rogers stuff, but high modernism. Space is clean. All those films and photographs the astronauts have brought back showed perfect edges and colors of unmediated light, a sense of edge, abstraction, and self-awareness in the midst of vast voids of metal and transparency, of utopias that look like architects' drawings. Space, it seemed, was gorgeously lonely, one big silent International-style plaza without even the heels tick-tocking across it. Then add the up-from-the-muck motif that Stanley Kubrick used in 2001 with the caveman throwing a bone up and up. Cut to space station, to all the other space movies that have come along since. Bring up the soundtrack music here, the synthesizer, the Berlin Philharmonic and the wordless soprano going ohhhhhhhhhhhhhhhh . . .

And the heroes of space: Henry Luce and *Life* magazine turned the first ones into marble gods. The result was boredom. In *The Right Stuff,* Tom Wolfe made them knights in single combat. The problem with the combat-hero thesis was: no enemy. It was as if Ulysses set sail and the only foe he had to fear was not Circe or Cyclops, but the shipwright. By the time of the last moon landing in 1972, the country was getting bored with astronauts and the space program. We no longer needed them to fight a symbolic war with the Soviets, thanks to Nixon's détente. Science was suspect, and the military was a basket case. And America was starting to have money trouble. Enter Everyman. Enter checkbook balancing, pay-as-you-go, middle-class space exploration. The shuttle. President Nixon, the Heifetz of suburban resentment, picked up his violin. The shuttle, the new song said, would "take the astronomical cost out of astronautics." He sounded as if he were about to propose shooting a Buick Roadmaster into space when he said that the shuttle would "make the ride safer and less demanding for the passengers, so that men and women with work to do in space can 'commute' aloft." The shuttle would be reusable and cost-efficient, and the astronauts would be commuters. In keeping with the new symbolism of the times, North American Rockwell Corp. got the contract for building the orbiter in part because it had more blacks, Hispanics and Asians in its work force than its competitors.

By 1986 the Challenger crew represented the tolerance, civil rights, technology, and the average citizen of America. That was its job, really. Along with whites Greg Jarvis, Mike Smith, and Dick Scobee were Japanese-American Ellison Onizuka, Jew (and Ph.D. engineer) Judy Resnik, black Ron McNair, and schoolteacher-citizen-mother Christa McAuliffe, who wasn't even a scientist. That was fine—by now, not just symbolism but science itself was on the line— the nuclear reactor failure at Three Mile Island, pollution, and the failure of technocracy to solve social ills, a failure summed up in the anvil chorus of liberalism: "If we can put a man on the moon, why can't we make the South Bronx a decent place to live?"

José Ortega y Gasset wrote in *The Revolt of the Masses* that the common man doesn't see technology as either risky or incredible. "The new man wants his motor-car, and enjoys it, but he believes that it is the spontaneous fruit of an Edenic tree. In the depths of his soul he is unaware of the artificial, almost incredible character of civilization, and does not extend his enthusiasm for the instruments to the principles which make them possible."

The sin of pride was a thing of the past. No more Icarus, no more Prometheus. Then Challenger blew up.

When Discovery was rolled out in 1988 to redeem the space program, the engineering had been tightened up and the symbolism re-
worked. There were no senators, Saudi princes, or Europeans along
for the ride. No more mention of a congressional proposal to put a
handicapped person in space, where weightlessness would prove
equality. Nobody pretended that shuttle flights are routine or ordinary, words favored first by Nixon and then NASA, as if they were
merely blasting a split-level tract house into space.

The symbolism had been drawn and erased so many times that it
was a gray smear. All you could say for sure on that day in 1988 was
that the shuttle stood on a piece of swampland in Florida. You
wanted the orbiter to be beautiful, but it wasn't. It looked like a toy
whose primary purpose is to be safe for toddlers. It was the product
of pure science and political squalor, or maybe pure politics and scientific squalor. It had all the charm of a freight elevator, which is what it
is. Before Challenger blew up it got called "Battlestar Bureaucratica"
and "The Flying Brickyard." There was something both noble and
hapless about its successor, like something way behind or ahead of its
time, or a sacrificial animal, or maybe a foster child who has to stand
there, overgrown and pathetic, while social workers argue over what
he should be doing, and is he worth all the time and money. If it was a
shuttle, what was it a shuttle between? It was designed to leave Earth
and go about 200 miles into nothing, then come back. It's as if
Columbus sailed out about 200 miles west of the Azores and heaved
to, let the sailors go swimming, caught a few fish, tried to live off rain-
water and porpoise meat and came back. And if the astronauts were
explorers, what brave new world were they looking for that not one
ship could sink or sailor could die without it being a national
calamity?

The tropical clouds cruised overhead like God's own spectator
fleet and shadows slid over the shuttle's mysterious ugliness. At night
there was the vacant glare of the xenon lights, an oil refinery bleak-
ness to things. Palmettos rustled and the pelicans shuddered on their
pilings. There were the alligators, too—NASA press handouts used to
stress the alligator angle, how the gators would have to be chased off

the runway before the shuttle landed, that kind of thing. The idea was to show how far we've evolved, biological destiny, homo sapiens transcending the muck. There's an alligator in the shuttle movie at the National Air & Space Museum, too, swimming in a creek as the shuttle broods in the background with an odd quality of looking monumental and transitory at the same time, like a portable cathedral or a secondhand pyramid.

But the noise:

A minute downrange, the Doppler effect sets in—the sound gets lower as the shuttle accelerates away from you in the manner of a train whistle rising and falling as it goes past. The shuttle is a silver point now, moving so fast that it has a flung quality. At two minutes, you see the mammoth amber cloud stacked just downwind of the launch pad. You hear the people around you clapping and cheering, and you realize that the shuttle by now is making no more noise than an airliner. The world looks new, the world looks old. Is that a rain squall moving in from the Atlantic? Is that the shuttle up there still, or just a piece of dust on your glasses, catching the sunlight, or just an idea, way beyond noise? For a moment, nobody asks what people have been asking for the life of the space program: why are we doing this?

fireworks

Here already. Like all holidays, the Fourth of July is a reminder of things not done: "I still haven't put out the hummingbird feeder or bought a bathing suit," you say. Soon enough the world will have a scrubby, mournful quality, like a high school athletic field between the end of baseball and the start of football. The dead of summer. But there are the fireworks. They get you through the dog days of summer the way Christmas propels you through the worst of winter.

All day long there are foretastes. The boy next door touches off a string of ladyfingers before you've even had your coffee, and the dog crawls under the bed and stays there. At the parade, the American Legion guys fire a salute. You remember a childhood of cherry bombs, M80s, Roman candles coughing out chunks of fire, Silver Salutes, a childhood in which your elders chanted of things lost—fingers, hands, eyes, lives. "Have a safe and sane Fourth," the radio keeps saying. You see a circle of kids squinting with failed astonishment at all-too-legal "snakes"—those little excrescences of ash that leave black spots on the sidewalk for months.

When it's twilight, finally, you assemble an expedition of who-ever wants to go, and you head down to the fireworks, past kids on bicycles with crepe paper woven through the spokes, a boy flinching as he draws circles in the air with a sparkler, the grandmas in pant-suits, the mayor in his necktie, everybody. The crowd has the peculiar character of Fourth of July fireworks crowds, complacent and excited at the same time. As darkness comes on, the noise of it acquires a den-sity, a heft—applause, soft-drink cans opening with a happy little slic-ing sound, the gasp of helium into balloons, a generator running someplace, the dry squeak of aluminum folding chairs, all the voices saying "Excuse me" as people tiptoe around blankets and coolers. And, "Well, it didn't rain after all." And, "Get one for your sister, too, and bring me back the change."

You spread an old blanket. The stars lower toward the treetops. Somewhere, blocks away, somebody sets off firecrackers—stones in Niagara, coals to Newcastle, a "codicility" to them, as George Plimp-ton put it in a book called *Fireworks*. The town concert band feels its way through popular favorites ("Just a Closer Walk With Thee," "If Ever I Should Leave You"), the effect being that of a small girl passing a large, full pitcher across a table, somehow breathtaking. A baby on the blanket in front of you waves its arms.

"You are reminded that the law forbids the sale, possession, or use of unauthorized fireworks," the loudspeaker says, adding, with the heartiness of officialdom that rues its necessary wet-blanketdom: "Enjoy the show!"

Will there be an opening salute, with no display but the kind of huge dark ripping crack as humbling in its way as the sound of a molar being pulled? Will there be the inspired American insanity that Jack Kerouac described when he wrote about both Americans and fireworks? "The only people for me are the mad ones, the ones who are mad to live, mad to talk, mad to be saved, desirous of everything at the same time, the ones who never yawn or say a commonplace thing, but burn, burn, burn like fabulous yellow Roman candles ex-ploding like spiders across the stars and in the middle you see the blue centerlight pop and everybody goes 'Awww!' "

Fireworks were invented by the ancient Chinese. By 1487 the English used them to celebrate the wedding of Henry VII. In 1613 James I marked the marriage of his daughter Elizabeth with an extravaganza over the Thames River showing St. George fighting a dragon. Peter the Great loved them. The French court watched them at Versailles. Handel wrote "Music for the Royal Fireworks" to accompany the celebration of the Treaty of Aix-la-Chapelle in 1749.

Fireworks were mostly amber until the nineteenth century, when potassium chlorate, discovered by Claude-Louis Berthollet in 1786, made colors possible. Magnesium and aluminum would create brilliant whites, and titanium was found to make magnificently loud salutes that leave a glittering white cloud. Charcoal and iron gave us orange. Strontium salts made red. Barium nitrate made green. A deep blue that is also bright has been the hardest to make. From the Japanese came the best examples of the round displays known as peonies or chrysanthemums. From the Italians (such as the Grucci, Vitale, and Zambelli families in American fireworks) came our taste for big booms.

Terminology varies from one company to the next. A peony can be fiery spokes in a wheel, whereas a chrysanthemum is one or more circles of stars, or vice versa. A tiger tail can be a variety of comet, the shell that leaves a thick trail all the way up from the ground, or it can be a trail cascading down from the "break," as the midair detonations are known. There can be any number of finales. To some pyrotechnicians, a finale is any huge and definitive eruption, as in "you start with the opening finale, then you work down all the mortars till you get to the closing finale." Shows rarely last more than half an hour; if they do, people's necks get sore from spasm of the trapezius muscle, among others.

The band is through. The raffle winners have been announced. You watch one of the musicians zip his bass fiddle into a canvas bag. The lights on the bandstand go out. Men with flashlights crouch by the fireworks mortars. There's a ground display. Will it say GOOD-NIGHT? Or be an American flag, hissing and melting in colors like circus costumes? Guys from the emergency squad stand on the running board of the ambulance to watch. The baby in front of you sleeps on its mother's shoulder. It's as if the whole crowd is accelerating somehow.

The first explosion of the evening: a dull, breathy grunt. The shell ascends with a deft wobble that gives off sparks like the incredibly slow rocket ships in the old Flash Gordon movies. Just as it starts to teeter toward extinction it explodes, making a noise so loud that the noise itself has brightness, like a blow to the head. Everybody goes "Awww!"

Shells chug into the air, giving proof through the night. Soon the sky is freaked with smoke, like veined marble. The flashing reveals it the way a match reveals a room at night, as if for an instant you're looking inside a mind, not a room—fireworks are an analog of certain kinds of thought: eureka, satori, aha! Pow. Pow. Pow. Peonies, chrysanthemums, hummers, serpents. They're so sharply drawn, like the sharpness of miniatures, but gigantic miniatures. Maybe it's just the acuteness of all aerial spectacle: lightning, flying champagne corks, shooting stars, confetti, rainbows, rings around the moon, hats thrown at Naval Academy graduations. Sparks fall into the trees. You feel exalted, a little dizzy with the same adrenalin that tightens the faces all around you. A bad shell sends fire scrambling across the grass. Was anybody hurt? No. There goes a willow, with great shaggy tendrils that give you the feeling they're not falling to earth as much as you're accelerating into outer space.

A flashlight guy by the mortars runs over and touches off the display on the scaffolding. It hisses and drips, an American flag. People cheer. In the age of laser shows, they still cheer a fireworks flag. The guy runs back and sends the closing finale walloping into the night. It makes people look fierce and happy, puts crazy square-eyed grins on their faces, except for the baby, who seems to be staring at the lights on a Good Humor truck. There is a salute.

"You are reminded that the law forbids the sale, possession, or use . . ."

Your wrists are sore from leaning back on your arms, and the heels of your hands have lines on them from blades of grass. Somebody sets off an absurd string of firecrackers, a long way off. Cars start. There are fireflies, you notice, and a plane way up high, drifting toward the horizon with its passengers no doubt asleep.

index